After Dickens is both a performative reading of Dickens the novelist and an exploration of the potential for adaptive performance of the novels themselves. John Glavin conducts an historical inquiry into Dickens's relation to the theatre and theatricality of his own time, and uncovers a much more ambivalent, often hostile, relationship than has hitherto been noticed. In this context, Dickens's novels can be seen as a form of counter-performance, one which would allow the author to perform without being seen or scrutinized. But Glavin also explores the paradoxically rich performative potential in Dickens's fiction, and describes new ways to stage that fiction in emotionally powerful, critically acute adaptations. The book as a whole, therefore, offers a radical new reading of Dickens through an unusual alliance between literary criticism and theatrical performance.

CAMBRIDGE STUDIES IN NINETEENTH-CENTURY
LITERATURE AND CULTURE 20

AFTER DICKENS

CAMBRIDGE STUDIES IN NINETEENTH-CENTURY
LITERATURE AND CULTURE

General editor
Gillian Beer, *University of Cambridge*

Editorial board
Isobel Armstrong, *Birkbeck College, London*
Terry Eagleton, *University of Oxford*
Leonore Davidoff, *University of Essex*
Catherine Gallagher, *University of California, Berkeley*
D. A. Miller, *Columbia University*
J. Hillis Miller, *University of California, Irvine*
Mary Poovey, *New York University*
Elaine Showalter, *Princeton University*

Nineteenth-century British literature and culture have been rich fields for interdisciplinary studies. Since the turn of the twentieth century, scholars and critics have tracked the intersections and tensions between Victorian literature and the visual arts, politics, social organization, economic life, technical innovations, scientific thought – in short, culture in its broadest sense. In recent years, theoretical challenges and historiographical shifts have unsettled the assumptions of previous scholarly syntheses and called into question the terms of older debates. Whereas the tendency in much past literary critical interpretation was to use the metaphor of culture as "background," feminist, Foucauldian, and other analyses have employed more dynamic models that raise questions of power and of circulation. Such developments have reanimated the field.

This series aims to accommodate and promote the most interesting work being undertaken on the frontiers of the field of nineteenth-century literary studies: work which intersects fruitfully with other fields of study such as history, or literary theory, or the history of science. Comparative as well as interdisciplinary approaches are welcomed.

A complete list of titles published will be found at the end of the book.

AFTER DICKENS

Reading, Adaptation and Performance

JOHN GLAVIN

CAMBRIDGE
UNIVERSITY PRESS

PUBLISHED BY THE PRESS SYNDICATE OF THE UNIVERSITY OF CAMBRIDGE
The Pitt Building, Trumpington Street, Cambridge CB2 1RP, United Kingdom

CAMBRIDGE UNIVERSITY PRESS
The Edinburgh Building, Cambridge CB2 2RU, United Kingdom   http://www.cup.cam.ac.uk
40 West 20th Street, New York, NY 10011–4211, USA   htt://www.cup.org
10 Stamford Road, Oakleigh, Melbourne 3166, Australia

© John Glavin 1999

First published 1999

Printed in Great Britain at the University Press, Cambridge

Typeset in Baskerville 11/12.5 pt [VN]

A catalogue record for this book is available from the British Library

ISBN 0 521 63322 2 hardback

Contents

Acknowledgments

The Dickens Project, University of California, Santa Cruz, begot the adaptations that began *After Dickens*. Indeed, the book itself was first the idea of the Project's two Directors, Murray Baumgarten and John Jordan. Dickensians, at least, will know what I mean, then, when I gratefully acknowledge them as my Chapman and Hall. They each read the entire manuscript in its earliest stages, and their prudent counsel turned a loose, baggy monster into something that had shape if not quite style. The former and current administrators of the Project, Linda Rosewood Hooper and JoAnna Rottke, made working bicoastally anything but a binary opposition. And the Friends of the Dickens Project have always been just that, heroically friendly, especially Barbara Keller, the Friends' dynamic leader during most of this book's gestation.

James Kincaid read the entire manuscript at a crucial stage, when his enthusiastic support renewed my depleted faith in its possibility. Even more than his advice, the bliss of his perfect frivolity has been a beacon ahead, showing me where and how criticism ought to go, even when I haven't had the wit to follow.

N. John Hall, Gerhard Joseph and Hilary Schor also read the manuscript, and generously guided its outcome. They taught me, in a dozen years of incomparable conversation, to recognize eccentricity as the most precious of a critic's commodities, and to treasure aberrancy as the only sure guard against a scholar's mere and dull competence.

And Regina Barreca has from the very beginning always been – quite unlike Agnes Wickfield – pointing upward, showing me, in her life and in her work, that if you're not angry, you are probably not thinking, and that if you are not laughing, you certainly cannot claim to have cared for the things of men. And if you are not generous without stint, then you have everything to learn from her example.

Among many others on the Project faculty I happily acknowledge my debt to: Janice Carlisle, Joseph Childers, Philip Collins, Edward Eigner,

Regenia Gagnier, Catherine Gallagher, Elizabeth Gitter, Albert Hutter, Wendy Jacobson, Jacqueline Jaffe, Fred Kaplan, Carol MacKay, Sylvia Manning, Joss Marsh, Patrick McCarthy, Helena Michie, Robert Newsom, David Parker, Robert Patten, Robert Polhemus, Norris Pope, Judith Rosen, Robert Tracy, and the late Elliot Gilbert.

At Georgetown, my colleagues Gay Gibson Cima and John Pfordresher persuaded me I had something to say, when that didn't seem terribly likely. The English department had four Chairs while I worked on this project: Paul Betz, James Slevin, Lucy Maddox and Leona Fisher. All of them made my finishing this book their own high priority. Lynne Hirschfeld, the administrator of the department during most of that time, listened patiently and counseled wisely though most of what she heard was merely paranoia. I am happy also to acknowledge the gracious support of the past and present Deans of Georgetown College, Royden Davis, S.J. and Robert Lawton, S.J.

Among my other Georgetown colleagues I owe happily acknowledged thanks to: Valerie Babb, Randall Bass, Edward Bodnar, S.J., Denis Bradley, Aimee Cooper, Maureen Corrigan, Bruce Douglass, Judith Farr, Keith Fort, Kim Hall, Lindsay Kaplan, Carol Kent, Joseph O'Connor, Patricia O'Connor, Victoria Pedrick, Michael Ragussis, Elaine Romanelli, Jason Rosenblatt, Nicholas Scheetz, Alexander Sens, Roger Slakey, Bruce Smith, Margaret Stetz, and Anne Walsh.

I am indebted to Josie Dixon at Cambridge University Press for a warm summer of welcome e-mail.

I have been buoyed by unflagging support from my friends: George Bear, P.-L. Bland, Gordon Davis, Patricia Dietz, Deborah Fort, Jane Jordan, Christine Smith, Judith Throm, Rebecca Tracy; from my family: James Glavin, Margaret Higgins Glavin, Joanne Parrack, Mary Joseph Pirola, Mark Pirola; from my son and daughter, Thaddeus Glavin and Cecilia Glavin, ecstatic that we are all now finally After Dickens; and from my wife, Margaret O'Keeffe Glavin, to whom this book is dedicated, and who makes everything that is good in my life possible.

Note on the text

For Dickens's texts I have, without apology, relied on a motley assortment of different paperbound editions, just those dog-eared ones I use to teach, because that's where my notes and markers are.

> For *Oliver Twist, The Old Curiosity Shop, Dombey and Son, David Copperfield, Bleak House, Little Dorrit, A Tale of Two Cities, Great Expectations,* and *Our Mutual Friend* I relied on the Penguins.
> For *The Pickwick Papers, Nicholas Nickleby* and *The Mystery of Edwin Drood* I used the Oxford Illustrated Edition.

Although I do not quote them in the text of *After Dickens,* for Dickens Letters, I read the multi-volume Pilgrim Edition published by The Clarendon Press and edited principally by Madeline House and Graham Story.

Introduction

After Dickens what? You well may ask.

Here's the exchange behind the title.

Two Italian art historians – Italians who also do Italian Art history – in an American museum, examining one of its Tuscan jewels.

"Pontormo," the younger skeptically asks, "or only After Pontormo?"

"After, *certamente*," confidently replies the elder.

"*Certamente*, it's certainly a Pontormo," hisses, from behind them, the collection's Curator. All along he's been silently trailing them through the gallery .

"Well, yes. Probably it was a Pontormo," the elder concedes, "once."

Safely away from the Curator's baleful glare, the older Historian explains – to me – what he meant. The original canvas has been so thoroughly overpainted that, whatever might remain beneath, nothing now visible on the surface can possibly lay claim to have been put there by Pontormo's hand.

Ironically, the correct art-historical term for that process of painting-over/painting-out is restoration. But if Pontormo had been a writer rather than a painter, the equivalent term would be adaptation. And – here's where I, and this book, come in – if Pontormo had been Dickens, that is a writer not a painter, there'd never be any question that he could ever be anything but, as my Italian friends would say, *in restauro*: under restoration. Or, in literary terms, under adaptation. For a fresco, a statue, a baptistery, to be *in restauro* means – as every tourist in Italy learns soon after arrival – that what you have come all this way to see is temporarily unavailable, out of sight, locked away from your inspection. (Probably indefinitely unavailable, since it's Italy.) But a written text, unlike a painting, never gets out of *restauro*.

We read only in so far as we restore. Painting can trace outlines; writing only leaves traces.

I

I know, of course, that paintings also can – and probably should – be read like texts. But there is a passive pleasure that painting shares with every other sort of spectacle, including theatre, a passivity that writing does not permit. Indeed, we can see that difference most clearly in the well-nigh desperate energy with which a figure like Brecht works against the passivity of theatre, to make theatre-going an experience something more like reading. If a novel, a poem, a play is to be read at all, it's got to be retrieved, put back together, refurbished. The pages may be there in front of us, but the text waits on our recovery. And just there, where restoration marks the only entry to reading, oddly the analogy to painting kicks back in. We can only do this work of restoration by overriding, covering over, erasing. My art-historical friends may reasonably stipulate for a way of seeing pictures that distinguishes between seeing a Pontormo – which is good – and seeing only after Pontormo – which is decidedly not so good. But we all come to Dickens only *after Dickens.*

What can we do about this inevitable lagging-behind? That's the question this book attempts to answer. If we can only, at best, and always, come after Dickens, how best can we stage that belatedness? Might we, as Pierre Bourdieu has suggested, somehow find "a way of producing an *aggiornamento*" of older traditions of reading in order to make possible a way "to redeploy a certain kind of literary capital" (Bourdieu 1990: 95). More specifically, how can we, in the twilight of what Joseph Roach has wittily labeled "the discipline that might still be called English" (Roach 1995: 45), "profit" from returning to the "literary capital" accumulated in Dickens's books? I understand and take full responsibility for all of the negative connotations in the metaphor of capital. Nevertheless, happily, I insist on asking: is there a way to navigate unscathed between the Scylla of canon-fetish and the Charybdis of canon-diss? Come neither to praise, nor to bury. Merely coming after, and glad of it?

After Dickens suggests one well-spent way to accomplish that *aggiornamento* can come from refocusing the relation between the page and the stage, between reading, adapting and performing. It's a way that positions reading as close cousin to adapting. A way that updates both of them as versions of performance. And that specifies such performance as modeling, fundamentally, what it means to find yourself coming *after* an original.

Of course, we come after Dickens in at least three ways. Most obviously, chronologically: he's gone, we're here. But we're also after

Dickens in the sense of seeking him out, trying to find him, tracing him through the pages where he himself has gone missing, constantly interpreting, striving for meaning, but catching instead only glimpses, versions, possibilities, accumulating readings, rereading. And that in turn means – to return momentarily to Pontormo – that we are also after Dickens stylistically, in the sense that echoes through so many second-level museums: an Epiphany "after Rubens," a Madonna "after Raphael." But where a better class of gallery may contain originals, the best of our readings can always only be "in the style of," never "by the hand of." To be faced by any sort of text at all, we readers of necessity become restorers – adapters *avant la lettre*. We overpaint to save, just as with the Pontormo, and in saving we overpaint.

I don't mean to imply that there's no sense in trying to distinguish between reading and adaptation, only that the difference between them is one of degree, not of kind. In fact, the more interesting difference separates, on the one hand, unproblematized reading and unproblematized adaptation, from, on the other, ways of reading and ways of adapting that recognize their common and problematic aftering.

Unproblematized reading insists that it can somehow make present to itself what Dickens actually said or even less plausibly what Dickens actually meant. It corresponds to the kind of "authentic" stagings of the novels, insistently faithful to every Victorian detail, that claim in hours and hours of performance or film to reproduce the novel under scrutiny. Both seem to me to involve similar sorts of forgery, copies which will not admit the altering in their aftering, which can not face up to the fact that the original can never be present to the consciousness of the follower, whether reader or adapter. Both forms function as pacifiers, fictions about fiction that attempt to console us for the inevitable depredations of time. Like the overpainting my art-historical friend so haughtily dismissed, they set out to hide the ways in which their recoveries inevitably obscure, replace, distort the originals they so earnestly claim to bring back.

On the other hand, reading and adaptation that problematize themselves take root in a common recognition of belatedness. We can see them agreeing companionably to blur the conventional distinction Bourdieu, in the same essay, outlines as a cardinal distinction between *lector*, one who "comments on an already stablished discourse," and *auctor*, one who produces new discourse. Obviously, *auctor* – author, prophet – is the privileged term of the pair, the one who writes out of "his charisma . . . the *auctor* of his own *auctoritas*." The *lector* – reader/

priest – holds only a delegated "legitimacy . . . based in the final analysis on the *auctoritas* of the original *auctor*, to whom the *lectores* at least pretend to refer" (Bourdieu 1990: 94). But in that "at least pretend" my argument squeezes its toehold.

The kind of reading and adaptation that interests me is the kind that problematizes itself, and thereby reveals readers and adapters as kin, reversing the conventional author-reader privilege. To use Bourdieu's terms, this is a reversal that recognizes that it's the priests who create the prophets, and prophecy. Prophetic charisma, whatever the faith, is conferred not by prophets on themselves but onto those prophets the scripture-redactors find they can use to suit their ends. (The other explanation is inspiration, but no one, I'm sure, wants to risk moseying down that particular path.) Prophets are those writers whom priests use to prove their points. The rest is heresy and schism. And, just as clearly, in our own after-words, it is readers who don't simply read-into, but much more crucially read-out, text.

Bourdieu's weakness, of course, is that he lumps everyone not a prophet into the category priest. That can't be true. Or at least it can't be true anywhere more than a mile beyond the left bank of the Seine. In any case, I don't want to go about multiplying Latin distinctions. I only want to make clear that, just as priests above all insist on distinguishing between priests and people, so also we must mark some significant distinction between two sorts of readers. Is it the distinction between readers and commentators – to redeploy Bourdieu's word – or readers and critics, or merely readers and profs.?

The words don't matter, I think, at least not here. What does matter is that we agree to see that those who read for themselves – rather than merely repeat others' readings – are in fact always "after" and always "aftering," always restoring, adapting, supplying, making texts and promulgating meanings. Some do that on the sly. I'm too much of a gentleman to name them. Others do it boldly, flagrantly, with panache. They are those who proudly up-date, re-invest, paint-over, paint-out, restore, adapt, and in the process take liberties with the narrow "manner of." They are those who will – I hope, by the end of *After Dickens* – be us.

While the reading side of this reading-adaptation equation may not find significant opposition, the adaptation-side is likely to face at first a fairly unfriendly audience. Despite significant recent defections, text-based critics continue generally to manifest a profound mistrust of theatricality – whether they are friend or foe to Foucault. Andrew Parker and Eve Kosofsky Sedgwick claim that the "theoretical convergence" of cultural and textual studies has of late "pushed performativity onto center stage" (Parker and Sedgwick 1995: 1). (Indeed, Eve Sedgwick, crossing Ziegfeld with Zelig, has been doing much of the best of that "pushing.") Parker and Sedgwick are probably right about the "fecund center." But in the wide margins which surround that center "crossings" of the page and the stage remain, to use another of their phrases, "under-articulated." Overpoweringly so, I would say. Off-center, most text-oriented criticism continues to insist that it "must protect itself from the performing artist . . . who is always the enemy" to language (Huston 1992: 129).

To demonstrate this point quickly – why dwell on the painful? – here are three recent readers of Shakespeare, surely an area where one might expect the most fecund crossings of language and performance.. *Staging the Gaze*, Barbara Freedman's 1991 study of Shakespearean comedy, sees performance as prime locale for Lacanian *Méconnaissance*, the "misrecognition" and "illusory identifications" through which the ego "is sustained" (Freedman 1991: 53). And text-centered Martin Buzacott demands nothing less than *The Death of the Actor* : "In this historically-bizarre modern theatrical age, the mythology of acting, suppressed for centuries and liberated with a vengeance, has attacked the authority of textuality with the result that the slave now claims the title of master as a natural birthright" (Buzacott 1991: 7). It's hardly a surprise then that Wolfgang Iser's attractively (to me) titled *Staging Politics* (1993) turns out never to speak at all of any actual staging, or acting, or actors, or theaters. All the world has become Iser's stage, literally, depreciating the stage itself into nothing but a convenient, toothless metaphor. For Iser the plays could be – we get the sense they probably would be – far better off being novels.

This mistrust of theatre and theatricality derives ultimately, I think, from an even deeper unease with affect. Here again Eve Kosofsky Sedgwick is in the vanguard. Her recent Silvan Tomkins reader, edited with Adam Frank, *Shame And Its Sisters* (1995), eagerly points toward rereadings of affect that could energize the entire field of critical practice. But whether Sedgwick will prove in this instance a prophet or Lot's wife, sadly saline with a pointless looking back, it is hard to say. Certainly, criticism as a whole seems now resolutely unwilling to let itself in for feeling.

But feeling is precisely what *After Dickens* intends to prompt, a "convergence of body and meaning" (Diamond 1995: 154) at the "crossing" between performance and critique. This convergence takes its source and pattern from a series of adaptations I staged for the annual conference of The Dickens Project, an international consortium of English departments, headquartered at the University of California, Santa Cruz. The Project scheduled these performances to parallel the longer conference papers on Dickens's fiction, not as curious or exotic complements to journal- and volume-based critique, – at least that's what the Project directors said – but as *supplements*, in the fully Derridean sense, to those more conventional forms. In a sense, then, the Conferences predicted the form of this book, this crossing of performance and critique, of acting and thinking, of body and mind.

The adaptations themselves stem from the theory and practice of Jerzy Grotowski, the widely acclaimed founder of Poor Theatre. (Movie-goers will remember Grotowski as the subject of the ecstatic rhapsodies that punctuate Wallace Shawn and André Gregory's film *My Dinner with André*.) Grotowski offers a critically generated model of adaptation which stages not a venerated image of the original, the parent text, but its probed and disturbing negative. Most of what now passes for adaptation on stage and screen represents a more or less "random historical pillaging" of the past (Wolin 1995: 57), displaying severed, deracinated members in misleadingly archival form, like blockbuster art shows in international museums. In contrast, Poor Theatre takes a scalpel to the parent-text and delivers from it the new materials folded away, disguised, denied by the original. Poor Theatre thus engenders from the source a new text, one that the adapter and the adapter's audience *feel* they must have, one that evades the traps of false consciousness or a culturally mandated subjectivity – imminence without immanence. Critique filters affect. Affect reinforces critique.

Through Poor Theatre we can *update* the Dickens we are *after*, to perform him belatedly as "present." We thereby re-make his fictions into something "comprehensible, usable and relevant to our own interests" (Orgel 1996: 64), understanding our "interests" as simultaneously theoretical and pragmatic, intellectual and emotional, the community's and our own. And in the process we move happily away from the terrible sameness of the field that has been English. We leave behind the numbing lock-step of the Theory Shop, and, refusing high-minded orthodoxies, look toward not only a stage but a world in which we can – there's no better word for it – act, a world in which we not only think but feel sharply. Worked within this frame, adaptation emerges as an instance – perhaps even a paradigmatic instance – of what the anthropologist Sherry Ortner has called a "serious game." Serious games, Ortner claims, play themselves out at an intersection of theory and practice, a cross of purposes "that embodies agency but does not begin with, or pivot upon, the agent, actor, or individual." Instead, they invite us to be agents-as-it-were, that is: *players*, who enter upon "webs" of already in-place social positions and ideological scripts, scenarios we can manipulate and modify just as long as we are playful, that is just as long as we move along and within those webs with "skill, intention, wit, knowledge, intelligence" and a serious commitment to the shocks of a serious game (Ortner 1996: 12).

I gesture here toward Ortner's feminist anthropology because I refuse to believe myself a solitary, the odd or only person interested in, still less capable of, the kinds of liaison on which my argument focuses. In a wide range of fields and activities we can easily recount the recent amalgamation of affect and agency: psychological studies of group conformity; forensic management of jury behavior; theological, philosophical, historical explorations of altruism, to name only three (Parrott 1993: 278). Certainly, I'm not the only person doing English stimulated by the challenge of Grotowskian transgression. Ten years at Santa Cruz taught me exactly the opposite. And I also hear or overhear at virtually every sort of professional gathering the costly, pervasive, and profitless, renunciation of creativity and feeling so many of my colleagues have enforced upon themselves as the price of performance in the Theory Shop. Why not transgress, then, not only the binding of theory and the boundaries of text but the boundaries that separate academic departments and the bindings that enforce the disciplines of critique?

After Dickens thus faces boldly and unafraid the nastily capitalist metaphor with which it opened – how to make a profit from coming After Dickens – because the ultimate restoration it seeks is not of the text, anybody's text, but of the restorer. We've got to get up off our knees from venerating the fetishized text – or down off the high horse from which we beat it, degraded and dethroned – and return to the fundamental understanding that we are writers too. We've got to remember that what interested us in the first place about English was the possibility of exploiting language to achieve a fullness, a richness, a density, of affect. And that a critique that doesn't take the restoration of that affect as its goal might as well be . . . well, what shall we call it? How about Sociology? We've got to become again prophets of our own charisma.

Of course, the enthusiasm of those last paragraphs betrays me. *After Dickens* has turned out to be, despite its academic credentials, in many ways a playwright's book. That's certainly not what I set out to write. But I am a playwright, as well as a literary critic, and in writing this book I've discovered that a playwright's way of thinking is more fundamental to me than I would have believed before I undertook this task. It's not just that the book's three parts insist on developing suspiciously like a script: set-up, flashback and resolution. Or that it would rather please than enlighten, though it hopes that in pleasing it might also enlighten. But *After Dickens* also insists, and this will doubtless disturb, that more than the usual combination of hands and eyes will be needed to read it well. It moves to a place where readers, shoeless, supine (but unobserved), are invited to stage themselves.

I get to that stage through three sets of paired chapters. We move from Dickens's exemplary resistance toward theatre (Set up), through an attempt to recreate what performance means in a shame-based psyche and culture (Flashback), to end with a pair of adaptations that transgress and transform their originals (Resolution).

Part I sets up the problem of the refusal of theatre, a refusal explored in detail in chapter 2 by focusing on Dickens's last completed novel, *Our Mutual Friend*. That chapter, generously, gives Dickens his only chance for a horrified rebuttal of everything we're about to do to what was literally his life's work.

Part II flashes back to the psychic and cultural origin of this crucial stage fright. Chapter 3, starting with *Pickwick Papers* and continuing into *Nicholas Nickleby*, locates anti- theatricality in the private and social shame attached to acting. Chapter 4, resuming in *Nickleby* but going on to spend a lot of time with *A Tale of Two Cities*, traces the ways in which Dickens arrives at a form for fiction which he fashions as a defense against that shame.

In part III, Resolution, Grotowski comes into his own and, as it were, gets the better of Dickens. Here we offer Grotowskian adaptation as resolution, dissolving Dickens's defense to show how we might retain and refuse him at the same time. Chapter 5 recreates an elaborately scaled staging of *Little Dorrit*. Finally, chapter 6, as a coda, invites you to begin to do the work of adaptation on and through your self, returning to *Our Mutual Friend* with a bijou staging as a blueprint for your own future adaptive performances.

Throughout this development, and despite the earnest advice of most of my brightest colleagues, *After Dickens* not only believes in but relies on that now deeply suspect notion, character, feeling's favorite tool. Obviously, any playwright's argument banks on characters to perform: specifically on characters I find in Dickens's texts, and characters I adapt from those texts. But by character here I also mean something more than merely figurative. I want to retrieve the original Greek sense of character, as a something pointed, sharp, jagged, menacing even. Remember that the original character is probably – at least for Sophocles – the serpent's tooth. Character here then stands for that psychic energy so enamored of its own fecund, if unhappy, agilities, that it eagerly courts even incoherence to baffle every readerly claim to competence – not don't tread on, but don't read on me. A notion of character I not only find everywhere in, but also everywhere as, Dickens.

This Charles Dickens is, inevitably, my adaptation of the man who lived between 1812 and 1870, my main character. This is a Dickens who feared the theatre. Who hated to write. Who constantly claimed center stage while refusing to be seen. The ultimate speaker, everywhere behind his figures and with such complete power that he could never be found out or trapped. This Charles Dickens is my familiar and my double, the necessary, inexhaustible through-line of my plan.

Three further and final caveats.

One. After this confession of predilections it can come as no surprise that I prefer suspense to any other structuring principle. These days the ill-omened byword for suspense is mystification. And we highmindedly treat all forms of mystification as bad: bad faith, bad thinking, even bad sex. But like the nineteenth century I find mystification, in the novelist Richard Ford's terms, "normal and even pleasurable" – normal indeed just because pleasurable. (Ford's word for mystification is "Dreaminess." It wouldn't be mine.) I love the nineteenth century precisely because it loved to mystify, and was indeed unsurpassed in trapping everything it made or saw or did within cloudy veils of mystification. How delicious and strange and witty to wrap a scarf around a piano leg and thus get everybody thinking about a phallus when they might only have been thinking about a piano. For my money, mystification keeps the emotion thrumming in emotional intelligence. And intelligence without feeling this book keeps insisting is just the intellectual equivalent of lunch-counter quiche, warmed-over experience sans texture and sans taste, sans sadness and sans pleasure. Sustaining, perhaps, to the saints of the latter-day Descartes, but scarcely fit food for citizens of a real, mongrel, if deeply flawed, democracy.

Two. I've tried to write *After Dickens* for both specialists and nonspecialists alike. Wherever they seem necessary I offer brief summaries of the novel under scrutiny. And I've put most of the more technical material in footnotes which the reader is free to ignore. I've done that, in part, because no one even among Dickensians (except for Michael Slater) remembers all Dickens's plots and characters precisely. But also because throughout the book I've tried to keep in mind W. H. Auden's advice: always write imagining yourself trying to cheer up a sick friend, all the while aware that the Postal Inspector won't pass the letter on unless he understands it. Here Auden's saying something like the psychoanalyst Robert Stoller's counsel that one should write a book so that those both inside and outside a field can follow it. Writing for insiders gives an argument rigor; for outsiders, clarity. I can't claim *After Dickens* achieves either rigor or clarity. But I have tried above all else to stay practical. *After Dickens* is a book about un-doing, un- doing Dickens, but, also and perhaps more significantly, about un-doing you.

Third and finally. Our bliss I believe to be of a very different sort from that of pure intelligence, of perfectly crystalline representation. I don't think – despite Dante – that His will is our bliss. I think His will is His bliss, and He is welcome to it. The bliss for which I root instead is that sort of cloudy unknowing which gets and keeps the juices flowing. So now you've been warned. Committed to affect, this book doesn't enjoy anything you can only know, and it doesn't want you to know anything you can't enjoy.

I

Set Up

"We have not outgrown the two great Theatres."
Household Words, January 1, 1853

Well before he became an author and Boz, Dickens, young, impecunious, and fiercely ambitious, managed to get himself that rare chance, a Covent Garden audition. He had been preparing sedulously for this opening, and capable judges thought he had a decent chance to be hired as a comedian. But when the day of the audition arrived, he bunked. He said he was ill. And he never rescheduled. Almost everything that follows in this book emerges from thinking about that no show.

I don't think this audition is the missing clue to reading Dickens, just as I don't think *Citizen Kane* is serious about Rosebud. The hidden clue lost in the early life seems to me just Welles's and Mankiewicz's *tour de force* satire about the over-easy Freudianism swamping pre-war Hollywood. And that's just as it should be. All I'm saying, to start, is that from the start Dickens was in not quite equal parts thrilled (less) and (more) frightened by the stage.

CHAPTER I

Dickens, adaptation and Grotowski

Winter of 1990–91. The gift shop of the Metropolitan opera is selling a beach towel. The top of the towel proclaims: "The Original Ending of Verdi's Aida." The middle displays a pyramid, some palm trees, and two figures in Egyptian dress, one male, the other female, peeking, suspicious and surprised, through an opening in the structure. And at the bottom: "Who would have thought there was a back door to this place?"

After Dickens is looking for that back door: to Dickens, to adaptation, to theatre, to theory. The back door that allows all four to escape, like Aida and Radames, from the nineteenth century, the century of the *liebestod*, the ecstatic union that relies on live burial. I want to adapt in a way that frees the originals from a regime which identifies bliss with death and insists on mere pleasure as the only real good: the greatest good of the greatest number, yes, but never the ecstatic. But on that retrograde threshold I also want to locate an even more encompassing "site of bliss," a moment and place for us as well as the characters (Barthes 1975: 4).

The "site of bliss," Roland Barthes says, is the place, the moment, where and when "the garment gapes," an *intermittence* "which is erotic: the intermittence of skin flashing between two articles of clothing . . . between two edges" (pp.9–10). This is the delight of taking what we want rather than accepting what we are offered, the bliss we spy rather than the pleasure we are shown. For me, that site focuses on the performance of adaptation. And what I emphatically reject is any form of adaptation that functions as memorial or monument, let alone masterpiece theater, any variation on Verdi's final pyramid tomb, the novel or the script as burial site. But in that rejection I want also to open a back door to current critical practice, to *theory*, opening a way out for the affect theory has bottled in, an outlet for the full range of feeling critique has boiled down to anger.

To open that way, I begin by defining my three crucial terms: Dickens, Adaptation, and Grotowski.

DICKENS

To begin, *After Dickens* reads Dickens generously, that is as a kind of idiot savant. He could do brilliantly one or two of the things that few of us can do at all – like write prose that actually improves when read aloud. But he couldn't do at all most of the things that most of us do without thinking, like think. The brilliant Winnicottian Adam Phillips has cannily observed that "psychoanalytic writing finds it difficult to show that everyone else is not like everyone else" (Phillips 1994: 36). And most kinds of non-psychoanalytic contemporary critical writing find it equally "difficult" to show that everyone is not like everyone else in some fundamental sort of group, linked by gender, or race, or class, or more recently by sexual orientation. This is because most of what we mean by thinking turns out to be some form of *slotting*, taking a category as more significant than the individual item being organized within the slot. It's slotting that makes it possible not only to organize, but to explain and to predict human behavior. Dickens doesn't think – actually I think that he can't think – precisely because he resists with all the force of unmitigated childish narcissism any and every claim of the slot on the self.

It's not simply that in life and in fiction Dickens separates from the group at every opportunity – the Inimitable Boz – but that he can't underwrite any sort of category as normative or determinative or even helpful. This insistence on unconditioned idiosyncrasy makes him, in all of his writing, and much of his life, remarkably, even absurdly, and certainly proudly *childish*. He did after all proclaim the goal of life to be finding ways to "preserve ourselves from growing" ("Where We Stopped Growing," *Household Words*, January 1, 1853) – a goal he largely succeeded in achieving. That's why George Orwell was right to say that Dickens had no ideas. And it is why his fiction has provided such a fertile field of incoherence for Derrideans a while back and more recently for Foucauldians. Seeing Dickens as an idiot savant, then, means that we should treat him not as a genius in the Romantic sense but as a *monstre sacré*, whose performance we'll use Grotowski to adapt, that is to desecrate (*sacré*) and gore (*monstre*).

Dickens himself is also deeply concerned with *adaptation*. Like Darwin, he is attracted to Nature's "sports" – the bizarre, unexpected, dazzling adaptations, the eccentric individuals marked off from the mass. Indeed,

Dickens's characteristic plot is very like Darwin's, the orphaned stand-out's story of rapid change and adaptation in response to the vicissitudes of a cruel and competitive environment. But where Darwin prizes adaptation *to* circumstances, Dickens insists on adapting *against* them. Generalized Darwinian adaptation is driven by the need to save a species. But about the species, or any thing of that ilk, childish Dickens could hardly care less. He is driven only and supremely by the child's care for self.

Look at *A Tale Of Two Cities*, written while Dickens was adapting himself to survive the flop of his domestic life by taking up a distinctly asocial liaison with the actress Ellen Ternan. The ostensible hero, Charles Darnay, returns altruistically to revolutionary France from his work as a teacher in England, confident that he can intervene for the private and for the general good. His blind choice virtually destroys himself and his family. Sydney Carton, his self-absorbed double, follows Darnay, cynically dupes the revolutionary authorities, and winds up turning himself into a sort of Messiah – "It is a far, far better thing" – redeeming not the fallen history of the French people or the more generalized cause of liberty but his own tarnished self-image, and in the process purloining Darnay's family to become, in effect, his own. Carton literally adapts himself into the progenitor to a line of adulating, eponymous followers, in a setpiece of megalomania simply staggering in its narcissistic grandiosity. "I see" Darnay's child, bearing "my name . . . winning his way up in the path of life . . . so well, that my name is made illustrious there by the light of his," and finally "bringing a boy of my name . . . to this place . . . [to] tell the child my story, with a tender and a faltering voice" (*Tale*, p.404) and so on through the annals of time. No greater love hath any Dickensian man than that he lay down his life for himself. If generalized adaptation means a forgetting, a leaving-behind, to make a different future possible, Dickensian adaptation means always remaking the future as a way of refinding that past, re-funding what the individual adaptor cannot bear to lose, the precious and individual self.

A Tale of Two Cities tells us then a tale of two sorts of adaptation. Darnay, the instructor in language, is a figure for thinking, for generaliz-ation, for those vulnerabilities to the slot that sap energy from Dick-ensian life. He is *gamous*, deeply invested in reproduction and genealogy: nephew, husband, father, son-in-law, in almost all of those relations disastrous and disaster-producing. And he is also deeply susceptible to the *mythic*, drawn by the appeal of historical change, to the illuminating narrative of cause and effect which the novel can only condescendingly dismiss as the Lodestone Rock. Finally, he is *theoretical*, no surprise in a teacher, that is someone who insists on yielding himself up to Law, in this case, both English and French law, someone who must permit himself to be identified, classified, imprisoned and condemned by in-eradicable marks of class and manner (the Frenchman, the aristocrat). In contrast, cannily *agamous* Carton centers a story that relies on features we can call *episodic* and *mimetic*. He not only survives but triumphs by his imaginative manipulation of discontinuities. His narrative depends on episodes, on the gaps that baffle rather than the seams that connect. And he wins by miming, by regularly and heroically pretending to be somebody else, competently basing his success in performance rather than identity.[1]

These three stances, agamous, the episodic, the mimetic, make a deep appeal to the adaptor in me, so deep that I'm eager to risk arguing that Dickens's enduring and essential claim on the attention of readers roots precisely in his *childish* rejection of thought. The agamous characterizes the actual child; the episodic and the mimetic seem to return us to something like the childhood of the race, to a moment before written language, before history, before culture. Reading Dickens, then, en-gages us in a determined turning away from what has become our dominant cognitive experience, the homogenizing culture of "the hy-brid modern mind" (Donald 1991: 359). His childish, pleasure-seeking eccentrics do all they can to refuse to be included in "the massive statistical and mathematical models and projections routinely run by governments" (p. 355). His episodic narratives can't be assimilated by the narrative-theoretical mind that produces science, law, economics and history. They catch us up – not in a conventional bourgeois idyll, but – in something deeply primitive and aberrant, in what he called in *Pickwick* "the delusions of our childish days" (xxviii: 375).[2]

While it may be easy, or at least easier, to feel this rapture could happen in reading the early and incomparably comic *Pickwick*, I want to make my argument more demanding and insist that we have the same experience when we read even the darker, later novels. Or to put it more accurately: we have to let ourselves have the same childish experience when reading the later novels if we want to feel glad we happen to be reading them. Clearly, a great many people who make their life's undertaking to study the Victorian novel don't feel that way, bringing to that undertaking something like an undertaker's frame of mind.

Let's look for a moment more closely at these three categories.

The agamous: There are people needing other people but, maugre

Barbra Streisand, there are people who need themselves more. How much harm we'd prevent if we'd get over thinking it's only the flawed or the weak who never get over preferring themselves. Another way to describe the agamous personality might very well be to call it "the unethical imagination . . . the creative spirit perverted by self-interest" (Stewart 1974: 67). But the moral view is distinctly not a view agamy would choose to embrace. Indeed, I want to argue that the line between the gamous and the agamous probably goes deeper and makes more of a difference than the more conventional boundaries between straight and gay or between feminine and masculine. Certainly, Dickens's protean imagination refuses to believe that loving men might be the only alternative to loving or to not loving women, or, of course, vice versa. Instead, with reckless and unrelenting perversity (a good term here) he continually retrieves and resuscitates eros in a dazzling range of eccentric forms, forms frequently forced to masquerade in what intolerant societies will accept as the real thing. But behind those masks, and sometimes out of them, Dickens gives his heart to agamy.

Agamy detests everything the marriage plot depends on. And it doesn't care very much for romance either. Agamy is the Shaker dream. Not necessarily averse to sex, agamy loathes and fears union. Thus, happy families in Dickens, unless they're very poor, have always first lost a spouse. Dickensian happiness is incompatible with regularized intercourse. It dreams the happiness of untouchables safely at play in the glory of *noli me tangere*, of egos who don't need solitude to feel supreme. Agamy's about being self-sufficient even while feeding one's appetites. Sometimes it's nasty, as in the myth of Narcissus, agamy's poster boy and the prototype not only of selfish Carton but of Dickensian alter-egos like Davy and Pip. But quite frequently, from Pickwick to Boffin, it's nice, avuncular, grandfatherly, and kind.

Nor is agamy unique to childish Dickens. Inevitably it pervades much of British Romantic and post-Romantic literature where an unassuageable nostalgia for childhood is virtually *the* literary subject. (The other great subject being snobbery. Which helps explain why any right-minded British adult would prefer to remain [even] a British child.) We find agamy coursing metaphysically through most of Wordsworth – how happy to be lonely as a cloud – and in the best of Shelley and Keats – Oh to be a wind, ah to be an urn, how simply lovely to be a bird. Unsurprisingly, it is everything to professionally chaste Hopkins: each man does the thing he is. *Wuthering Heights* is its charter. You find agamy nowhere determinative in Charlotte Brontë or George Eliot, who can't or won't imagine unmediated happiness. But it's all over Conan Doyle and Carroll and Kipling. Nor is it a merely a Victorian phenomenon. Agamy is key to Shaw, to Joyce, to Woolf, and – it's too obvious to mention – to Barrie: to anyone whose ideal of happiness is a room – or a land, even a never-never land – of one's own. And it remains the driving force in the fiction of Iris Murdoch and Muriel Spark – both of whom, not coincidentally – have written terrific continuations of *Peter Pan*.

The episodic A gamous culture is also, necessarily, rigorously continuous. It can't admit a kiss is just a kiss. It won't let time go by. Instead, it keeps on insisting we'll always have Paris, until it manages to squander all the succulent lubricities Casablanca might sustain. The episodic, in contrast, entertains the delicious possibility of forgetting without loss. Sternly it stares down the psychoanalytic project: the transformative necessity of recovery and recuperation. Adam Phillips sees two sorts of narrative: Freud's and Proust's (Phillips 1994: 13). Freud views everything as stemming from the individual's desire, acknowledged or unacknowledgeable. Proust insists, on the contrary, that only accidents and the unforeseen can create genuine possibilities for epiphany. Phillips favors Proust. But both are narratives of remembrance. And both kinds of narrative the episodic imagination finds suspect. Where and as it can, it refuses them both.

That is why, in part, you can never actually remember a Dickens novel (unless you are Michael Slater). A test: think of the one you know best and try to repeat exactly in order everything that happens. You can't. How could you? And why should you? Dickens offers not a coherent, unified world but (in William James's phrase) a multiverse: particulars, innumerable, unconnected, intensely vivid, a collection of moments rather than a train of events.[3] *Adam Bede*'s narrator undertakes in her opening words to "show" the "reader," "With this drop of ink at the end of my pen," "far-reaching visions of the past." In one sense or another that's exactly what virtually every Victorian novelist offers, except Dickens. Indeed, far from being its typical voice, Dickens turns out to be a highly unlikely Victorian writer, as unlikely a novelist for his time as, say, Arthur Miller is an unlikely playwright for ours.

Childish Dickens, proud master of parts publication, always sides with forgetting, even when he finds that forgetting is not humanly possible. Those who persist in remembering victimize either themselves, like Miss Havisham, or others, like Tulkinghorn, or both, like Miss Havisham and Tulkinghorn. In *A Tale of Two Cities*, most of the harm gets done when people become involved with the Bank, the site of accumulation, accounting, storage, where the present draws on the past. Outside its London office the beheaded are paraded on Temple Bar. In the courtyard of its Paris premises, the Terrorists sharpen their knives. History can only mean repetition. And the Terror merely recreates the horrors of the *ancien régime*. The Terror is all about remembering. When episodic Dickens drops his ink, it's to blot the past out.

The mimetic The *mimetic* is the furthest thing we have from Mimesis. Mimesis makes a cult of the original, of the prior real that can only be examined and then copied in some way that is irretrievably second-hand. But the *mimetic*, as I'm defining it here, refuses the priority of any sort of origin. Carton makes a much more interesting and effective Darnay than Darnay ever could. *Déclassé, arriviste* Dickens always knows that origins contaminate. If you honor them you'll only reach deadlock. Pretending opens the sole path toward presence. All the memorable Dickens characters specialize in pretending. Little Dorrit, Esther Summerson, Pip, they are all first-rate pretenders. They save themselves, and even others, by the skill with which they make believe.

And that mimetic skill is the antithesis of writing. It is not too much to say that Dickens hates writing. His letters make it clear that very shortly after he began his career as a novelist he began to find writing a virtually intolerable burden. And that burden increased beyond toleration as he grew older. I would even claim that his mature life took shape as a flight from writing, a flight, from which he was repeatedly recalled by the necessity to earn his and his increasingly expensive family's, living. There's only one novel in the last decade of his life, when he was at the height of his powers and of his fame, and also when he had the widest possibility for opportunities to earn money apart from writing. What Dickens loved of course was speaking, turning writing into reading aloud. That's certainly what he meant when he claimed at the 1858 Royal Theatrical Fund Dinner that "Every writer of fiction, though he may not adopt the dramatic form, writes in effect for the stage." Not that he loved the stage – which I believe he feared almost as he hated writing – but that he loved speech.

For Dickens, writing and speaking mean entirely different linguistic feats, and all of his sympathy yearns toward the latter. Recent research not only supports the difference between phonological and ideographic alphabet use, but may also provide neurological and sensory grounds for Dickens's preference of the former. The phonological connection between sign and meaning seems more immediate and powerful than the ideogrammatic. Evidence "drawn from studies of the genetically deaf and of both deep and surface dyslexias make it clear that alphabet-based writing . . . follows a parallel but quite different visual or ideographic route [from speech], a route between sign and potential reference more diffuse and various" (Donald 1991: 303–304). Reading calls upon different parts of the brain than hearing, pathways that lack that strong sense of immediate affect produced by responding to speech.

Speech is episodic and individual; writing cumulative and impersonal. Speech relies on the visual/mimetic; writing on the phonetic/symbolic. Speech is expressive; writing merely suggestive. Speech points; writing replaces. Hence those most characteristic features of Dickensian prose: onomatopoeia and paronomasia; parataxis rather than conventional syntax; the increasingly audacious manipulation of the fragment as opposed to the grammatical unit; a rhythm so regular it frequently approaches blank verse, and a persistent reluctance to generate any form of coherent reference. In a prolepsis of that high modernist poetic cliché, Dickens's prose wants to be, not mean. He elides writing for sense into the sheer play of sound. As much as possible within the constraints of narrative, he writes a prose that wants to signify only itself signifying, a prose that refuses to refer.

This inimitably rich play of Dickensian signifiers is always in riot against the constraining claims of the signified, the signs in gleeful revolt against the demands of written representation. In Dickens there is literally no there to imitate, or, rather, the only there in Dickens is a literal there, a word-play there, a trace. At the end of a long passage of Dickensian description, you only think you know what you've seen. Go back and try to draw it; you find the street, the building, the room spontaneously combusts. Its lines won't come together or hang true. Instead, language delightedly, delightfully, dissolves identity, solidity, value in just about every thing and person and place the ambient culture expects to value, name, and prize. In Dickens, then, what you see is what you, inevitably, don't get, can't get because it's just some version of mirage. And if you're naive enough to think you've got something, you are, just as inevitably, a dupe. You're Copperfield letting the wolfish Steerforth into the happy family at Yarmouth. You're Pip trusting Miss Havisham. You're the howling mobs on the Place de la Concorde bloodlusting after Darnay, while a smugly self-congratulating Carton takes his place.

Inevitably, speech is the weapon against the world Dickens's child-heroes most skillfully deploy: Paul Dombey, and David, and most poignantly Pip, whose "infant tongue" refuses the patronymic and therefore "Called myself Pip, and came to be called Pip" (*Great Expectations* I: 35). But writing is the club of the Goliaths, most powerfully instantiated in the law writers of *Bleak House* whose collective name is Nemo, and who busily, endlessly inscribe the tyrannies of Chancery. Against their depersonalized world and the impersonal narrative that describes them, *Bleak House* sets its second, its other, its preferred voice: Esther's narrative which imagines itself not to be writing but speech, direct and immediate address.

Finding it "a great difficulty" to begin to "write [her] portion" of the novel's pages – an instant indication of Dickensian virtue – Esther immediately displaces the act of writing for the recollection of speech. "I can remember, when I was a very little girl indeed, I used to say to my doll, when we were alone together, 'Now Dolly, I am not clever . . .' And so she used to sit . . . staring at me, . . . while I busily stitched away, and told her every one of my secrets" (I: iii, 62). Speech here and everywhere in Dickens belongs to a culturally prior and therefore – to the *childish* mind – a more authentic oral-narrative mode of cognition-representation. Unlike writing which is always in and of the past, speech takes place in a continuous present and offers at least the illusion of real presence, of an affective liaison among speaker, subject and audience. Esther knows her doll is looking at Nothing but that does not disenable her from the verbal tasks at hand, in the nursery or in the novel.

Writing, however, is trauma. Writing, inevitably, betrays the promise of language. It longs to lapse entirely into an *infinite caricaturing of woe* (*Tale* I:xiv, 189), a prime instrument of Terror, sorting not only subject but speaker within the deadening realm of the theoretical, the legal, the external and the collective. That certainly seems to be how we are asked to read the crucial episode of Dr. Manette's memoirs in *A Tale of Two Cities*. Imprisoned in the Bastille, Manette has written down and hidden away the true story of his persecution at the hands of the Evremondes. Much later in the novel, he succeeds before the tribunal of the Terror when he speaks movingly for life of the Evremonde heir, now his son-in-law. But that release is immediately reversed when the Defarges produce the written history, snatched from concealment by Defarge during the Fall of the Bastille. Suddenly, nothing Manette can do or say in the present can save his family from the deadly writing of the past. Writing has rendered him literally speechless, enrolled him in the lists of the "dumb" (p.322). The inscribed word, separated from the speaker-audience bond, takes on a perverse life of its own, a life of the theoretical and impersonal system the Terror delights to generate. His own writing comes back upon Manette like Laocoön's serpents, writhing, coiling, crushing his life and the lives of his children, overwhelming any effort he can make against their sinuous claims. Only the improvisational comedy of Carton's silent mimesis can save the Manettes from the consequences of their tendency toward prose.

But nothing can relieve Dickens himself from the burden of writing. He must write though he longs to speak, longs for the other position even as he is repeatedly forced to recognize his insuperable dependence on the form he views not merely with suspicion but with disdain and fear – hence the inexhaustible, exhausting obsession with the public readings. If he's got to write the damned stuff out first, at least he will redeem that compromise by endlessly, exhaustively reading it aloud. Speech making up for past print. But it doesn't. The reading aloud is always a reading of what has been written. In the same way the parts become volumes. The episodes construct plot. And the agamous routinely surrenders itself to be swallowed up in some version of marriage and reproduction.

Carton is Dickens's only completely successful agamous protagonist, and he has to die to achieve agamy's completion. Dickens's usual story is more likely to be some version of Pip's. Pip starts off dreaming himself a sort of little god who can name his own I Am. He believes he inhabits a world where language has the immediate clarity of pointing, thus approximating the earliest stage of writing (lists) where the symbols and what they express seem one. "The shape of the letters on my father's [tombstone], gave me an odd idea that he was a square, stout, dark man, with curly black hair. From the character and turn of the inscription, '*Also Georgiana Wife of the Above*,' I drew a childish conclusion that my mother was freckled and sickly" (*Great Expectations* I: 35). Nothing is arbitrary where the look of letters, their sound, their meanings are all the same. There is no significant lack or gap. But that *childish* world is in fact a grave. Over it Pip immediately finds himself, pulled upside down by Magwitch, even as he attempts to read further. Magwitch not only robs and starves him but seems to castrate him as well, emptying his pockets. The child cannot resist. He becomes not only enthralled but even made the unwilling son to that superior adult power, which the world reads as the Father and which Dickens reads as Shame.

Virtually everything in Dickens turns on shame, or, rather, on this contest between shame and bliss, a contest bliss always loses (except, patently, in Carton's "Tale") but which shame also never quite wins. In this contention, shame names the internal, apparently insuperable drive that insists the Child become a Father in order to be a Man, that he enter the ritualized scenarios of courtship and reproduction that allow organized life to deploy him as it wills. Conversely, bliss names the possibility that the Child is not Father to but the Man Himself, that he retains into adult life the power to disrupt the all-encompassing scenarios of cause and effect – subordinating, integrational, teleological, to remain indomitably selfpreferring and proudly solo (if not precisely single). It's this notion of bliss that's always out there beckoning from Heights like Emily Brontë's. But Charles Dickens is no Emily Brontë. He is too committed to making it in the world, to making it big in the world, to permit himself that dubious flight onto the moors. Those moors, his moors, he's terrified must inevitably turn out to feel, if not look, a lot like the Marshalsea. (Isn't that the main thrust of the Alpine episode in *Little Dorrit?*) And yet, at the same time, and with the same passion, he's too thoroughly invested in this childishness (a more technical term for which is, of course, narcissism) ever to surrender easily or entirely to the canons, mythic, theoretical, gamous, of realism. He compromises instead.

One way to describe that compromise is to say that Dickens *adapts*. Outlining the form of that adaptation will take us much of the remainder of this book. Suffice it to look here at the recurring Dickensian version of playing Happy Families. What we see is that it's never the case that Dickens speaks "for" and "from the hearth," if hearth means the ordinary bourgeois experience of a traditional domestic order (D. A. Miller 1988: 82). No, the intact family hearth invariably means misery in these novels. From Dingley Dell, to – preeminently – Bleak House, and finally to the Nuns House at Cloisterham, Dickens prefers instead a career-long series of parody-hearths, hearths-as-it-were, hearths under adaptation. All these places function more like cloisters than homes, with Mothers and Fathers to be sure, but these are reverend mothers and very reverend fathers, superiors in the rituals of agamy rather than parents engaged not only in but by reproduction. At these parody hearths, "deeply damaged characters whose core sense of self is devastated or almost nonexistent" play at parody families (Kohut 1985: 158). There they fulfill that most Dickensian of desiderata: they Stop Growing. They enclose themselves in bliss apart from the adult world, erecting elaborate and "destructive defenses" not only against their own "drives" but also against all those "adult" characters driven by instinct who might assert against their fragile fantasies the imperatives of shame.

ADAPTATION

But must we go on to performance? Why can't we stick with the page, with critique, with argument? After all, isn't acting merely artifice, the sugar-substitute when the real sweetness of experience has already been abjured? No, that's the Puritan notion of acting, the idea of acting common to all those isms that have misread the importance of being earnest. Done well, acting is, as Hollis Huston claims, the closest thing we have to the examined life (Huston 1992: 6). And we can't stick to the page, critique, argument, for exactly the reasons that prevent us from cutting directly to the therapeutic cure without going through all that messy business of transference. We can't settle merely for thinking because, sadly but bluntly, no one has ever been changed only by an idea. We can be interested in and by an idea, of course, but we are only changed by an idea in performance.

The triumphant rise of therapy in our culture roots largely in the corresponding decline of our theater. "Must you be so theatrical," we ask self-righteously, equating theatricality with excessive and inauthentic feeling, and vice versa. No clearer sign alerts us to the continuing Utilitarianism of our post-industrial era than this deeply conditioned, self-defensive dread of extreme emotion. But emotion must be siphoned off somehow, banned from public and authentic expression increasingly into secret sessions of private shame. Theatre, and what theatre used to express, have become for us the compost on which therapy thrives.

We operate now within a public culture trained to get over grief as quickly as possible, taught to cope rather than to mourn, and, as Harry explained to Sally, to go home as soon as possible on the morning after the night before. We learn to keep our distance, in order to keep our selves intact. Deep feeling ties you down. And rather than being tied down, gain the advantage by putting down the other guy first. Billy Crystal: the implicit master of all the ceremonies of our contemporary lives. The put-down: *Aporia*'s popular cousin. It is as though we are terrified that feeling, any sort of strong feeling, can and must in the end lead only to a post-cathartic emptiness. Feeling finally can only let you feel let down.

Without access to affect we are left – and we have left those we train – without either the stimulus or training to respond with complex feelings to complex texts. Not a problem if human beings could be moved to live well, to behave generously, to seek justice, through disinterest or abstraction. I am not thinking here only of the great public choices but of the perhaps even more significant choices that foster healthy and durable intimacies, choices that are perhaps even more at risk the way we live and read now. Choice always follows from feeling. Complex choices from complex feelings. And that shaping of complex feelings has been from the beginning of culture, not only Western culture, the particular province of literature.

Of course, if I want to dude things up, I can try to defend these assertions by identifying my position with what Mary Louise Pratt has called a "linguistics of contact," her phrase for the endeavor to gain "a linguistics and a criticism whose engagement with the social world is not confined" either to the "utopian" or the "dystopian" (Pratt 1987: 64). Her "linguistics of contact" calls for an essentially intra- and inter-cultural contact, a way to connect severed communities now almost exclusively focused on their differences, and on the history of outrages that have generated those differences. However my kinds of contact, between text and performance, between author and adaptor, between actors and audiences, are far less global. Nevertheless, my notions of adaptation do overlap Professor Pratt's in a kind of shared horror at criticism's vertiginous fascination with the Frankensteinian specter of *aporia*.

Yearning toward *aporia* slants academic effort and prestige heavily toward a poetics of lamentation and denunciation, a more or less exclusive focus on the impasse, the dead-end, the stone that keeps a crypt a tomb. It's a focus that risks doing to literary studies what logical positivism earlier did to – at least, British – philosophy, submitting discourse to a hermetic critique so rigorous and scathing that the discipline itself ceases to matter to anyone outside the professional field. Obviously, there's an urgent need to unmask and frustrate the hegemonic asymmetries persuasively, sometimes invisibly, seeping from the texts of both elite and popular culture. But what really requires resisting, I think, is not literature itself but a model of literature, common to both older and contemporary criticism, that generates *aporia* by mistakenly treating literature as a branch of epistemology.

Literature is, of course, not an epistemology, as Plato acknowledged when he banished the artists. He understood, in his inimitably mean-spirited way, that far from being a part of philosophy, art is philosophy's implacable foe. The offspring of sly craft and idle play, literature always sides with rhetoric against philosophy, sides with doing against thinking, feeling against reason, acting against mere knowing. Of course, no one would ever have forgotten this were it not for the Cartesian curricula of the French lycées.

Literature always prefers a way to a truth, any day, even when the way leads only to trouble. That means literature constitutes an instance of what the Greeks called a *poros*, literally "a way," which "unlike contemplative philosophy" – as Bruce Robbins has argued about *poros* generally – offers "a practical and professional know-how associated not with universals but with particular local situations of conflict, danger and rapid change, like those of the navigator, the doctor, the athlete, the politician, and the sophist" (Robbins 1990: 229). Literature then is a *poros* in two senses. One way, as a craft, is the "know-how" to do ingenious things with words, as navigators do things with winds and tides, or doctors with blood and muscle. The other way, as a style: literature is *poros* that offers a practical guide to mistrusting wisdom, doubting knowledge, suspecting counsel, sidestepping understanding, and generally keeping out of the way of oracles, a way, then, of constructing sturdy plots and of being, as actors say, in the moment.

Literature opens this *poros* by persuading, inciting, exciting, moving, enchanting, all the stances philosophy loathes, cold, remote, disdainfully theoretic philosophy. (By philosophy I mean here, it goes without saying, the post-Heideggerian, anti-humanist, largely French amalgam that angles so eagerly for what Peter Dews following Max Weber has recently called "the disenchantment of the world" [Dews 1995: 159].) Like philosophy literature makes us think, but entirely unlike philosophy it does so because first it makes us feel. And mostly it makes us feel how little we learn or accomplish when we, only, think. Certainly literature loses all potential to make any kind of real difference to its readers when denied the power to provoke strong response.

But strong response is precisely what the Theory Shop seems determined to contain. Affect, as Elin Diamond says about catharsis, always "situates the subject at a dangerous border," a border where being is in some way "seized," seized by the text, or its subject, or our own vulnerabilities, causing us to "suffer a disturbance in the totalizing vision that affirms consciousness and mastery" (Diamond 1995: 154). Of course, never before has criticism been so absorbed in defending that "totalizing vision" of its own autonomous mastery, even as it works to defenestrate any viable notion of the individual subject. Inevitably, then, never before has criticism felt so threatened by the dangers that lurk at the crossing between thinking and feeling, knowing and being known.

Richard Wolin has recently written illuminatingly of the way so much of the most advanced theoretical argument, in literary, historical and cultural studies, clings to the "inordinately dispirited images" that derive from "Foucault's cheerless image of a 'carceral society'." Repeatedly, he shows, the most advanced thinking prefers to align itself with "a vision of utopian possibility that resides beyond the fallen and desolate landscape of the historical present," rather than "to activate elements of the past for the sake of an emancipated future" (Wolin 1995: 57). Obviously, this is not the place to get into the vexed business of Habermas v. Foucault, so I will limit myself here only to asking whether Wolin does not seem to be pointing in this willed bleakness to a choice that adumbrates the classic Freudian forking between eros and thanatos. We seem to be torn between a demand to feel which forces us under the other's sway and an overpowering need to feel nothing at all rather than giving way to that which we can't predict or predicate. Reread in this way, criticism's anti-feeling defense seems to imagine as our only effective, not to say affective, alternatives the interclasped terms that will shape much of the argument that follows: self-protecting narcissism or empty-hearted shame.

In moving away from this dilemma toward annexing affect to thought, we have to realize that not every sort of adaptation will do equally well. Brecht warned that "Literary works cannot be taken over like factories" (1964: 108). By that he did not mean that "literary works" should not be taken over at all, only that they are harder to take over than gas and similar sorts of works. But the adaptor's challenge remains profoundly revolutionary as Brecht understood revolution: to expropriate the original owner of the work, the author, and thus free up its hoarded resources for a different sort of distribution.

Obviously, that sort of adaptation works toward goals very different from the adaptations we are used to: alright I'll be brutal, by the sort we tend to import from the United Kingdom. I'm by no means making a blanket charge against all British-based adaptation. The Glasgow Citizens' Theater has recently shown exactly the kind of innovative, provocative, radical reading adaptation should produce in its brilliant mounting of Giles Havergal's all-male, four-performer adaptation of Graham Greene's picaresque *Travels With My Aunt*. Nor would I wish to leave the impression that the contemporary American theatre offers no models for the kinds of adaptation I'm endorsing. The contrary is clearly demonstrated by work like Mary Zimmerman's extraordinarily inventive adaptation of *The Arabian Nights* for twelve performers, originally at Lookingglass Theatre in Chicago, and later at the Manhattan Theater Club. Of course, it is not incidental that the production originated in Chicago, the real home of innovative theatre in the USA.

And I'm certainly not thinking here of unpretentious, clearly commercial enterprises like the musical versions of *Oliver Twist* and *Edwin Drood*, or the endlessly spun-out versions of *A Christmas Carol*. No, scandalously, I want to impeach the virtually hypercritical status of adaptations like the ambitious and high-minded, not to mention long-winded, RSC *Nicholas Nickleby*, as well as comparably monumental screen and video presentations like the Alec Guinness–Derek Jacobi *Little Dorrit* and the Diana Rigg–Trevor Howard *Bleak House*. These standard-setting adaptations are all far more colonizing than revolutionary. They intervene to subsume, not to subvert, to profit from rather than share out the resources at hand. They eagerly do the work of shame.

But the RSC *Nickleby* is explicitly Brechtian, you have just said! It's got *Verfremdungseffekt* you can eat with a spoon. It's about the Poor! For what more can one ask? My answer is: we want an adaptation that remembers most clearly what Dickens seems to be struggling hardest to forget – bliss, and an adaptation that forgets just as energetically what Dickens insists on remembering – shame. Adaptations that are themselves insistently agamous, episodic, and mimetic. Adaptations that release the heroic energies of the self-loving self to perform its self-inventions in whatever arrangements it chooses to contrive. Or, if it can't manage that – and none of the adaptations in this book do – then we want an adaptation which might mark off clearly for us how much we lose when we buy into what Dickensian shame has to offer. An adaptation that understands that the mimetic gives life, and that mimesis kills.

Aristotle famously insists that effective drama requires both mimesis and catharsis. But adaptation regularly, and often even obsessively, fetishizes only mimesis. Conventional adaptations, like the ones I've just named, *imitate* the original text's *imitation* of life, imagining that it's in that imitation that the text's bliss resides. They solidify a fiction's figures and spaces and plots into bodies and places and lives. But these real bodies in apparently real settings inevitably "naturalize" fiction into specimen. They can tend either toward *verismo*: "Did you know that every one of those extras is wearing authentic period underwear; can you imagine the itch." Or toward the stylized: "Oh look! How well they are pretending to be people riding in a crowded carriage! And it's only a kitchen table. Isn't that amazing!" Either way: we see the plot's pain but we feel only admiration. In conventional adaptation particularly our interest becomes monopolized by a simulation of life so life-like it stops us from wondering if life, on these terms, should be liked at all. That's why of course the favorite American slot for adaptations like these is TV at the end of a Sunday evening, preferably in winter: the Cocoa hour.

A doubled mimesis invariably cripples catharsis. It forfeits those elements in the original form which stimulated feeling without feeling free to invent new and dramatic forms which can stimulate the production's own specific affect. The successful, in the sense of powerful, adaptation knows – since it is exchanging spaces – that it must in fact change the space, particularly the space of fiction. Theatre takes shape as fiction's foe. Even with writers far less evasive than Dickens, it is the business of fiction to elude crystallization, to distend, to postpone, to submerge. That's both the fascination and the glory of its form.[4] Indeed, as Bert O. States claims, "part of the liberty of the novel form" roots in its ability "to put perspectives on top of perspectives, to reach out in philosophical, biographical, societal, and most commonly, descriptive directions that lie behind the scene and the action" (States 1985: 136). In fiction such digressions and delays usually feel interest-enhancing and theme-enriching. But in the theatre they just as usually feel digressive, tangential, drifting. The general, indeed the generic, business of the stage is to embody, to clarify, to present: to stand and deliver.

This is a matter of epistemology as well as of affect. For all the misreadings of the Aristotelian unities, there is a sense in which Aristotle was right. Drama must observe a unity of action. It is so hard to pay attention to as it moves along. We can't slow down, let alone stop. We can't check back. We can't pause to ponder. We can't clarify or refer. And so even in the most experimental and avant- garde sorts of play we require a clarity and intensity of focus on action, so that we can begin the process of interpretation with some degree of assurance that at least we know what is happening even if we do not yet, or never will know, what it means. And it's only that sort of clarity which will provide the foundation for a strong audience response. It is hard to care in any way about that which we find merely baffling. What in the novel is all suggestion in the powerful emptiness between the markings on the page must, on the stage, make itself seen to be felt.

But what I don't want to feel is what Henry James liked to get from St. Peter's in Rome. "You think you have taken the whole thing in, but it expands, it rises sublime again, and leaves your measure itself poor." As his friend Clover Adams joked, James always enjoyed chewing more than he could bite off. But even for appetites less gourmandising than James', there's a way in which, when any master's work *expands*, the rest of us seem to wind up feeling somehow diminished. For the work of this book, therefore, I prefer a spatial model very different from either Aida's pyramid or James' St. Peter's.

Here's what I like. "Twined round the grand apartments in the Ducal Palace at Mantua is a series of smaller rooms where a person of normal height must stoop and finds beautifully chiselled doorframes awkward to get through. These rooms butting on ones of normal size were constructed for the court dwarfs" (Harbison 1988: 28). Obviously, as Dickens's adapter, I play dwarf to his superb Duke – though this dwarfing may be a back way to Verdi, to that other Mantuan Court freak, the insubordinate Rigoletto. But I am also Duke (dux, leader) to the *childish* Dickens who Stopped Growing, and to all those dwarfish characters he styled in his self-image, selves "that have stayed behind . . . deliberately . . . a heroism like that of Carroll playing with his schoolgirls" (Harbison 1988: 22).[5]

The "inter*twining*" of the two kinds of space establishes a paradigm of adaptation. Harbison rightly keys on the dwarves' beautifully chiselled doorframes as the defining objects in the complex space. The framed doors refuse to cut off dwarfed from ducal, refuse to polarize along the lines of the Jamesian poor measure and the Petrine sublime. Instead, they enforce beautifully a need always to be moving in and on, what Harbison notes as the crucially double rhythm of the doubled space, *growing* and *shrinking, tightening* and *relaxing*. The doors open each series into its continuation and its antithesis. They demand our own ongoing negotiation of a never less than awkward passage. That negotiation insists bliss comes from refusing to settle in the norm, ours or another's. Mantua thereby models both the bliss and the task of adaptation: eagerly remembering what one is choosing to forget, all the while forgetting what one has decided keenly to remember.

This doubleness means that Mantua's exquisitely carved, always inviting doorways refuse *aporia*. They insist instead that we adapt: outgrow, intervene in, modify, adjust, redeploy the original. We get Dickens to outgrow his own, enclosed, great theatres of shame. At the same time we open ourselves to the opportunity of bearing a witness that we can find more satisfying, challenging and inaugural than anything we can achieve with a strict and faithful copy. To generate that witness, we turn to the radically alternative performance agenda developed as Poor Theatre by the great Polish director Jerzy Grotowski. We construct this agenda by combining accounts of Grotowski's own adaptations (1960–70) with the theoretical arguments in his epic *Towards a Poor Theatre* (1968). Together they offer the most powerful and persuasive contemporary model I know for capturing the goal at the core of this book's project, the bliss that seeks to move beyond theoretical *aporia*: to retain the enormous affective power of Dickens's episodic and mimetic inventions, but at the same time to refuse his deep investment in the disenfranchising structures of shame.

AND GROTOWSKI

Introducing their collection of essays on *Performativity and Performance*, Andrew Parker and Eve Kosofsky Sedgwick ask: "When is saying something doing something? And how is saying something doing something?" (Parker and Sedgwick 1995: 1). Interesting as those questions may be, I think we're likely to get more useful answers for performance, certainly for adaptation, if we revise them to ask something like: "When is telling something doing something? And how does telling something get something done?" Telling may be a form of saying but it is not the same as saying. Saying can happen in a void, it requires no audience. Telling, however, always assumes a told-to. There is always a response to telling, even if it is only the very response no teller wants – You lie! I don't believe you! Anyone trained for the stage, any stage, knows that only poor actors only *say*. Knowing actors always *tell*, their scene-partner, if they have one, but in every case, the audience.

Failing to mark that distinction between telling and saying is what causes the usually keen J. L. Austin to get theatre thoroughly wrong in his famous dismissal of stage-speech as parasitic. He sees the actors speaking to each other on the stage and knows that, in that narrow room, they make nothing happen. But he refuses to see that their speech is actually directed at an audience, and, in so far as they are skilled at what they do, those actors must of course be producing affect. Masters of perlocution, they are stirring, rousing, thrilling, exciting, irritating, angering, appeasing – the list goes on – the audience. Affect, we may well claim, is the intended effect of all their telling. If we doubt this, we need only think of the long history of theatre riots. Or of theatre censorship.

But my point here is not the obvious one that stage-speech stirs. We've known that since Aristotle. I'm interested in the more telling point that successful stage speech, entirely perlocutionary, inevitably affective, can never guarantee the effect at which it aims. The audience not only always can, but frequently does, resist. Think of poor shamed Henry James at the curtain call to *Guy Domville*. Or Yeats at the Abbey

Riots. Nor do theatre audiences think and feel as one. It is different of course in the much more deliberately manipulative experience of film. Film apparatus not only makes us see as one, it also induces us to feel as one. But stage audiences rarely bond. That divergence results from what Timothy Gould calls "perlocutionary gap," the gap between the intention and effect of a speech act (Gould 1995: 31). In terms of theatre, it's the gap between saying and telling. Cinema works to make that gap as narrow as possible. But the conditions of stage action make perlocutionary gap an inevitable feature of all live performance. Indeed, perlocutionary gap is the problem much of drama theory sets out to overcome. But, for our purposes, perlocutionary gap is the break through which adaptation arrives.

And that's precisely why, for its model of adaptation *After Dickens* must turn, regretfully, away from Brecht. No figure in twentieth-century theatre argues more intelligently or wittily for the necessity of critique than does Brecht. It is his greatest achievement to have resoldered the long-rusted link between theatre and thought. Why, then, isn't this chapter called "Dickens, adaptation and Brecht"?

Of course, as co-heirs to the reformation of theatre begun by Stanislavski and Meyerhold, Brecht and Grotowski have an enormous amount in common: Grotowski, as he explicitly claims, completing Stanislavski's reformation of actors' training; Brecht continuing, indeed plagiarizing, Meyerhold's contrary theatre of alienation. (But, then, again, whom didn't Brecht plagiarize – except, perhaps, Stanislavski?) All of these reformers work to secure the theatre's position within modernism, by repositioning the spectator within the theater. They break from a theatre of "the fourth wall," rigidly typological, relentlessly presentational, a theatre that is – only – watched, the "evident meeting . . . of story and picture" (Meisel 1983: 3). In this new, modern theatre, not only do the spectators become part of the work of performance but the key goal of that performance becomes the spectators' transformation. Of course, nineteenth-century theatre aimed to move its audience, but it always kept its audience moving more or less in place, passively stimulated, unchanged, indeed unchallenged, in feeling or belief. A theatre of the churn. But self-consciously modern theatre set out to make things not only new but different, to make something happen, in the audience even more than on the stage. And that is where Brecht and Grotowski part company. Both passionate advocates of transformation, they nevertheless mean by transformation radically different sorts of change.

Brecht's theatre is fundamentally indicative, a theatre, as he so often said, of quotation. Its transformations are public, political, ideologic. Top-down, Socratic, Brecht aims to take the spectator, not merely figuratively, out of him or herself to a position Brecht knows is better. He is "concern[ed]," as his notes to *Mother Courage* explain, "that the spectator should see" (Brecht 1955: 120). See what? The reverse of "those who look on at catastrophes wrongly" (p. 119). Brecht's theatre teaches us then to see the (Brecht's) truth, and that is a truth that not only suspects but demonizes every sort of affect. For Brecht, affect merely confirms the individual in mirage-like, deleterious subjectivity, "in an imaginary coherence . . . the condition of which is the ignorance of the structure of his production, of his setting in position" (Heath 1992: 234). Affect keeps "the masses" passive, "objects" of stimulation, and "so long as the masses are the *objects* of politics they cannot regard what happens to them as an experiment but only as a fate" (Brecht 1955: 120). If the audience is to be transformed, the theatre must break from this misleading realm of feeling by a ceaseless process of distanciation, a distancing from all that is private, personal, interior, individual, from everything the self might (mistakenly) label and cherish as its own.

It's that same self that Grotowskian transformation labors not to repudiate but to mobilize. Grotowski's theatre, fundamentally affective, is also fundamentally interrogative. It has no answers, only questions. In fact, it asks only one question, repeatedly, powerfully, even savagely hurled at the spectator: how do you feel about this? To that question it has no answers of its own. Indeed, it repudiates the notion that any one answer would be the goal of any such process of interrogation. (And here, if we are still looking out for forebears, we should claim that Grotowski is even more the heir to Freud than he is to Stanislavski, just as Brecht is even more the heir to Marx than he is to Meyerhold. Or better: that each ephebe continues the work of the predecessor largely by mobilizing a theoretical vision to which the pioneer lacked access.) To be truly transformative, Grotowski's theatre insists, each answer must be an individual spectator's own.

That is my position also. Auden, who almost never got anything wrong, surely didn't get it right when, entombing Yeats, he insisted that poetry makes nothing happen. Anyone who knows a certain sort of undergraduate – or Helen Vendler – understands that poetry often makes too much happen. It's theatre that *makes* nothing happen. Theatre does not convert, nor does it prohibit. That's why Grotowski abandoned theatre after 1971, devoting himself thereafter to paratheatrical research in a series of nontheatrical venues around the globe (in theory-crazed spaces like Irvine, California: What could Grotowski himself have thought when he found himself landing at John Wayne International Airport?). Like Brecht, Grotowski wanted to see change effected not merely prepared for. Indeed, Brecht himself, always pragmatic, spent most of his time at the Berliner Ensemble trying to figure out ways to make his plays entertaining, *à rebours* all those theories of alienation. At its best, theatre prepares the ground for action. It prepares that ground by rehearsing – in a phrase recently popularized by Daniel Goleman – our adjustment of "emotional intelligence," an individual's nuanced, continuously jeopardized, constantly tasked capacity to modify emotion by thought, and thought by emotion. It's in the playhouse, supremely, that we get to practice this delicate, endlessly difficult, always imperfect balance. Simply put, theatre prepares us to care intelligently about life. And it's more or less up to the rest of culture to manage the outcome. The preparation alone is task enough for theatre. Thus I find myself, paradoxically, more loyal to Poor Theatre than its inventor. Where others later sow, I'm happily content to harrow.

So I don't mind that Grotowski is likely to seem *vieux jeu* to many in the contemporary theatre (as *vieux jeu* as saying *vieux jeu*). He is generally thought to have made his contribution, largely to actors' training, twenty years ago, and has pretty much vanished along with other gurus of the late 'sixties and early 'seventies. Grotowski himself contributed to that eclipse by abandoning theatre just as he achieved an international reputation. Complicating that choice, his retirement coincided with the notorious failure of the 1968 revolutions to generate the wholesale transformation of bourgeois culture that had seemed the logical next step in the development of modernism. (As a counter, it's tonic to examine a work like Laura Jones's *Nothing Except Ourselves: The Harsh Times and Bold Theatre of South Africa's Mbongeni Ngema* [1994], to gain a sense of how Grotowski can contribute to a society in which theatre continues to play a vital part.)

Even aside from seeming dated, Poor Theatre does not lack its own intrinsic problems. As a director-manager, Grotowski seemed unable to center a play on a woman; indeed, he invariably staged women as those two stale types, the temptress and the whore. And his insistence on transgression (about which more in a moment) can border dangerously on the masochistic. Finally, both his productions and his theories are profoundly anti-historicist, suffused with dubious notions like the "timeless" and the "essential." That essentialist, anti-feminist, masochistic slant I try to correct in the adaptations I advocate. Thus, as you will see, I deliberately re-center *Bleak House* and *Our Mutual Friend* on the women whose stories the narratives suppress rather than on the ventriloquized women their patriarchies endorse. And I look for every chance to use comedy to counter Grotowski's (not to mention Dickens's) celebration of pain. In effect, I adapt by adapting Grotowski. Nevertheless, I retain, indeed blazon, my loyalty to Poor Theatre. I do so because of the way in which Grotowski heroically preserves that adherence to the individual that seems to me basic to all theatre: unique player connecting powerfully to singular spectator.

This connection relies on two cardinal features of Grotowski's method. He trains actors to make themselves malleable rorschachs within which each spectator uncovers whatever he or she specifically needs – or refuses needing – from that performance. And he constructs performance out of roles not characters, thereby shortcircuiting conventional theatre's fetishistic focus on the idealized subjectivity of a heroic histrionic self. (Which is how he managed to escape the trap that bagged Stanislavski: equating a naturalism of surface with an authentification of inner life.) As a result, rather than striving for unity, Poor Theatre revels in the perlocutionary gap. It designs performance that provokes different, shifting, particular struggles in each spectator, struggles against one's self, one's cultural history, and the cultures that produce those histories, struggles made possible by, but not overdetermined by, affective stimulation. Each audience member "reads" the play for him or herself. Each watcher feels a unique, and intimately personal, response.

The core value here is transgression. (My preferred word, as I've already suggested, would be harrowing.) It is transgression that promotes the goal of transformation. Grotowski's adaptations stage three sorts of successive, and successively interdependent, transgression: of the text, of the performer, of the audience. Indeed, part of Poor Theatre's attraction for this book draws on Grotowski's insistence that the greatest theatre, from the Greeks onward, has always depended on the re-vision of a prior text. His own practice purloined a range of sources from plays by Marlowe and Calderon to chapters of Genesis and The Gospel According to St John. These prior texts the audience should know in advance, yet in the theater they experience not their continuation but their transgression. The adaptations freewheelingly reverse or invert these sources even as they work to retain the original emotional resonance. In turn, the performers transgress their own inhibitions, performing without reserve their deepest and most private feelings. And, finally, the audience members, responding to these violations, experience a profound transgression of their individual and communal self-regulation.

In other forms of modernist theatre practice, Stanislavski's, Brecht's, or – most notably – Artaud's, the performers sustain all this burden of self-transgression, laboring on the audience's behalf: Artaud's famous metaphor of the actor as martyr signaling to us from within the pyre's flames. And, of course, this is the tradition that also generates the theoretical basis, at any rate, for most of contemporary Performance Art. But in Poor Theatre each participant, on stage or off, is called upon to mount in some way his or her own scaffold. The performers' self-transgressions mark merely, sublimely, the inciting incident that sets off an ongoing chain of comparable transgressions incomplete until the entire audience, individual by individual, has shared the affective burden of the performers' task. As Stefan Brecht puts it: "Grotowski's theatre . . . intensely individualist" is concerned "not with an individual but with individuality," not with the received but with the forged or forging self (S. Brecht 1970: 187).

Across the spectator, then, as across the actor and the text, Poor Theatre thus deftly traces a *scalpel*, a key metaphor for Grotowski, to cut away whatever is "banal and stereotyped" (Grotowski 1968: 43), all the dodges, equivocations, prevarications that dare not name their speakers. That anatomizing goes beyond any customary, mere, or safe critical analysis. Even (or perhaps especially) the most advanced sorts of criticism regularly turn out to be something like versions of telephone-sex. They risk nothing for or of the critic, except for the impersonal gestures of reason and resistance. (Criticism does, that is; not telephone sex). But Poor Theatre gives us a model of performance which insists that the scalpel must be wielded not only toward the parent-text but also, effectively and affectively, against the scalpel-wielder. That is: dangerous and necessary, it brings working on texts back into the spectators' main, if bloody, stream.

In Poor Theatre no audience member can hold back, can enforce any emotional limit beyond which she or he will not let the performance reach. Like the actor, the spectator must permit the adaptation to take her or him as its target. In effect, the spectator must permit the self to be adapted also. Eric Bentley, for example, wrote of responding to Grotowski's *Apocalypsis Cum Figuris* in a way that had never happened to him in the theatre before, with feelings so intimate, indeed secret, that he could not without severe embarrassment reveal them in his review. A true Brechtian, he even doubted whether such feelings could be experienced appropriately in the theatre (Kumiega 1985: 149). That's exactly the transgression Grotowski intends: the power of a performance to pierce to a level of affect not only contained, reserved, held back by cultural norms, but in effect reinforced by standard cultural performance.

In his magisterial study of *The Audience* (1990), Herbert Blau argues that Grotowski's own audiences were "not so much instructed as constrained to bear witness." Though the spectators were "close enough to see the actors sweat," "the actors were not playing with or to" the audience (p.34). That is exactly right (and marks clearly Grotowski's break with Brechtian "instruction"). Grotowski demands "the actor must not have the audience as a point of orientation, but at the same time he must not neglect the fact of its presence . . . the essential thing is that the actor must not act *for* the audience, he must act in confrontation with the spectators, in their presence" (1968: 213–214). Grotowski thus wants his audience not merely to witness but to bear witness to what it watches, as one bears witness in attesting to a will or giving an affidavit or contributing evidence. In those instances, as in Poor Theatre, one doesn't simply see, one becomes, knowledgeably and acknowledgeably, part of what one sees. Poor Theatre insists we interpret simultaneously from and against our selves. From our selves because we must respond to performance affectively out of our own private limitations, our own unique sorts of emptiness. Against our selves because the frontiers of our own history are precisely what Poor Theatre aims to transgress. But "In this struggle with one's own truth," Grotowski insists, "this effort to peel off the life-mask," we will "cross our frontiers, exceed our limitations, fill our emptiness."

A phrase which lands us squarely back with Dickens.

AND BACK, THEN, TO DICKENS

To achieve these goals, *After Dickens* traces a genuinely *critical* process of adaptation, perfidious not faithful, transgressive rather than imitative. We show why and how to coax from Dickens's texts something like the performance Lacan argues that therapy must coax from the subject: a radically different sort of witness, the better, more reliable story lurking behind the plausible one that first gets told. Adapting Lacan, we can claim that, like the analyst, the adaptor must beware not to bear false witness. Obviously, the Dickens text is calling on us powerfully and persuasively "to bear witness" (Lacan 1975: 50). It wants us to believe, support, adhere. But warily we should take all such original versions as a kind of "empty speech:" Lacan's term for an account "in which the subject loses himself in the machinations of a system of language, in the labyrinth of referential systems made available to him by the state of cultural affairs to which he is a more or less interested part." Instead, from "this empty speech" we budge the subject (the text-being-adapted) toward a "full speech," the speech that "realises the truth of the subject." For that truth, of course, adaptation can claim no more ontological warrant than can therapy. Truth here simply means, for therapist and adapter alike, that which the subject is hell-bent to evade.[6]

What would that turn out to be like, you well may ask.

Let me try to answer that question, and in the process make concrete much of the tiresomely abstract speculation that has preceded, by briefly outlining how we applied this process in adapting *Bleak House*.

We centered our staging of *Bleak House* on a character from the novel who adapts herself into a character from the stage. Before *Bleak House* begins, Lady Dedlock's sister changes her name to Barbary when she cuts herself off from the world, to raise in secret her sister's bastard, the novel's other heroine and demi-narrator, Esther Summerson. In fact, we never do learn the sisters' maiden name. But why does this recluse call herself Barbary? Not a usual English name. In fact, so unusual a name that it seems to cross purposes with her ostensible desire for absolute anonymity. A Miss Smith or Jones or even Pym faces a fair chance to pass unnoticed, but a Miss Barbary? You're likely to remember the extravagance, the sheer staginess of its self-conscious theatricality. It sticks out like a signpost, a symptom, a name that asks for attention, that asks to be read. And in that name I think I hear Lacan warning me to hear Dickens inadvertently signaling me not to recreate his work. I believe I hear Dickens cautioning me instead to unwrite it and thereby to revive what he dares not openly name, the novel's "sufficiently censored dreamable dream" (Phillips 1994: 24), to finish it as adaptation – that is, in a phrase I adapt from the inimitable Barthes: "To be with the one I love and to think of something else" (Barthes 1975: 24).

I think I'm witnessing in Barbary one of those names that work to conceal an origin while at the same time setting it up in lights: a stage name. The stage named, of course, is *Othello*. Barbary must be naming herself – or, if you wish, Dickens has to be naming her – after the maidservant that Desdemona recalls so pitiably as she is preparing for her death-bed. The only other Barbary I can think of is Richard II's "roan Barbary," the horse Bolingbroke usurps along with the crown. Richard: "Rode he on Barbary? Tell me, gentle friend, / How went he [Barbary] under him [Bolingbroke]?" (*Richard II* V:5.81–82). Others may make much of this. "That jade hath eat bread from my royal hand? / . . . Would he not fall down, / Since pride must have a fall, and break the neck/ Of that proud man that did usurp his back?" (85. 87–89). Jade was a demeaning term for women. The horse Barbary betrays one who loves him – the former king – as the aunt Barbary seems to betray gentle, trusting Esther. And Pride leads Bolingbroke as it does Miss Barbary. You can begin to imagine what others might do with all this. And therefore, no doubt, you think I'm right to shun it, and return to *Othello*.

Here is how Desdemona remembers Barbary.

> My mother had a maid called Barbary.
> She was in love, and he she loved proved mad
> And did forsake her. She had a song of "Willow."
> An old thing 'twas, but it expressed her fortune,
> And she died singing it. That song tonight
> Will not go from my mind; I have much to do
> But to go hang my head all at one side
> And sing it like poor Barbary.   (*Othello* IV 3.28–35)

Now that seems to turn out a lot more promising than the equine business.

Like Desdemona, Miss "Barbary" can't get *Othello* "from [her] mind." Which means, in effect, that Miss Barbary can't get Desdemona from her mind: that she and Desdemona both see Barbary as their common type and as their future fate. But surely Miss Barbary is even less like Desdemona than she is like Desdemona's mother's maid. Gentle, trusting, married Desdemona is about to be betrayed to her death, like the maid Barbary, by a lover who has in effect proved mad with jealousy. Miss Barbary, peremptory, repressed and repressive, refuses out of wounded pride the only suitor, Lawrence Boythorn, she has ever had. And what won't go from her mind is not some old lovelorn ballad but the sternly apocalyptic warnings from the Gospel of Mark: "Watch ye therefore! lest coming suddenly he find you sleeping. And what I say unto you, I say unto all, Watch!" (I: 3, 67 – Mark 13: 35, 37). Beyond that, she rigidly preserves her silence.

Her silence, or Dickens's? *Bleak House* fiercely castigates Miss Barbary for her attempt to silence Esther. Miss Barbary, it insists, has tried as hard as possible to prevent Esther's story from entering the field of narration. Her own "cruel words" told Jarndyce – who later tells the adult Esther – how "the writer [Miss Barbary] had bred her [Esther] in secrecy from her birth, had blotted out all trace of her existence, and that if the writer were to die before the child became a woman, she would be left entirely friendless, nameless, and unknown. It [the letter] asked me, to consider if I would, in that case, finish what the writer had begun" (VI: xvii, 290). But doesn't that word "writer" invite us, ironically, to think about Dickens's own role in this project of suppression. Isn't that entire erasure, after all, exactly what Dickens does to or for Miss Barbary? Hasn't his writing "bred [Miss Barbary] in secrecy . . . blotted out all trace of her existence, and . . . left [her] entirely friendless, nameless, and unknown?"

In fact, when you think about it, Dickens silences Miss Barbary far more effectively than Miss Barbary comes close to silencing Esther. Esther, after all, not only finds her voice and writes, she writes almost half of *Bleak House* – no mean feat for someone who was intended to have had "blotted out all trace of her existence." But we can learn nothing about Miss Barbary: nothing of her own "story" apart from a bleakly drawn outline of its intervention in the fully, indeed fulsomely, narrated stories of her sister and her niece. Her would-be-readers can scarcely start, let alone "finish what the writer had begun." May we not conclude, then, that Dickens is warning us, despite himself, that he is the real Miss Barbary, if being Miss Barbary means rendering "a woman . . . entirely friendless, nameless, and unknown." And if that's so, doesn't it also mean that we somehow have to consider Dickens as the real, if reluctant, Othello, to Miss Barbary's Desdemona-Barbary: the forsaking lover, who should love but who instead, somehow struck mad, betrays, betrays in fact exactly as Othello does by stopping his beloved's voice.

The answer to this is No, but Yes, and then No again, and therefore finally Yes-and-No.

Here's No, the first time.

Dickens doesn't love Miss Barbary at all. That's right, isn't it? She is the bad mother, in D. W. Winnicott's famous binary, repressive and denying, juxtaposed against the good and loving, would-be-nurturing but deluded, "real" mother, Lady Dedlock. Isn't that polarity literally the matrix of the novel's ongoing fantasy, Esther's fantasy and Dickens's? Overcome the bad mother's forced separation of the child from the good mother by inventing the polymorphous pre-Oedipal Jarndyce, at once mother, father, and lover, who unites all the potential objects within an ideal of impossibly powerful, agamous benevolence? Of course that's the story the novel tells if, by reading, you want, like Jarndyce, to "finish what the writer had begun." But perhaps you suspect, like me, what volunteering to continue that project might entail: the surrender of bliss in favor of mere, snug comfort.

What if you think, instead, that this kind of writing, the writer's unfinished project, parallels what Miss Barbary calls "sleeping?" What if, instead of writing, we "Watch!"? Can we tell a different, transgressive story, if we keep our eyes open for other plots inside the novel competing to be seen? – Not only different but better stories, or at least fairer, than the one the writer has begun.

This brings us to Yes, the first time.

Yes means reading Miss Barbary or, at least, her "choice" of name as a sort of symptom. Symptom is a key element in D. A. Miller's extremely influential reading of *Bleak House*. Central to his complex and incisive argument is the rejection of " 'contradiction' in the text" as "in a certain Marxist manner . . . the 'symptom' of an ideological bind, obligingly betrayed to our notice in the text's taken-for-granted 'distanciation' from its own program" (D. A. Miller 1988: 65. OrIG. 1983). Ingeniously, Miller argues instead that incoherence marks "a positively advantageous *strategy*" for the text's intervention "in the ideological 'conflict' " that surrounds it (p. 66). Unpersuaded, Dominick LaCapra has responded to this argument by stressing the ways in which "symptomatic, critical, and possibly transformative forces interact in relating a text to its various contexts (or subtexts)" (LaCapra 1984: 117). My post-Freudian use of symptom obviously proposes no intervention in that argument. In a sense, transgressive adaptation wants to cut the Gordian knot of ideology by treating the text not as already-processed but as still-and-indeed-endlessly-raw material. I'm interested therefore in using symptom in a different and earlier, more as it were raw, sense.

In the Greek, symptom meant literally a mishap or mischance. Medically, it thus came to mean a sign or a reminder of a mishap we might otherwise overlook. With those meanings in mind we might then ask: what misfortune does a sign named Barbary remind us we have overlooked, or, better still, remind us of what Dickens is having trouble forgetting? There are a number of answers to that inquiry. All of them invoke the word betrayal. And all of them circle back on the fact that, by calling the character Miss Barbary, the novel like a screen dream alludes to, or reminds us, of a narrative that something or someone has attempted to obscure, the kind of tell-tale self-accusation the accuser appears to prefer to believe that he has not let slip. We begin then to see Miss Barbary as a sort of rock in the narrative stream, catching and withholding that which might otherwise rush past us unnoticed.

Desdemona's Barbary tells of a woman who dies from neglect because the man she loves is incapacitated from loving her back; her word is "mad." That's also, of course, Desdemona and Othello's story; their word is jealous. It's also Miss Barbary and Dickens's story, as we've seen; their word is Bleak. But it's also a story that *Bleak House*, like *Othello*, feels compelled to retell in manifold. Repeatedly, the novel returns to women whom their lovers abandon to madness, degradation and death, "entirely friendless, nameless, and unknown." All of these Dickensian *stories* focus like Shakespeare's on a literally lethal hero, insisting that virility is viral because of an innate male incapacity to discover or deliver bliss. The stories of not only Ada and Richard, or Honoria and Hawdon, but also of Lady Dedlock ruined by the sadist Tulkinghorn – who clearly adores her – and the impotent Leicester Dedlock – who also loves her as best he can. And, of course, Miss Barbary herself. The novel may pretend these are not its preferred fictions, telling them from a safe, censorious distance, but that distance it continually betrays by the savagery with which it indicts any woman who like Mrs. Jellyby would try to remove herself from the plot of heterosexual subjugation and neglect.

Another way to say all this – our preferred way – is to claim that *Bleak House* can find no viable mode for agamy. It wants to, it's got to, show "the romantic side of familiar things" because the familiar seen straight on is just deadly. We are encountering here, I think, a middle-aged and ageing male narcissism, as frustrated as it is demanding. (Narcissism will come up again, at great length, later on.) Dickens seems doubly disabled: unable any longer either to love being a man, or – being a man – to love. That second inability, to love women, drives the novel's theme, its obsessive repetitions of Barbary's story. But the first inability, to love being a man, shapes its form, the famous bifurcation into a second, female voice. In effect, Dickens evades the shame in failing to love women by permitting himself, as Esther, to imagine instead what it might be like to be one. After a succession of best boys, from Sam Weller to David Copperfield, he has turned to – and almost into – the incomparably best of girls.

We might well frame this reversal by contrasting the doubling in *Bleak House* (1850) with an apparently comparable move in the earlier *The Old*

Curiosity Shop (1840). *Curiosity Shop* also divides into a male and female fiction, although both are narrated in the same voice. Doomed Nell centers a horrific, heterosexual plot of predatory desire and ruthless persecution. But hobbledehoy Dick Swiveller memorably provides the novel with an engaging counter-focus, spinning out its agamous comic plot of mutual liberation, in which Swiveller and his beloved Marchioness intervene to save each other and themselves. Ten years later, the genders have switched genre. The male is now both deadly and dying; it is the female alone that seems viable. Alone is the operative term here. Men who desire women both give and catch death. Women, women who preserve themselves from wanting men, promise the only mode of preservation. And they are the only women the novel finds worth having. It would seem as though Dickens can now only endlessly re-narrate his sex's, his own, need to desert and destroy those whom they love. But as a woman he senses that he might get to tell a story that permits him not only to save but to love himself. Between *Curiosity Shop* and *Bleak House* he appears to have to become something like that archetypally bold coward, the guy who gets off the sinking ship by huddling inside a shawl.

This *travesti* means that *Bleak House* need not hang its head and sing "Willow." It can *express* instead the peculiar and bizarre model of a cheerier *fortune*: contrasting eros-seeking, betrayed, abandoned Honoria and Ada against virginal Esther whose happiness is secured by transference from unworthy suitors (Guppy) to non-contaminating patriarchy (Jarndyce) and its passive surrogate (Woodcourt). The novel goes out of its plot's way to reassure us that this bleak eros is virtually non-carnal and therefore reliably non-lethal. Esther loses even her meager claims to physical attractions. Woodcourt is repeatedly sent to sea with scarcely the suggestion of a proposal, let alone a proposition. From Jo to the shipwrecked colonials, everyone is dead and dying all around Woodcourt. He's Doctor Death, incapable of supporting or renewing life, and, inevitably then it would seem, Jarndyce's ideal of a husband. And Jarndyce enters the marriage plot only so that we can see him withdraw in time, an epitome of the eros interruptus which leaves this novel giddy. Both Bleak House south and its copy Bleak House north are reassuringly prophylactic against any contaminant libido. Erotic bliss they literally "blot out." And in its place they supply bespoke lives in a bijou residence, what Adam Phillips might call a "banal replacement-memory" (Phillips 1994: 24) or what Roland Barthes would term a text of *pleasure*: one that, expunging the reckless avidity of desire, guarantees

Dickens the "consistency of his [threatened] selfhood" (Barthes 1975: 14). We might call this agamy-without-(even the shadow of)-a-vengeance: a renunciation of erotic bonding so sterile that it guarantees to do no one harm, by insistently refusing to do anybody any sort of good.

But this novel's alternative is never entirely or convincingly the conventional banalities of pleasure. And that gets us back toward, if not yet exactly at, No, again.

In all the novels of the middle period, Dickens reliably finds mere pleasure insufficient, despite his strenuous efforts to endorse its comfort. (That is another way, I suppose, of saying that Dickens is both a writer who endlessly renews his right to canonical status, and a typical Victorian.) He continues to gesture, never more poignantly than in this middle period, with longing and regret toward the earlier male sites of bliss he now finds himself constrained from incorporating: for example, in Copperfield's notorious love and admiration for Steerforth, especially in his final refusal to condemn his errant friend, or in Sir Leicester's final pairing with Trooper George, a partner far more faithful than Lady Dedlock could ever have been, a pairing which perhaps gives us one last privileged glimpse into the final days of Mr. Pickwick and Sam Weller.

And it's that palpable longing which leads me to prefer Richard Carstone as the best informed reader of the novel, its preferred adaptor because its most resistant character. Richard urges Esther and us "to take an interest" and "To look into" Jarndyce, and then to see how he becomes "quite another thing" (XII:xxxvii, 581) from what he pretends. Bliss may kill in this novel, Richard shows us, but pleasure surely mummifies. Jarndyce's Bleak House is a kind of proto-Ibsenite Doll's House, in which Esther figures as Trilby to Jarndyce's ventriloquizing Svengali, or as key-wound Coppelia to his Doctor Coppelius in a bleak house that holds no possibility for either bliss or flight. Listening thoughtfully to Richard, we begin to realize we should pay more attention to Barbary, and very little to Jarndyce. We should at least entertain, despite all Dickens's claims to the contrary, the possibility that good Esther Summerson may very well be her mother's "shame," the pleasant alternative that both damns and disguises access to women's bliss. In effect, we should refuse, like Richard, to believe that *Bleak House* "works."

If *Bleak House* "works," the reader commits to that fundamental bifurcation: that it tells two contrasting stories, narratives that not only differ from but counter each other – Esther's endorsed "amateurish, slowly dilating 'circle of duty' as a paradigmatic alternative to Chancery's expansive 'circle of evil'" (Robbins 1990: 214). The Chancellor centers a public story of illimitable desuetude. Jarndyce pulls together around himself and his house the opposing story, a private narrative of consolation and reconstruction – to which Richard Carstone proves the stiffnecked exception that underscores the necessity for the Rule, Lucifer to Jarndyce's omniscient Patriarch. But Richard insists there's not two stories but only one: "I do declare to you that he becomes to me the embodiment of the suit; that, in place of its being an abstraction, it is John Jarndyce" (XIII:xxxix, 609). Richard anchors this reading in the novel's double play on *suitor* (p.580). Most of the characters are in one way or another *suitors* to Chancery, refused, postponed, manipulated, cheated suitors. But many of those same characters, and certainly the younger ones, are also *suitors* in erotic plots, suitors refused, postponed, manipulated and cheated by Jarndyce. When the young Richard could feel "utterly regardless of this same suit," that is the Chancery suit, then he and Jarndyce "got on very well." But when he grew into manhood "it was quite another thing. Then John Jarndyce discovers that Ada and I must break off, and that if I don't amend that very objectionable course" – but there are two courses now, the suits for the will and for Ada – "I am not fit for her" (p.581).

The impersonal narrator makes us see the horror of the Chancellor, that soft-spoken, middle-aged, gentlemanly person, in his cozy chambers, the robes thrown aside. But Richard insists we see the Chancellor doubled not denied in that other middle-aged, snuggery-loving dominator, Jarndyce, whose vampirish needs fasten on the sweet young things in his care, keeping them from young men who might provide them something like bliss. Richard thus reads for us scenes or moments that Esther repeatedly wills us to not mind. Jarndyce's initial, terrifying encounter with the child Esther in the carriage. His solipsistic trust in Mrs. Jellyby and Mrs. Pardiggle. His blind indifference to the misery of the Jellyby and Pardiggle families and of the unemployed families who neighbor his estate. His delighted, constantly defended harboring of Skimpole. His bizarre choice of the emotionally retarded Boythorn as best friend. Richard asks us to see that Esther is wrong when she, blindly loyal, insists that Jarndyce has "kept himself outside the circle" (p.589). Far from being outside, Richard claims, he shares the circle's center. Jarndyce, not Krook, is really the Chancellor's "brother." As Richard wittily insists, it is only "wise and specious to preserve that outward difference" (p.581).

The novel now seems to be compelling us to rewrite it, to let Barbary sing the Willow her betrayer has silenced, to say Yes and No. Barbary is the memory that resists the novel's imperative forgetting, the ghost in the machine of Dickensian repression. And Richard has all along been, we suddenly glimpse, a would-be best boy, an agamous lover, terrible at marriage no doubt, but then that's what agamous lovers are supposed to be, and – we have Ada's witness for this – wonderfully satisfactory at all the other things one might desire a lover to be. Even prune-toned Esther can't manage to resist his charms. If only Jarndyce had loved Richard early and well, we begin to muse, as Pickwick loved Sam, or the Cheerybles loved Nickleby, what a quite different story, what an un-bleak story, we might have read. And even without that love we can still read inside *Bleak House* a novel which insists on our resistance, which time and again implores us to look where it mutely points, away from what it seems to say. It is after all Dickens who authored Richard. It is after all Dickens who named Barbary.

But here we have strayed to the verge of a reading. We've probably even overstepped that boundary, entering a territory next to the one so carefully policed by Jonathan Arac, Terry Eagleton, D. A. Miller and Bruce Robbins. From all of them we already know well "Dickens' complicity with the social structures he deplored" (Robbins 1990: 226). And right next to that we've found a field where Dickens deplores his misery-making complicities. But neither field should distract us now. That way's aporia, and we remain committed to *poros*. We only offered this reading, really, as a sort of dumb show, like the prelude to *The Mousetrap*, just a little something to adumbrate the harrowing that is to come. The play, that is: the adaptation, remains the thing at which we aim. But to get there, we've got to swerve now away from reading and toward theatre, toward, specifically, the theatre that Dickens himself would urge us, dangerously, to adopt, his as-it-were theatre that shudders at any hint of adaptation.

CHAPTER 2

. . . *as upon a theatre*

This chapter lets Dickens proffer his counter-model of theatre. It centers on *Our Mutual Friend*,[1] but, just to give you a feel for the difficulties ahead, it starts in *Nickleby*. Later on I deal with *Nickleby* at considerable length, in chapters 3 and 4. Here I'm only interested in that relatively early section where Nicholas works in a theater. And I'm deploying it simply to show from the start how entirely misleading it is for anyone to argue, or believe, "that Dickens loved theatre" (Rubin 1981: 18).

We encounter Nicholas just as, having failed at the pre-scripted roles of private secretary and school usher, he unexpectedly finds himself snatched into the raucous, subversive world of the Crummles Theatrical Company in Portsmouth. Of course, Nicholas turns out to be a prepossessing young leading man; even his sidekick Smike emerges as a more or less acceptable clown. But Nicholas soon learns that his sister Kate, left unprotected in London, has become the target of an aristocratic seduction. He immediately denounces the damnable fooling that keeps him apart and impotent, returns to London, and successfully attacks the instigator of the intrigue, Sir Mulberry Hawk. So much for the stage.

And so much for the novel, because now we're going to imagine that Dickens, sensing there's money to be made, decides to rival the RSC and adapt *Nickleby* himself. In this staging, Nicholas discovers at Portsmouth not only that he has a pronounced histrionic gift but that the profession recognizes and rewards him lavishly for using it. As if in confirmation, his mother suddenly writes to tell him of how, when pregnant with him, she dreamed of Shakespeare and was at the same time "very much frightened by an Italian image boy" (xxvii, 353). This communication is taken by the entire Crummles Company as a portent – that Nicholas will be a great British, but not (mercifully) an *Italian* actor.

On the strength of that interpretation, Nicholas immediately determines to rescue his sister Kate from the put-upon life of milliner and

47

lady's-companion. She joins him in Portsmouth. After valiantly struggling against an initial shyness, and a slight problem with vocal projection,
Kate begins to realize that she too has a capacity for performance.
Brother and sister become a well-known, well-loved pair: she's Miranda
to his Ferdinand, then Juliet to his Romeo, later Hermione to his
Leontes (and later still Adele to his Fred). Together they climb from
provincial to metropolitan renown. As Kate grows more famous and
sure of herself she successfully defends herself against her earlier suitors.
Her *froideur* leaves the cad Sir Mulberry Hawk permanently doubting his
manhood. But she chooses to make a real man out of Lord Frederick
Verisopht, and in the process turns herself into a real Lady. Nicholas
himself becomes an idol of the town, rich, feted: ladies of the chorus on
every chaise longue, while countesses by the dozen wait near the stage
door discreetly expectant in their private broughams.

Surely, by this point, we hear the dour voice of some Victorian
showman warning: "I knew Becky Sharpe, sir. Becky Sharpe was my
friend. And you, Mr. Nickleby, are no Becky Sharpe." That sour voice
recognizes that my version of Dickens's revision can only emerge from
someone who respects acting and loves theatre. Dickens could no more
write that plot than, taking up his early chance at the Covent Garden
audition, he could attempt to live out the fantasy we've just described for
Nicholas. Indeed, could someone who did not "love the theatre" write a
novel more dismissive, condescending and disparaging toward theatre
and theatre-folk than *Nickleby*? Well, one might add a Svengali in the pit,
or a Dorian Gray in the stage-box. But what – short of the absolutely
criminal – could be added to his already acid account that would make
the theater any more completely a site of shame? "Oh! that I should
have been fooling here!" (xxx, 398).

Dickens is no friend to performance.

And, as we're about to see, when we turn from *Nickleby* to *Our Mutual
Friend*, he's not all that fond of adaptation either.

QUOD SCRIPSI SCRIPSI

Stalwartly, ingeniously, *Our Mutual Friend* refuses adaptation, as stalwartly and ingeniously as it subverts performance. (For my resistance to that
refusal, see the concluding chapter of this book.) Self-protecting, the
novel insists that what has been written has been written. Tampering
with texts can never be innocent. To adapt is a kind of literary treason:
lèse-textualité.

But wait a minute, you are saying, if you know *Our Mutual Friend* at all. It's a novel that cries out for adaptation. The Boffin about-face is notoriously unacceptable, too easy, too complete, quite simply too good to be true. And it's not just the Boffin business. The entire novel, and especially its second half, seems a virtual compendium of things which ought to send us, like the infant Inexhaustible, "screaming among the rainbows" (IV: xiii, 849). Just think about what happens to Jenny Wren, abused child, dolls' dressmaker, stunted Sybil. Which of us wants to accept as a model happy ending the notion that this highly intelligent, talented and brave survivor can find not her best but her only chance for happiness with Sloppy, the genial idiot who in proposing offers to ornament her crutch? Surely she deserves better and more, even admitting the fact that Sloppy's a talented woodworker.

Here's my own *short* list: what any adaptor of *Our Mutual Friend* – even one not committed to transgression – must want to change, or, in most cases, drop.

> That *faux*-philo-Semitism which invests, and degrades, Riah;
> That "discovery" of a meritorious female erotics which turns out merely to recycle masochism;
> That disdain for individual merit and distrust of intellectual training which toadies to establishment models and claims of class;
> That "pious fraud" which claims that:
> (a) Child and Father are the only terms in any sort of discourse, and
> (b) the part of the Father has always already been cast.

All of these must go, right? Now you can add in the margins your own suggestions for out-takes (if this is not the library's copy).

But it won't do you any good.

The novel warns against, plots against, and systematically undoes all late-coming attempts at subversive modification. No surprise: its chief villain, Silas Wegg, turns out to be a professional adaptor, though Wegg titles himself (as all adaptors must) "an official expounder of mysteries" (I: v,97). Actually, Wegg turns out to be a sort of performance artist *avant*, as well as *contre*, *la lettre*, a reader who refuses to let any text alone that he can twist to serve his own needs. He doesn't just sell ballads, he adapts them, personalizing them to be always about the only personality he finds interesting, himself: "my eldest brother left our cottage to enlist into the army . . . as the ballad that was made about it describes. 'Beside that cottage door, Mr. Boffin'" (p. 96). Such familiarization Dickens insists we find not only funny but criminal (which already says some-

thing determinative about this fiction's powers of resistance). Adapting
the ballads is the faux-innocent symptom and snare, behind which
lowers all that mean-spirited, destructive tampering with wills and
legacies that finally gets Wegg cast out into the deep night-soil.

But it's not just Wegg. We can hear the same alarm sounding (at its
most convoluted) in the cautionary tale of Robert Baldwin, one of
Boffin's eccentric misers, whose story he instructs Wegg, and us, to read
and take warning from. Briefly summarized: a Mr. Baldwin arbitrarily
leaves his wealth away from an elder (Baldwin major) and to a younger
son (Baldwin minor). But Baldwin major suppresses that will and enters
irreproachably into the property. Baldwin major marries a second wife,
at seventy-eight. He then decides to disinherit *his* elder son by his first
marriage. (His own experience, you would have thought, might have
suggested a certain prudence here.) Irrationally, Baldwin major confides
this notion to his younger son, the disinherited fellow's younger brother.
But this second second son reverses the usual procedure in such matters
(see Jacob and Esau *inter alia*). "[I]n order to preserve the property to his
brother . . . [he] broke open his father's desk, where he found – not his
father's will which he sought after, but the will of his grandfather, which
was then altogether forgotten" (III: vi,547), leaving the property to the
original Baldwin minor.

Dickens insists that those latecomers who break and enter, seeking a
text they'd prefer, merely and inevitably disinherit themselves. There's
no possibility of recuperation. In the Baldwins' world, and in the world
they model, no "desk" contains or conceals a better text, a document
that can give us what we want, what we think we need, or what we
believe we are owed. Indeed, the final phrase about grandfather Baldwin's will – "which was then altogether forgotten" – can imply, if *then*
means after the break-in, that even the original will now no longer
applies. We are being given to understand that no writing, even the
father's, can withstand the vicissitudes of greed, desire and history, the
interplay of family. The novel seems here to want to insist, in a remarkable prevision of Freud's account of the roots of civilization, that writing,
its production, its transmission, its retrieval, starts from and routinely
returns to an act of dynastic violence, of expropriation: fathers against
sons, brother against brother, son against father. And, in the end, all of
it: intention, betrayal, discovery, will only be "forgotten," both the
original transgression as well as all those subsequent, repetitive violations. Nothing, not a page, not a word, shall be lost. But, then, nothing
will remain to be gained, either. "As-ton-ish-ing!" as Boffin says. Best

then, the book seems to warn us, to leave what's written well enough, or poor enough, alone. The text we've got is bound to turn out better than the one we go discovering. The text you break in to find never can turn out to be the text you want, the text that fulfills your needs for empowerment, reversal, or release. Any and all transgressions of the text leave you with "rotten paper."

Indeed, literacy's best pleasures seem to be just those of feeling "dead." Lizzie and Jenny, on the rooftop reading, call out in delight "Come up and be dead" (II:v,332). *Dead* when the gravestones, at St. George's Covent Garden, look "as if they were ashamed of the lies they told" (II:xv,451). *Dead* where even the New Testament's "sublime history" amounts to little more than a dusty mound of syllables, leaving its assiduous conners "as absolutely ignorant . . . as if they had never seen or heard of it" (II:i, 264). *Dead* as Bradley Headstone, hanging miserably around the terminus to read bills which describe Eugene's murderer, only to discover instead that he's escaped detection because – the very thing he was trying to prevent – Lizzie and Eugene will wed (IV:xv, 863). A reading that destroys his sanity.

Literacy imperils not only the morally ambiguous like Bradley but the clearly innocent as well. Its costs range from the self-suppression of the good Miss Peecher and her little Mary Anne, through the betrayal of Georgiana Podsnap ensnared by the Lammles' "prompt-book" (II: iv,315), to the would-be seduction of Lizzie, made literate and potentially demirep in the same seductive ploy. Throughout the book writing, and reading the written, pushes individuals of every sort ruthlessly toward the margin, no matter their claims on justice. It pushes nasty Charley Hexam away from his sister and out of his home, and into rock-hard selfishness. And it thrusts the more sympathetic Headstone, fatally consenting to write his name on the black board, into Rogue Riderhood's power, and into the Weir.

Stick then, *Our Mutual Friend* insists, to the writing we have. Stick to reading the already written. Stick to *Our Mutual Friend*. What you receive in these pages, whatever its limitations, is the best you're likely to get. Night and year are "closing in." We can't chart beyond our ineluctable confines "of iron" and "of stone" (I: i,43). "Print . . . now opening ahead" only seems to promise "a new life" (I: v,95). In fact, print leads to "Scarers" (p.104), the iron "Gospel according to Podsnappery," and the stoney "Returns of the Board of Trade" (III: viii,566). Of course, Wegg-like you can try to revise, refuse, resist but, in the end and again Wegg-like, you'll only deprive yourself in the process. Tampering with the text will leave you nothing. Nothing but torn and terminal pages. "In these times of ours" (I: i,43) we must accept the ostensible text as transmitted, no matter how spurious, no matter how implausible. If we acquiesce in our "odd disposition to dispute" this fiction as "improbable," Dickens insists we show ourselves as nothing less than "Idiotic" ("Postscript"; 894–895).

HALVING A MUTUAL FRIEND

But what happens if we actually try to be Idiotic? What if, for example, we idiotically follow a notion of James Kincaid? He divides the novel in half, setting "the increasingly moving Wrayburn-Hexam plot" over against "the increasingly silly and trite Wilfer-Harmon plot" (Kincaid 1971: 228). Of course, in a typical gesture of self-contradiction, Kincaid insists that we can't actually halve the book; we are "forced to pay for" the richness of the one half with the tedium of the other. But why is that so? Why can't we read Dickens exactly as Dickens has Boffin read Plutarch – by halves? Wouldn't that lead to an adaptation we could stomach?

Our Mutual Friend does actually seem to trace lines along which we can cut: a *parvenu* fiction of radical *possibility* and a contrasting *plebeian* fiction of equally radical *dearth*. Fictions of possibility detect no end of wonders to be displayed. (Here "possibility" comes from Mrs. Boffin's response to Bella's sensible objection that her current husband can't also be her long-dead fiancé: "Why not, deary, when so many things are possible?" (IV: xiii,841). Possibility insists that the Meek shall inherit the Mounds, as long as they agree to receive the story like Bella, thrilled to abase herself before its narratives as "stupid," "silly," and hard-hearted (p. 846). Fictions of dearth, however, find virtually nothing possible. Ultimately consigned to dearth, Bradley can't get away with bludgeoning Eugene. Nor can Rogue get away with blackmailing Bradley. The best marriage-plot dearth can deliver offers only the somewhat impoverished consolation that Eugene the bridegroom "might not be much disfigured by and by" (IV: xvi,883).

As though to encourage us in exactly this partition, the novel even invents for each type of fiction an ironically rueful artist-figure, and a corresponding mode of material production and consumption. To supply the *parvenu,* Jenny Wren produces upscale *objets de luxe*, spectacularly displayed behind flaring gas in the best shops in Bond Street (III: ii,495), toys that are snapped up by consumers who, as she knows so well, "don't like to be made melancholy" (IV: x,804). These shops target women, as do all fictions of possibility, offering models, or more precisely, modes, which interpellate and then station women, especially young women, within the politer classes. But while you may find Mr. Venus's skeletons "at the West End" (I: vii,127), you won't find Venus himself there, but in shabby East-End Clerkenwell, behind "a dark shop-window with a tallow candle dimly burning" (I: vii,122). There the dyspeptic "articulator" of dearth produces for a distinctly plebeian clientele "popular" *objets d'art*: stuffed dead pets priced at "three and ninepence," dispensed from a dirty, dingy shop, lit by tallow. And Venus's custom appeals only to boys and men: the little boy who comes for the canary; Wegg; the Belgian and French gentlemen who lend their bones to make up his miscellanies. This pairing thus opens up what Venus would call a "general panoramic view" (I: vii,126), not simply two Londons, east and west, plebeian and parvenu, but two contrasting types of fiction, two highly polarized ways of representing, entering, and critiquing, the prospects of urban experience at mid-century. For women a fantasy of conformist upward mobility. For men a crippling counter-fabrication of dispersal, dismemberment, destruction.

Of course, both these artist-artisans are Dickens, or figure parts of Dickens. Forster was the first to notice how Venus's duelling frogs (I: vii,122) echoed the bronze group in front of him when he wrote. That borrowing clues us to see how Dickens's Venus-like labor articulates the dearth of the world, its "dismemberment . . . separation of classes . . . separation from wholeness in work" (Hutter 1983:154). But doesn't Jenny's Lady Belinda Whitrose-doll also reflect Dickens's doll-in-train-ing, Bella Wilfer? Admiring her "rainbow" semicircle (III: ii,495) isn't Jenny advertising her connection to her creator's final "nursery gar-nished as with rainbows" (IV: xiii,849). Making wholes out of parts, piecing together fragments, prettifying them into significance: that's his kind of task as much as it is hers.

It's all so perfect, so ample, how can we not try to cut along the perforated lines? We'll refuse Jenny, or rather refuse to echo the Jenny-in-Dickens. We'll refuse the nuptial fantasies of *parvenu* spectacle. In-stead, we'll go with dearth's harsh story of plebeian males disem-powered and destroyed, a story which most of us, looking both back and around, can't help but credit. What does this adaptation turn out to look like?

Faust. Not Marlowe's, obviously. Gounod's: the opera which had recently made so marked an impression on the Dickens who was

simultaneously carrying on his own Faustian seduction of the Marguer-
ite-like Ellen Ternan (Johnson 1952: 502–503; Kaplan 1988: 416, 462).[2]
Like Marguerite's, Lizzie Hexam's story centers on deception, disfigure-
ment, murder and suicide. The benefactor is also the seducer; to trust
his love is to be betrayed and shamed. But Lizzie's story is also tinged by
the all-possible *parvenu*, more than tinged, contaminated by it, like all the
women's stories in this novel. She manages to revise, indeed to gut,
Faust, first evading and then converting her seducer, Eugene. A more
satisfying plan might then be: stick to Bradley Headstone, the excluded
middle figure of the plebeian triangle. That way our adaptation could
look, or at least sound, a lot more dramatic and intriguing even than
Faust. It might look and sound like *Macbeth*.

Little-Hans-like, Dickens drops lots of crumbs to outline such a path.
After Mr. Dolls' fumigerous visit (II:13,604), Eugene quotes from the
banquet scene (*Macbeth* III:v). And after Doll's funeral the narrator again
alludes to Banquo's undiplomatic drop-by (*Our Mutual Friend* IV:ix, 801).
But those lines are just *jeux d'esprit*, literary cartouches. The parallel
really makes narrative sense as it takes over and inflects Bradley's fall
and death. When Rogue suddenly materializes in Bradley's cheerless
classroom, the scene crisply derives itself from the oft-quoted Act III
banquet. Headstone-Macbeth confronts the irrepressible evidence of his
crime, the "secret'st" man of blood, this truly rogue-Banquo, before a
group of subordinate boy Thanes, who see this *ghost*, but not their
master's doom, their "blindness" ironically deepening the horror, and
the pathos, of the encounter.

Shakespeare's banquet is notoriously unstageable, like much if not all
of *Macbeth*. The audience is always too fascinated with the mechanics of
the Ghost's entrances and, trickier yet, exits, to pay much attention to
what Macbeth is saying, let alone feeling. "There he is, Gladys, look:
coming in behind those guys in plaid!" "Which guys in plaid, Donald?"
Dickens does it much better, as he invariably manages to do when he
remakes heroic drama into something banal. (And as he routinely does
not, when he exaggerates the already elevated: turning an already
almost impossible Cordelia into an over-the-top Little Nell.) Thus, when
Bradley "slowly wipes his name out" from his blackboard (p. 867), the
deliberate, mute, eloquent gesture more than matches the great spoken
scenes of the higher-status drama. He realizes here, and enacts, what
Macbeth will later say: that all language is merely sound, most poignantly the hard-won language of the self-taught schoolmaster; all plots of
ambitious self-improvement merely versions of an Idiot's tale.

It's even tempting here to go over the top ourselves, and cast the role of Lady Macbeth upon little Miss Peecher over the way. But, of course, the real Lady Macbeth here turns out to be Lizzie Hexam, the instigator of all Bradley's crimes. Or at least her instigation seems to be what he's claiming in the churchyard where she refuses his proposal. "Yes! you are the ruin – the ruin – the ruin – of me. I have no resources in myself, I have no confidence in myself, I have no government of myself when you are near me or in my thoughts" (I: xv,452). Here Bradley speaks what every reader of *Macbeth* knows about the influence of the Lady. But Lizzie has been pre-claimed from this sort of accusation by the *parvenu* story of possibility. That villainous parallel must be refused and blocked. And so she is immediately rescued not by one but by two interventions, Eugene's, then Riah's, and swept off from any further association with Headstone. It is exclusively to the men, the focus of dearth, that this most dire of plots pertains.

The plebeian story, to its credit, will stage no divinely-righteous Malcolm, captained by an avenging Macduff. Instead, Rogue, having been Banquo, reemerges, as in some understaffed provincial company, to play Macduff on the ramparts of Plashwater Weir. That's not a bad idea actually. In performance *Macbeth*'s wide and constantly shifting range of hostile Others costs the play's last half much of its emotional and even narrative coherence. But collapsing Banquo and Macduff into Rogue concentrates the Bradley plot admirably. And of course Rogue has a comparable, carefully-prepared-for, parodic boast to match Macduff's brag that he cannot be killed because his mother had a C-section. Headstone can't drown Riderhood because he's already been drowned once. But Macduff is right about his immunity and Rogue is wrong. Macduff concludes tragedy; Rogue ends up in, and as, dearth.

Read as *Macbeth*, more specifically: read Romantically as *Macbeth*, Bradley's story emerges as one of trapped and thwarted ambition. The play: "They have tied me to a stake. I cannot fly, / But bearlike I must fight the course" (V: vii, 1–2). The novel: "To these limits had his [Bradley's] world shrunk" (IV: xv, 868). The parallel becomes even more solid when we recall that ambition keyed the nineteenth-century's prodigious admiration for Macbeth. He was Macready's "favourite character," his signature role (Macready 1967: 292). He saw the part as "lofty, manly . . . heroic;" insisting that "the grief, the care, the doubt, was not that of a weak person but of a strong mind and of a strong man" (172). And here Macready was at one – for once – with a Romantic theatre which reread the regicide as "a man of feeling, extremely sensitive to assaults upon his inherent courage and devotion, highly susceptible to imaginative stimulus . . . valiantly but unsuccessfully struggling against mental processes he cannot control and exterior forces he cannot understand" (Donohue 1970: 214). Those features, virtually term for term, describe Dickens's Bradley, extremely sensitive, courageous, devoted, imaginative, unsuccessful against exterior forces he certainly cannot understand: "enough that in certain smouldering natures like this man's, that passion leaps into a blaze, and makes such head as fire does in a rage of wind when other passions, but for its mastery, could be held in chains" (II: xi,396).

So far, so good: Bradley's story is, clearly, the one we want to stage. Of course, the schoolmaster's story is not that of a nobleman scheming to be a king, but of a boy plodding the harsher road from the lower to the lower-middle class. His enemies are not witches but gents. In fact, Bradley's turns out to be the story Dickens has been teasing for thirty years, the suppressed, avoided continuation of *Oliver Twist*: how hard, indeed impossible, it is for a good boy to get over a bad past. But Bradley is grand, tragic rather than pitiable like Oliver, because, unlike Oliver, he stalwartly, paradoxically, refuses to internalize the novel's class-driven register of plebeian emptiness and unworthiness. (In contrast, the well-born Eugene, with much less at stake, easily accepts the fundamental rightness of his own battering.)

Bradley consistently refuses any form of social self-abasement. He refuses to abase himself early on in the face of Wrayburn's taunting and humiliation (II: vi). He refuses it later in response to Lizzie's rejection (II: xv), even as he confesses his torment and obsession. Finally and fatally, he refuses it when Rogue's blackmailing discovery has apparently left him no alternative but a surrender even more abject than Bella's. He would rather erase the writing he has labored so hard to master, than cavil or cringe before the blackmailing scoundrel. Headstone may be merely "the miserable master" (IV: xv,865). And Schoolmaster may sting as the worst of Wrayburn's jibes. But to the end, and especially at the end, Bradley is, like Milton's Satan to whom he is also compared (p. 863), perversely masterful.

He can refuse abasement because he knows what we also believe: the pious parvenu fraud of possibility comes down always to an impious cheat. "He thought of Fate, or Providence, or be the directing Power what it might be, as having put a fraud upon him – overreached him – and in his impotent mad rage bit, and tore, and had his fit" (p. 863). Like Macbeth in the famous Act V soliloquy, Bradley comes finally to recognize "possibility" as a lure, the profitless dangle by which a hostile governing principle subverts individual worth and denies earned merit. Macbeth tells about foul means to seek a fair prize, the throne and a crown. Bradley speaks of something more dire: the prize itself, middle-class respectability, is not only unattainable, it is not worth the soul-sickening price it demands. Of course, completely externalizing pleni-tude leaves him no option except to embrace dearth heartily. Yet, even as he thrusts himself and his adversary into the slimed and deadly pit, he cries out his own final, haunting, heroic version of "Lay on, Macduff": "I can be!" (IV: xv,874).

But what can he be? Indeed, can he "be!" at all? Bradley may indeed be "lofty," but the novel will scarcely allow him to be "heroic" – and not "manly" at all. He can try as hard and ingeniously as possible to submerge the tell-tale bundle of working-man's clothing, but like the Freudian repressed it will irrepressibly and incriminatingly return to mark him. Nothing can annul the original "pauper lad," certainly not the parody of education available through popular extension schemes. Bradley might have found his proper place in a ship's company, we are told, but having left or never found his correct milieu, that proper place can never be relocated. Forever the "mechanic . . . in . . . holiday clothes" (II: i,266), Bradley must inevitably return to his proletarian dress to live out and die from his resurgent, unmastered emotions. In Dickens's novels, origins always out.

But, in brutal fact, it's not just the world but Dickens that's against Bradley. Both agamy and class conspire against his chances to emerge a hero. And yet even that "both" misleads. In Dickens sex and class are always profoundly intertwined. He appropriates virtually intact Bal-morality's sexual regulation of women: all erotically responsive women are *a priori déclassée*. (Calling that Balmorality is probably unfair to Victoria, who seems not only to have had a great deal of [admittedly quite legitimate] sex, but also to have enjoyed it mightily. Balmorality stands rather for what her subjects thought she stood, or perhaps better, wouldn't stay still, for.) But men Dickens seeds up and down a kind of agamous, class-runged ladder.

Actively sexual lower-class men are invariably comic or disgusting or both. Even if their desires are unconsummated, they are either dismissed or destroyed. This novel is full of them: Venus, Boffin, Rogue, even Gaffer.

Sexually active upper-class men are reprehensible but glamorous, perhaps more attractive by reason of their class than their gender. In this novel, Eugene or Lammle. Steerforth is the pattern. They can be saved if they remain unzipped. Otherwise, they, generally, drown, lamented.

Middle-class men – the nice sort – fall easily in love but it's always the love of the pantomime: principal boys, even as they age, oddly androgenous and certainly unphallic. In this novel, most clearly, Harmon. In other novels: Arthur Clennam and Allan Woodcourt.

Middle-class men – the *not* nice sort – usually Dickens's most interesting male characters, epitomized by Carton. In other novels: Copperfield, Pip and John Jasper. Consumed by envy of another man's virility, they are Dickens's idea of a hero. Relentlessly agamous, they successfully purloin the fruits of the rival's sexuality, or, at least, interrupt the rival's coital plot. Oddly absent in this novel, which to a great extent accounts for what Kincaid finds trite and silly.

Why these steps should spread in exactly that way we will argue out in the two following chapters. Here let it suffice to say that Dickens must endlessly renarrate the story of plebeian men as other and as failed, just so he won't be forced to reenact it. He'll have no truck with the notion that a man's a man for all that. All that, in Dickens, always makes all the difference.

Which is why, in *Our Mutual Friend*, the further the plebeian man is articulated, the more "small you . . . come out" (I: vii,126). Seen or displayed by upper-class men, he comes across as something less evolved: "the passion-wasted nightbird. . . the worst nightbird of all" (III: xi, 618). We even catch an allusion to the five-year old *Origin of Species* when we read of Venus's "head and face peering out of the darkness, over the smoke . . .as if he were modernizing the old original rise in his family" (I: vii,126). This satirically anti-Darwinian stance generates generally comic or fantastical metaphor along the model of the Jonsonian humors: Gaffer the Bird of Prey; Rogue the Fox; Venus the sparrow; Wegg the fly. But it also functions in more disturbing ways. Thus, when Eugene taunts Bradley, and goose-chases him through the dark streets, the narrator invites us to recognize the "ill-tamed wild animal" in the "hunted" Bradley, "wild-eyed, draggle haired" (III: x,607–609). Lizzie does exactly the same thing in the terrifying proposal scene in St. George's Churchyard. She makes us feel – and the narrator makes us feel she is right in so doing – that Bradley's sexuality carries within him

the seeds of destruction. He is like the new "railways" which "still
bestride the market-gardens that will soon die under them" (II: i,267).
Blood literally pours from his proposal. In fact, Bradley does kill Rogue
Riderhood in a kind of mortal version of the missionary-position,
pushing Rogue backwards into the Weir as he grapples his enemy in an
iron embrace – Rogue who has made himself into Lizzie's unwanted,
parodically sexual surrogate: "You can't get rid of me, except by coming
to a settlement. I am a going along with you wherever you go" (IV: xv,
873).

Eve Kosofsky Sedgwick sees Bradley's attack on Rogue as anal rape
(Sedgwick 1985: 169). But that's not how the novel actually positions
them. Although Bradley does initially grab Riderhood from behind, he
then "got him [Riderhood] round, with his back to the Lock, and still
worked him backward" until "Riderhood went over into the smooth pit,
backward, and Bradley Headstone upon him" (IV: xv, 874). Straight, or
perhaps not so straight, missionary. I don't think this can be considered
"Sphincter domination," nor that Headstone is here, or elsewhere,
being "used as a woman, and valued as a woman, by men with whom he
comes into narcissistic relation" (Sedgwick 1985: 169–170). It seems to
me to be just the reverse: if anything, Bradley is using Rogue as a woman
in a kind of desperately symbolized revenge-substitution for the union
with Lizzie he believes Eugene has usurped.

Yet, though I disagree with this reading of the rape, I accept completely Sedgwick's account of the "chain of Girardian triangles" reach-
ing through the novel "from the lowest class up to the professional class"
(p. 165). That chain's another version of my ladder. With it we uncover
the-all-but-culmination of Dickens's career-long anxieties about representing a healthy, fully sexualized masculinity, or rather a fully hetero-
sexualized, that is reproductive, masculinity. (Unfortunately, *Drood*'s
Jacobean murder plot sketches but never works through those anxieties
it renders in such memorable grotesquerie.) Excluded from the *parvenu*
realm of marriage, plebeian men have no erotic choices except unwel-
come homosocial scenarios. Indeed, Bradley, Charley and Wegg transfer finally all their frustrated passion to fascinatingly sadistic all-male
triangles: Bradley–Eugene–Rogue; Charley–Bradley–Gaffer; Wegg–
Venus–Boffin. But I don't read these triangles as the revelations of a
closeted homosexual drive. It is class more than libido that is operative
here. Lower-class men can only interact erotically with other men not
because they desire men but because their class prevents them from
realizing their heterosexuality. (The parallel in our own culture seems

clearly to be men, generally underclass men, incarcerated in our prisons.)

The novel warns all plebeian men well off its erotic premises. Sexual passion is either wasted on or wasted by them. Only upper-middle-class men and the women they fancy can enter the marriage plots. Rogue and Hexam are widowers, dependant on daughters whom upper-class men force to betray them. Venus cannot marry except as a boon from the *parvenu* Harmon–Boffin menage (IV: xiv,853–854) and as a result of betraying his lower-class confederate. But Bella can easily become the grandest of ladies, even though she is merely the daughter of a permanent junior clerk. And that in a novel which relentlessly satirizes the self-seeking of the nouveaux-riches. Harmon can marry even though he works as a secretary, because he is first recognized as the true heir to a fortune. And Eugene marries not only well but supremely well, even though he is throughout nothing but an idle louse.

But Bradley, our would-be Macbeth, Bradley can know none of those joys, despite the fact that he is a hard-working and (until he has the misfortune to fall in love) an entirely respectable schoolmaster. Plebeian men find themselves emblematized instead as the emasculated plaything the novel thinks it a good joke to call (George) Sampson. For them, Venus's shop functions as a sort of generic erotic metaphor: dead babies in jars, missing male parts, a dim place where women prudently refuse to be seen in "a boney light," a place of bones where boners are unlikely. A mere Secretary has no claim on mercenary Bella. The successful articulator of human warious cuts no dice with grasping Pleasant Riderhood.

But this doesn't mean the novel is simply or predominantly parvenu in its allegiance and narrations. It's much more complex than that. And here we arrive at the core of its resistance to adaptation. And, of course, the core of what makes it a very great novel indeed. *Our Mutual Friend* is always delighted to prove the *parvenu* fiction of *possibility* unutterably shallow and stupid in practice. It never permits us to forget that parvenu means Chicksey, Veneering and Stobbles. It means Podsnap. It means the Lammles and Lady Tippins, and the Lady-Tippins wanna-be's, Mrs. and the younger Miss Wilfer. Possibility means the parvenu reflected in all their philistine narrowness through the poisonous clarity of the Analytical Chemist, another of those lower-class characters who make the parvenu display possible. It insists we feel how cruel it is for frozen, crippled Jenny to be forced to "plod" outside the shop window, admiring dolls she has made but which she will never be able to possess. Poor

Riah can, it is true, break momentarily from the enslaving fictions of Pubsey & Co. But his subsequent career almost immediately settles back into the patterns he has just so bravely broken. Working for Harmon and Boffin at the end, he is sent to tell Twemlow that the old arrangement for paying the debt may be resumed. The impoverished aristocrat must continue to fork over to Riah the interest he can scarcely afford just as "heretofore," to "appease his Jewish rancor" (IV: xvi, 875). Riah may seem "no longer ravening but mild"; nevertheless, no real change in the way the world sees him is possible. He is manipulated by his kindly new masters, Harmon and Boffin, as he was by the vicious Fledgeby.

And, of course, *we* don't believe for a minute in Bella's aviaries and her ivory casket of jewels or in any other sign of the magic transformations the Boffins manage for themselves and others. But the real point is: the novel doesn't believe in or trust the Boffins either. That skepticism regularly pops up from within the Harmon–Boffin plot itself, the ur-fiction of possibility, "Wrapped," like the Baby Bella's doll, "in new Bank notes" (IV: xvi,883). It's all over the satire that accompanies almost every one of Mrs. Boffin's appearances. "Mrs. Boffin fairly screamed with rapture, and sat beating her feet upon the floor, clasping her hands and bobbing herself backwards and forwards, like a demented member of some Mandarin's family" (IV: xiii,845). Boffin's generosity flatters Wegg. And it corrupts Bella. It more or less kills Johnny Higden, and Betty Hidgen as well. Even Boffin himself, just at his moment of triumph, can't restrain his sense of the absurdity of his wife's "pretty picters" (IV: xiii, 849): "Mew, Quack-quack, Bow-wow!" he exclaims, hurrying away downstairs. He knows. And he lets us know: Boffins are all bosh.

Well, there went our adaptation. Our neat plebeian-parvenu division dies under us, just when we thought we had got its two sorts of fiction satisfactorily severed. The novel noxiously insists it won't go halves. Adapting it begins to look something like partitioning Yugoslavia. No matter you rearrange the parts, you can't make it make (your kind of) sense. Not because the parvenu has colonized the plebeian. Not even because the novel alternates inhabiting a *parvenu* and a plebeian vision of its materials. You can't carry it off because Dickens refuses to commit himself to, or be trapped within, any logic beyond the wish-fulfillment of the fictions he's devising.

We come face to face now with where this book started: Dickens won't, can't, in any case, doesn't, think, if thinking means, fundamentally, slotting, patterning one's thoughts in common categories. Thinking requires relinquishing the world I desire in favor of a world others know. That's not just a sacrifice Dickens won't allow, it's the sacrifice all his fiction is constructed to refuse. (Has there ever been a novelist more intent on constructing – sheer – *fiction?*) At the beginning of this book we said that there's no there in Dickens. But it's more accurate to say: there's no here there, if here's where we live, and there's what Dickens imagines.

Dickens constructs these novels as chamber theaters, closed in upon themselves, performing Dickens's scripts for Dickens's pleasure. Enamored of their own fecund, if unhappy, agilities, they eagerly court even incoherence if that's what's needed to baffle any readerly claim to competence. Not don't tread on me, but don't read me, when reading me requires I submit to categories we must share. There's nothing for us to carry away from reading texts like these, except the memorable pleasures of having read them. If we are the kind of reader who takes pleasure in reading texts so terrified of bliss they read all change as mutability. Texts which believe that a difficult liberty is always well surrendered in exchange for an enclosed and counter-civic regime. Texts, that is, which offer as more than sufficient the swoon of hallucination.

Of course, we do find the Law here. From what Victorian novel can it be absent? But we don't find here anything resembling D. A. Miller's *Police*. Despite his very impressive first scenes (I: iii, 66–74), Mr. Inspector turns out to be no Mr. Bucket. And by the end of the novel, he's more like a figure out of *Pirates of Penzance*, except he finds his lot a distinctly N'appy one (IV: xvi, 875).

The Inspector and the Law have no regulatory connection to the dynamic of this fiction. They neither prevent Eugene's bloody battering nor prosecute his assailant – the latter simply because Lightwood and Wrayburn, the lackadaisical lawyers, don't want it done. In this novel Law seems more concerned with the trajectories of plenitude than with plebeian enforcements – for obvious reasons: there are cash prizes to be had for solving its puzzles. But here the Law, and its enforcers, are routinely impotent. It/they never solve the Harmon murder. It/they get to Gaffer's drowning too late, for all the patient watching on the rainy shore. And it/they have nothing to do with the exposure and expulsion of Wegg. The Inspector is given a chance, during the extended finale, to nab the secondary crooks in Miss Abbey's bar (IV: xii,830–836). But that sequence is really managed by a cool, unflappable Harmon-Rokesmith, who treats the Inspector throughout as a sort of amiable but dim upper-servant. Even the dreaded Poor Law surfaces within the novel (though quite differently in the Postscript) only as the paranoid delusion of an ignorant old woman. We never see its horrific mangling. Instead, we are made repeatedly to feel that Betty Higden is wrong, if thoroughly pitiable, to destroy herself fleeing from its imagined (imaginary) terrors.

Emptying from the Police both power and prestige does not mean, of course, that there is no crisis of *discipline* in the world of this novel. Rather, it means that the crisis has assumed such monumental proportions that even the Police cannot manage it, either through action or through the intimidating threat of action. Indeed, the only thing that can be done in the face of so monumental a crisis, is to withdraw from it into a chamber of one's own.

This is it, then, our core idea: the Dickens novel flees from adaptation, because it first flees from comprehension. Once we grasp that, we begin to understand why it so thoroughly loathes and fears (and inevitably, therefore, envies) theatre.

ENTERING THE DICKENS *CAMERA*

It's in the Postscript to *Our Mutual Friend* that Dickens most clearly defines this model of writing and reading.

> When I devised this story, I foresaw the likelihood that a class of readers and commentators would suppose that I was at great pains to conceal exactly what I was at great pains to suggest: namely, that Mr. John Harmon was not slain, and that Mr. John Rokesmith was he. Pleasing myself with the idea that the supposition might in part arise out of some ingenuity in the story, and thinking it worth while, in the interests of art, to hint to an audience that an artist (of whatever denomination) may perhaps be trusted to know what he is about in his vocation, if they will concede him a little patience, I was not alarmed by the anticipation.
>
> To keep for a long time unsuspected, yet always working itself out, another purpose originating in the leading incident, and turning it to a pleasant and useful account at last, was at once the most interesting and the most difficult part of my design. Its difficulty was much enhanced by the mode of publication; for, it would be very unreasonable to expect that many readers, pursuing a story in portions from month to month through nineteen months, will, until they have it before them complete, perceive the relations of its inner threads to the whole pattern which is always before the eyes of the story-weaver at his loom.
>
> (Postscript; 894)

These paragraphs push a line that goes something like this. Read this novel not for truth but for pattern. Your delight derives from the novelist's pride of craft: from his *devising* successfully carried through. The author holds all the "threads" of his almost infinitely diffused "pattern," despite the "difficulty" in sustaining such an extended, intricate project, and certainly despite the inevitable impercipience of the "many readers." Those readers can unwisely insist on their meager sense of the probable, in exchange for that which "god-like" is "always before [Dickens's] eyes." But if they surrender their meager thinking to his idiot savoir, they receive in return an "account" that is "pleasant and useful," "useful" because "pleasant," rather than useful because relevant. Beware then of joining that "class of readers and commentators," like Wegg and the youngest Baldwin, who doubt the authoritative "design" of the "story-weaver at his loom." If you read like Wegg and Baldwin, you'll most certainly, as they do, lose any hope of getting from the text either what (Dickens thinks) you want or what you think you can use: usable if temporary pleasure.

But this image, the "whole pattern . . . always before the eyes of the story-weaver at his loom," doesn't that suggest that we've arrived in the territory of Shalott? Arguably, Dickens could be thinking of the men who actually did work at looms. But the emphasis on aesthetics rather than mere trade taken together with the sketching of a solitary artistic chamber, in which the novelist weaves, makes the Tennysonian allusion difficult to avoid. Both Dickens's Weaver and Tennyson's Lady are *cameral* figures – the term is Gerhard Joseph's. Each works in a special sort of solitary atelier, a "room that brings into focus a crucial vista in the outer world" (Joseph 1992: 63).[3] In her upper room, the Lady-weaver feels at first "half-sick of shadows," and then so sick of them that she causes her mirror to break, her design to explode, and, finally, her life to end. In death she becomes – having been the maker of a beautiful object – that object itself, the focus of Camelot's admiring, indeed necrophilic gaze. Reversing the figure, Dickens stresses his narrative delight in the pattern he is tracing. Now it is not he but we, the "class of readers and commentators," who dwell in the land of shadows, incomplete, fractious, ignorant, dependent on the clarifications and consolations that he in his solitary, artistic chamber arranges for us. Where the Lady is torn between her frigid, exogenous design and the exterior, sensuous world alluringly reflected in her mirror, the novelist delights in his enclosure, his privacy, his self-sufficient supremacy. "I devised . . . I foresaw . . . Pleasing myself with the . . . ingenuity . . . in the interests of art . . . trusted to know what he is about in his vocation." He doesn't need to see, to know, to recognize what's outside himself: "the whole pattern . . . is always before the eyes of the story-weaver at his loom."

That means that the Lady's and the Weaver's cameras differ radically. The Lady's is a panoptical tower. The Weaver's is much more a *camera obscura*. The Lady sees (the pattern she weaves) because she knows (the world it images), and she becomes known to that world because she has seen it first. Slowly, inexorably, she is pulled by what she sees out into the world, and despoiled for its inspection. But the Weaver weaves a pattern available only to the Inner Eye. He *knows* (the pattern) because he *sees* (the pattern). The world does not intervene. His "whole pattern" represents neither an object disclosing itself to, nor an idea teased out from, the Weaver's mind. Instead, the design appears as a sort of shadowy middle ground, different from both the subjective and the objective realms, just as the fluid images refracted by a convex lens colorfully *move* – and that is crucial – in clarified and complex selections across a *camera obscura*'s interior, prepared field. This is not Freudian dream-work. It's the work of the pre-Freudian dream, of reverie. It constitutes "an optical regime that will a priori separate and distinguish image from object" (Crary 1992: 37), and image from author. This regime provides no usable information about either the world or the novelist. Just the reverse. It grants him an impermeable autonomy.

Indeed, privacy may well furnish the obscure *camera's* greatest charm. The Dickensian Weaver delights in third-person language: the artist, the story-weaver, a language that playfully suspends his attachment to or responsibility for the text, all along, of course, asserting his superiority over the bewildered reader. And therefore nothing in that pattern should suggest to us, readers, commentators (adaptors), that we have glimpsed something of the Weaver's self when we have traced out the pattern the Weaver winds. No. The camera's "orderly projection" may be "made available for inspection by the [reader's] mind" (Crary 1992: 46), "pursuing a story in portions from month to month through nineteen months" (Postscript). But nothing in this projection should suggest that we've achieved intimate contact with the author's actual self. He defines himself only as a recording device, an optical instrument. And devices, notoriously, do not have selves. (This is not by any means someone to confide, "Reader, I married him.")

The Weaver is simply and supremely the absorbed servant of the pattern: his privacy, and his superiority, inviolable. There is no hint here of lack or shame, nor of guilt, although much of what follows in this book connects Dickens's counter-theatricality to shame. On the contrary, it is hard not to feel that Dickens is mischievously playing out in the Postscript (as he does in the plots of the novel) the pleasure-seeking dynamic of that hidden, doubled life he was currently carrying on with Ellen Ternan. That suggestion gains further support from the dangerous hint at the end of the Postscript where he alludes to the Staplehurst railway accident, an accident which came dangerously close to revealing the Ternan liaison. Here Dickens can't seem to prevent himself from teasing us with the hints of self-exposure we might get, only to hold back the information we would need to use the clue.

This "story-weaver," "Pleasing myself," indifferent to everything but "my design," demanding to "be trusted," never critiqued, how can he – why indeed should he – submit his notions to our slots? That would mean submitting his judgment to what the Postscript dismisses as "the odd disposition in this country to dispute as improbable in fiction, what are the commonest experiences in fact" – in fact as Dickens feels fact to be (p. 893). Such a submission can only seem "Idiotic," "nonsense" (p. 894) to a writer whose novel is "a kind of toy with which to dazzle himself" (Newsom 1980: 45).

And what of the reader? What is our connection to this cameral fiction? Our job, clearly, is to allow ourselves to be dazzled also, and dazed. Dazed first, dazzled later. The Postscript seethes with a commination of readerly sinners against this text: who find the Harmon–Rokesmith plot both tedious and unpersuasive, who think the multiple wills too mechanical a contrivance to bear the weight of so much plot, who find it strange that Betty Higden should run herself to exposure and death when any number of cozier alternatives were within reach. That kind of thinking is anathematized because nothing in our experience can be brought to bear against the self-evident supremacy of the story-weaver's "device." Ours not to reason why, let alone why not. Ours but to passively respond to the passing show. Which makes us an awful lot like the nouveau-riche Boffins as they discover London's "transparent lucidity" (Hillis Miller 1958: 307). They "derived an enjoyment from the variety and fancy and beauty of the display in the windows, which seemed incapable of exhaustion. As if the principal streets were a great Theatre" and they "constantly in the front row, charmed with all they saw and applauding vigorously" (III: v,528). Applauding vigorously, that's the work of the Dickens reader.

Of course, we are meant to feel superior to those naive consumers, the Boffins, and the precarious pleasures of their "great Theatre." Indeed, Theatre more or less warns us off the premises. As we'll see, in Dickens theatre always implies some sort of delusion. And it's illusion the Weaver wants us to accept. No, this Weaver offers his audience not the London Stage, or London as a stage, but something much more *ingenious, artful*, and *enhanced* (p. 893). If we will only stop carping, if we will just sit back and trust the Weaver to know best, we will get, "available to vision, focused and framed as a unity for the man with binoculars" (Clark 1985: 62), a theatre that is, in Dickens's own phrase, merely, and wonderfully, "as upon."[4]

That phrase, "as upon a theatre," comes from one of the final chapters of *Our Mutual Friend*. The chapter, "Two Places Vacated" (IV: ix), functions as a kind of theatrical manifesto, the parallel to the Postscript's anatomy of fiction. In sum, it argues something like this: *theatre is good, theater isn't*, when theatre names what happens in a theater. Theaters house, stage, produce theatre: the intersection of performers and spectators. Dickens believes, at his most optimistic, in a theatricality that can not only exhibit, but can actually generate self. (That's why people get the sense that he loves theatre.) He also believes that theaters surely kill. (That's the part people tend to miss.) What's more, and here comes the paradox: life will degenerate without theatricality quickly, and terribly, into mere, and destructive, theatre. This means that theatricality can only transpire "as upon a theatre," never as what really works on a stage. How does the chapter work this paradox through?

"Two Places Vacated" attempts to pay a long-postponed debt. It apologizes for and tries to retract the outrageous anti-Semitism displayed in his famous early villain, Fagin. In a key moment, the venerable Jewish money-lender, Mr. Riah, explains to his young friend, the dolls' dressmaker, what we learn earlier in the novel and what she has begun to suspect. Riah has been made a victim of living theatre. He has been made to "play the Jew" by the real moneylender, Fascination Fledgby, the malevolent power controlling the legal and economic fiction of Pubsey & Co, a bill-discounting operation in the ominously named St. Mary Axe. Fledgby can move undetected in *nouveau riche* society, while Riah, his agent, is thoroughly vilified. The British public are prepared to believe anything bad of "one of the Jews" (p. 795).

When Riah comes to realize that his compliance with Fledgby's nasty-minded fiction has harmed not only himself but the Jewish people, he breaks with his "master" and contributes to the exposure of the now rapidly unravelling money-lending enterprise. This conversion Riah describes as a form of theatre, but he also depicts it as, inextricably, the conversion and cleansing of theatre: casting out Shylock from the available repertoire of Jewish performances.

Riah explains that he began to comprehend the damage he was allowing himself to do when he reflected on a "theatrical" scene earlier in the book (III: xiii, "Give A Dog A Bad Name, And Hang Him"). There he had allowed Fledgby to force him to play Shylock toward the tremulous aristocratic pauper, Mr. Twemlow, while his master, delighted, and Jenny, appalled, watched. In the later chapter, he tells Jenny what happened to him afterwards:

I reflected, I say, sitting that evening in my garden on the housetop. And passing the painful scene of that day in review before me many times, I always saw that the poor gentleman believed the story readily, because I was one of the Jews – that you believed the story readily, my child, because I was one of the Jews – that the story itself first came into the invention of the originator thereof [Fledgby], because I was one of the Jews. This was the result of my having had you three before me, face to face, and seeing the thing visibly presented as upon a theatre. Wherefore I perceived that the obligation was upon me to leave this service. (p. 796).

In this "painful scene," Riah outlines a kind of proto-Brechtian theatre that makes not only a difference to himself but also to each member of that original audience – "I perceived that the obligation was upon me to leave this service."

Surely this is theatre with a difference, but so great a difference, in fact, that it tends to become almost unrecognizable as theatre. If Riah did not deploy the metaphor so explicitly, would any of us call theatre this Wordsworthian scene of emotion recollected in tranquil solitude – *as I reviewed that painful scene many times sitting in the garden on my housetop?* Doesn't theatre happen, we want to ask, in a theater, on a stage, and not afterwards in, as it were, the study? Doesn't theatre happen in company?[5]

After all, drama generally tends to work some variation on the formula: Making the Inner the Outer for the Other. Theaters are places where we, as spectators, go to see rise into plain and moving sight what someone else has carefully, even obsessively, hidden away. A well-known etymology even derives theater/theatre from the Greek word to gaze at, to behold. But we spectators always retain the right to recognize or deny that hidden as something of our own. We remain inviolable: only the characters are at risk. *Pace* Brecht, to be at all effective theatre, we insist, must be vicarious. Aren't we then more likely to call this as-upon theatre something like therapy: 'Making the Inner the Outer for the Self"?

But it's precisely this spectatorial distance that Dickens brands as vicious and corrupt. To make this argument, the chapter juxtaposes Riah's conversion with a contrasting sequence of what it calls "gratuitous drama" (p. 799), everything that makes theatre monstrous. This gratuitous drama entails the drawn-out, terrifying death of Jenny's drunken father, Mr. Dolls (who occupies the second of the chapter's two places vacated). At the end of a harrowing trail of abuse, he is carried, feverish and hallucinating, into an Apothecary's shop where, watched through a window by the curious, the man becomes by dying merely "it" (p. 801). The horror of this remorselessly sadistic sequence roots as much in the within-the-chapter audience's drawn-out delight as it does in the dying man's torment. Dickens always refuses to sentimentalize or celebrate the carnivalesque. He needs to keep us always aware of, and fearful about, the revelling crowd's deep need for a butt, a raree, a cock-shy, the need for someone even less fortunate than themselves to cement the communal frolic. Here, typically, he insists we see the mob's thrilled response to Dolls' collapse as not only grotesque but dehumanizing: "the window" through which his tormentors watch the dying drunk "becoming from within, a wall of faces, deformed into all kinds of shapes through the agency of globular red bottles, green bottles, blue bottles, and other coloured bottles" (p. 800).

This "ghastly," and clearly theatrical, illumination refocuses the scene away from the sight of the dying man and onto those who are ghoulishly drawn to turn the sufferings of a fellow human into the stuff of spectacle. In other words, to turn themselves into a great – read: excited, responsive – audience. That is in large part what makes this drama so bleakly and complexly "gratuitous." The spectators get it for free. They pay nothing. And the show is all the better, they feel, for its cheap and easy accessibility. But Dolls' death is also gratuitous because the audience gets nothing in return for watching. The drama makes no difference to anyone watching except for the dying man's daughter, who hides her face, refusing to be part of the audience. Dolls' "gratuitous" death is then the scene that doesn't signify, a non-sign, the horrible meaningless reduction of a human death to nullity. His drama degrades its protagonist to no end, only an ending, and it degrades its audience even more meanly.

Stated most bluntly, for Dickens gratuitous dramas shame, annul, even kill because the performer allows himself, or is forced, to become a spectacle, seen, used, "written" and therefore inevitably disregarded. As Shylock, Riah is entirely legible, and therefore completely misread.

When he compassionately tries to warn Fledgby's clients of what they have in store, his auditors can only hear threats, the assigned text, just further, confirmatory evidence of his "Jew's" bloody-mindedness. Dolls' role as cock-shy forecloses even more unbearably the chance to tell the self or the self's true story. To the hungrily watching audience, his performance reveals an all too easily and immediately legible imprint, indistinguishable from the blunt markings of tatoo and stamp: "a strange mysterious writing on his face, reflected from one of the great bottles, as if Death had marked him 'Mine'" (p. 800). Entirely visible and entirely (and therefore falsely) legible, he must also be entirely isolated, and entirely dead, the terrifying victim of a demonized, obtuse and counter-narrative Gaze. Visible, misread, isolated, dead: that regress spells theatre in Dickens.

We begin to grasp what's most deeply at stake in this stage fright when we see that for Dickens the subject of gratuitous drama is inevitably male. Theatre almost always abuses a him. Of course, Dickens also regularly subjects his women to the rigors of a specifically, and frequently, theatricalized Gaze. But, running counter to much of contemporary theory, his actual theaters threaten women less with macho power than with papier-maiche. In *Nicholas Nickleby*, for example, Kate Nickleby is tricked and trapped into a theater box. There she is subjected to the unwanted attentions of the upper class seducers, Mulberry Hawk and Frederick Verisopht (xxvii). But theater, stages and boxes alike, house fashion, that is vanity, superficiality, farce: Mrs. Nickleby's meandering reminiscences and Mrs. Wittiterly's addle-brained vainglory. The callous aristocrats merely fluster and annoy Kate rather than raising any serious threat to her virtue. The evening concludes safely with the soft-witted Lord Frederick's frustration. Kate's real danger comes from dining in her uncle's house. And it is her brother who finds in a theater the place of shame.

In *Bleak House* (xiii), a comparable persecution, this time with a distinctly lower-class gazer, redounds entirely against the male. Esther Summerson can not evade the languishing gaze of the socially climbing junior clerk Guppy: "we never went to the play without my seeing Mr. Guppy in the pit . . . I really cannot express how uneasy this made me . . . [it] put such a constraint upon me that I did not like to laugh at the play, or to cry at it, or to move, or to speak. I seemed able to do nothing naturally" (p. 222). Like Kate, Esther is embarrassed and uncomfortable. But she also, unlike Kate, makes the scene continuously funny. She deploys her arch sympathy completely to disempower an admirer whose "prepared expression of the deepest misery and the profoundest dejection" gives him only an air of "general feebleness." Far from being overpowered by Guppy's unwanted attentions, Esther claims she can't help "thinking of the dreadful expense to which this young man was putting himself on my account" (p. 223). In fact, the usual dynamic of seduction and ruin is pointedly reversed. She won't complain to her guardian because she fears "that the young man would lose his situation, and that I might ruin him" (p. 223).

The theaters in this scene and *Nickleby* are comic. But the male gaze turns back on the gazer in more crucially freighted scenes also: like the key confrontation between Lady Dedlock and Mr. Tulkinghorn later in *Bleak House*, as well as in the remarkable voyeuristic sequence between Eugene Wrayburn and Lizzie Hexam early in *Our Mutual Friend*. In both scenes the female object of the gaze seems paradoxically to grow stronger, or at least more resistant, in response to the demand that she decline into spectacle.

Neither scene seems to follow the outlines of either fetishistic or voyeuristic scopophilia, as these have been magisterially delineated by Laura Mulvey. Lady Dedlock imagines her treatment by the blackmailing Tulkinghorn as a dramatic performance, one in which the stage as scaffold neatly, bleakly converts into the scaffold as site of execution. "I am to remain on this gaudy platform, on which my miserable deception has been so long acted, and it is to fall beneath me when you [Tulkinghorn] give the signal?" (xiii, 637). Like Riah's, her life and career merge in an entirely and deliberately deceptive performance. But strikingly unlike Riah, and certainly unlike Dolls, Lady Dedlock has complete control over that performance. She has designed its scenario. And, when she is unmasked, she will, as she and Tulkinghorn agree, disappear. Lady Dedlock has perhaps more "floor-scenes" that even conventional Victorian melodrama would require, but, as Mary Saunders has shown, she never loses face in public (Saunders 1989: 73). Except for the first tell-tale, and very private, faint that puts Tulkinghorn on the scent, no one ever sees Lady Dedlock as anything less than fully composed and entirely in control. First lady of her social sphere, she knows superbly how to resist the inquisitorial gaze. Thus, when that gaudy platform does ultimately fall, her in some ways equally degraded death in every detail reverses Dolls' public dissolution. When her body is finally found (xviii, 59), she has already died as privately, indeed as mysteriously, as she lived. And only her child is permitted to approach her.

In *Our Mutual Friend*, illiterate, laboring Lizzie Hexam gets no such class-generated protection. Just the reverse. She is so entirely view-mastered that she has to flee London and the novel's plot for most of the second half of the book simply to save herself from being constantly traced and nastily accosted. That makes her scopic susceptibility even more illuminating for our purposes, particularly in the scene where she becomes "a sad and solitary spectacle" for her would-be, upper-class seducer Eugene Wrayburn (I: xiii, 211), a scene from which Lizzie emerges almost as enhanced as Lady Dedlock does from her comparable moment with Tulkinghorn.

Eugene's insistence on peering through a small, uncurtained side-window rather than a larger, curtained one not only clarifies his project as voyeuristic, but it also resonates for our argument with the peculiar, mysterious Apothecary's window giving on to Mr. Dolls' death. In this brief scene, paragraph by paragraph Lizzie is rendered, by the voyeur's eye and the narrator's prose, more and more the subject and stimulus of male scopic pleasure. She moves from being an almost invisible silhouette, through several stages, until Eugene and the reader can respond to her as a dehumanized aesthetic-erotic *gestalt*, a "deep rich piece of colour," the prose, his breathing, her breath all rapturously moving together with "the rising and the falling of the fire." So completely does Eugene's eye encompass the sequence that the male (heterosexual) reader feels himself almost the inevitable referent of Eugene's final, ambiguous remark: "If the real man feels as guilty as I do . . . he is remarkably uncomfortable" (p. 212).

Eugene feels guilty because Lizzie can break his attempt at ocular control to assert herself against her observers' (the apostrophe is correctly placed) predatory claims. She foils Eugene's and the prose's trance-like concentration by suddenly starting up – we have a sense that perhaps she has heard her silent trespasser. She leaves the room, comes outside where Eugene hides by his peep-hole, and calls out several times for her father. When she goes back, Eugene feels he has no choice but to drop away from the window and return through the mud to his friend. If anything the male gaze seems to have made Lizzie an even more powerful figure than she was in the earlier sequences of assisting her father and protecting her brother. But her expansion is not one which the male gaze can successfully go on to fetishize. Instead, Eugene is forced to drop the observer's stance, to abandon guiltily the scopic project, "Guy Fawkes in the vault and a Sneak . . . both at once" (p. 212).

In contrast to all these women, the male body in Dickens is routinely, and successfully, voyeurized. This switch completely inverts Victorian custom. As Tracy Davis has shown, nineteenth-century theaters featured prime displays of female flesh. But even when men like the step dancer W. P. Carey stripteased, they revealed nothing. On stage Carey went so far as to unbutton his trousers. He then went off stage to remove them and returned "attired in long black drawers (Davis 1991: 121–122). Carey went about as far as he could go, because striptease is something men can only parody. The classic Freudian explanation for that difference follows, of course, the classic Freudian explanation for every sort of difference: the woman's lack of penis makes her the mesmerizing object of the terrified male gaze. With no lack to reveal, the stripping male can (censurably) expose himself but he can never be (powerlessly) exposed. Nevertheless, Dickens regularly produces scenes of successfully voyeurized men. Men voyeurized by other men. Voyeurized men who must therefore be, the novels anxiously hint, cock-shy. If stage fright is male–male, can castration be far below?

Consider *Our Mutual Friend's* hero, John Harmon. The Harmon plot roots in a voyeur's project. Harmon has resolved to return home from South Africa secretly to spy on the fiancé of his arranged marriage. He finds that project foiled almost as soon as he touches shore. He becomes the one betrayed, by his fellow, male conspirators. They turn him into a theatricalized figure, undressed, drugged, duped, beaten in ways that powerfully echo the story of the unfortunate Dolls. But Harmon, unlike Dolls, sees and feels what is happening to him. The assaulted, battered, shrunken voyeur becomes himself voyeurized. He feels himself shrinking into a powerless target while "to my sense of sight he [the mate Radfoot] began to swell immensely" (II: xiii, 426). The other's tumescence signals the sexual trauma at the core of this scopic inversion. As a result of his "rape," Harmon loses not only his name and identity but his right and power to marry. In the Dickens world, to be seen, specifically for a man to be entirely seen by other men, is to be literally and entirely unmanned, alive or dead.

Dickens renders this castration-by-viewing nowhere more poignantly or more powerfully than in the downfall of the novel's anti-hero, whose subversion we traced earlier, Bradley Headstone. Ironically, but inevitably in Dickens, Wrayburn can spy much more successfully on the male teacher than he can on the illiterate female. He tries once to turn Lizzie into show and fails miserably. But repeatedly he reduces the schoolmaster to spectacle, exposing Headstone not only to Wrayburn's own gaze but also to that of his sidekick Lightwood, enhancing his pleasure by explicitly theatricalizing it. And this theatricalization in turn emascu-

lates Bradley, "cancel[ling]" his "figure," comically reducing him to a
merely enormous but anguished head. But it is a blind head. Bradley
cannot see: the sight he seeks, Lizzie, is always denied him. Nor can he
in any way protect or conceal himself from his tormentor's gaze. Night
after night he leaves the arena "torturing himself with the conviction
that he showed it all and they exulted in it" (III: xi, 608). But that all he
can show is only weakness, lack. Indeed, he is helplessly available not
only to sighting from above by well-born men, but also to low-born
villains like the murderous scavenger, Rogue Riderhood. Headstone
must "show it all," to the exulting hilarity of both stalls and pit alike.

Watched by Wrayburn, that vulnerability produces merely but exquisitely extended humiliation. Watched by Riderhood, exposure
means death. Riderhood moves from ditch to ditch, "and holding apart
so small a patch of the hedge that the sharpest eyes could not have
detected him" eagerly watches Headstone undress, bathe in the river,
and dress again (IV: vii, 775–776). This climactic voyeurism ironically
inverts Eugene's failed attempt to steal a glance at Lizzie. The same
motifs recur, crossing the ditches, watching through the smallest aper-
ture, but now the male–male gaze entirely inverts the outcome. Lizzie
demolishes effortlessly, even unconsciously, the attempt to see her
unawares. But Bradley – Susannah without a Daniel to intervene –
succumbs without defense to the salacious, exploitative male gaze. He
has gone to elaborate lengths to conceal not only his body but his
purpose and his actions from Riderhood. But this novel insists that it is
virtually impossible for any but the best-born men to conceal themselves
from the prying gaze of other males. In that eager watching Riderhood
can not only see Headstone completely but he effortlessly learns from
that watching how to destroy Bradley's life, to turn him like Dolls into
gratuitous drama. He discovers the clues that will drive a disgraced
Bradley down into the fatal pit.

To survive the Dickens plot the Dickensian male performer must find
a way to turn gratuitous drama into as-upon theatre, to use, rather than
be used by, the onlookers. He must turn those eager prying audiences
into a mirror of himself, the audiences he needs rather than the audiences who prey upon him. Thus Riah has "a look of having lost his way in
life" (p. 798) as he closes down his performance as Shylock, and shuts up
Pubsey & Co. Yet almost immediately he transmutes that earlier,
overdetermined, pseudo-Shakespearean performance into an acutely
renewed life now opening before him. He manages that change because
he "had you three before me, face to face," making them mirror himself

back to himself, "seeing the thing" – that is, the self – "visibly presented as upon a theatre." This as-upon-a-theatre he turns into an intersubjective arena for the forging of a new and usable self. No surprise that the chapter ends with Riah accompanying Jenny home to fill the place vacated by Dolls, gratuitously gazed to death, who could only be a common figure of fun and no real father to her. As-upon theatre confers (private) life just as surely as gratuitous drama delivers (public) death.[6]

Riah's intersubjective development of self strikingly prefigures arguments of the influential American phenomenologist Bruce Wilshire. Wilshire argues that theatre enables us "to see thematically and acknowledgeably what previously has simply engulfed or blinkered us" (1991: 33). In that very nice phrase to "see acknowledgeably" I hear what happens when Riah sees himself as seen by the trio of Jenny, Twemlow. and Fledgeby. At that moment a self emerges before him as it is "performed" with, toward, among those others who recognize, perceive and respond (in quite different ways) to that self. Wilshire is working here on foundations laid by Kant and by Hegel. He is following up Kant's crucial insistence that we can know something only in a context, by placing it against, as it were, its other or opposite. And, more significantly, he is also following up Hegel's dialectic insistence that a human being can become itself "only when it makes its own what others have made of it" (p. 152). But Wilshire – and Dickens – go beyond that foundation. They insist that human beings searching for individuation must meet what Wilshire calls the "actor's challenge," and what Dickens means by behaving "as-upon-a-theatre."

An individual meets the actor's challenge when he "disclose[s] the other incorporated in him *as* other, as character, but he can do so only in the presence of others for whom he is another who mimetically enacts their common life" (Wilshire 1991: 24). Here Wilshire reads the self as doubly theatrical. It derives from, is originally part of, and never significantly departs from, a "common life," a repertoire of human positions and possibilities [from cockshy to Shylock, as it were] which culture holds in repertoire for all its members. Those characters the self then mimetically reproduces in itself and for the others.

We are far away here from the Lockean notion of "a primal and sovereign inwardness . . . the autonomous individual ego that has appropriated to itself the capacity for intellectually mastering" its world (Crary 1992: 47). And just as far from a world in which the difference between true and false identities corresponds to the difference between an accurately perceived object and an optical illusion. Thus, Riah's "conversion" does not move from false to true self, or from role-playing to true self. We might prefer a sentimentalized, authenticist scenario where Riah, having been cast in a theatrical (read: false) part, Shakespeare's moneylender, eventually escapes from theatre into life by publicly discarding and renouncing role-playing altogether. But that's not what happens in this novel. Instead, Riah's solitary (read: sovereign, autonomous) mental operation aligns others' views for review (review is Riah's own term), and then synthesizes or fuses these "dispersed and multiplied" signs into his own "aggregation of disjunct elements" (Crary 1992:129, 126–126). But those "elements" are continuous with the original role. In effect, Riah moves from an unflattering to a kindlier version of the same role. In a world where performance is all, you only can be how you manage to seem.

This Dickensian appraisal of identity, like Wilshire's, sticks resolutely to an index of mimetic performance and common roles. When Riah converts, he can only convert from a role "as a Jew" to a role "as a Jew." Riah's psychic and personal break-through depends entirely upon the ways in which that change happens "as upon a theatre," that is: as and from a repertoire. He's explicit about the renewed sense of ethnic-religious identity that urgently drives this change. "But doing it as a Jew, I could not choose but compromise the Jews of all conditions and all countries" (IV: ix, 795). He's clarifying a role, not something personal or individual in him, a Lockean self. Life is for him what a career is to an actor, a perpetual, usually frustrating search to be cast in sympathetic parts.

Does that limitation shape all of Dickens's para-theatrical project, or does it simply and more starkly uncover only Dickens's thorough participation in his culture's historic refusal to credit any form of Jewish conversion?[7] I would say both.

I find it deeply disturbing that Riah maintains the fiction of Jewish rancor when he resumes dealing with Twemlow, this time as Harmon's, not Fledgeby's, agent. Why can't Riah just come clean with Twemlow? What use can that fiction still serve – except the uses of anti-Semitism? For that matter, why can't Harmon–Boffin just pay the debt? It's a piddling amount of money. Does the novel keep the money-lender in operation, we need to ask, because that is the only role from the common stock it can imagine a Jew playing? The novel certainly seems able to conceive an alternative. Admirable, middle-class Jews own the mill to which Lizzie transfers mid-way through the novel, in all respects an apparently successful, tolerant, enlightened couple. But they are invisible. Though we hear about them, we are never permitted to see them, despite the fact that it would be very easy, and splendidly Dickensian, to extend the comedy of Mrs. Milvey's unconscious prejudice by having the Rev. and Mrs. Frank actually encounter Lizzie's employers, rather than rendering them only in Lizzie's hazy description. Nevertheless, hazy description is all they get. The mill-owners have no presence in *Our Mutual Friend*. They make no impact. The only Jew we see is the Jew prejudice has constructed: the money-lender, gabardined, broad-brimmed, staffed. It begins to seem the only kind of Jew Dickens can write.

Is that why Jenny Wren can't see that the real villain at Pubsey & Co is Fledgby (III: xiii 638)? Ultimately, she does ask Riah's forgiveness for her error (IV: ix, 795), but, disconcertingly, she almost immediately suggests that of course she couldn't help misjudging him. "It did look bad; now didn't it?" Indeed it did, Riah agrees. And the text concurs. Jenny is the patron of Mrs. Truth, astute at sizing up (Christian) men. She knows and loves Riah, loathes Fledgby, and has every reason to trust her 'godfather' (he has saved Lizzie from her suitors and assisted in the delivery of the exculpating documents to Miss Abbey). Nevertheless, she's quite all right, the novel maintains, to deny and unhesitatingly betray this entirely admirable man. We are unlikely to believe in a lurking anti-Semitism just under the surface of *her* friendship, since she hasn't given the slightest hint of anti-Semitic feeling or awareness before this point. Rather, the prejudice seems to root in the fiction itself, in its sense that the stereotype is so irresistibly likely that even an astute well-wisher like Jenny can accept and act on it without incurring narrative censure.

But it's neither supple nor subtle enough to call all of this merely anti-Semitism. Rather, anti-Semitism shapes the particularly toxic expression, for this character, of Dickens's relentless sense that role supremely determines all male identity. In Dickens's fiction, origins will always out, and origins always play themselves out in the calculus of socially assigned, male roles. Thus Rogue can never be anything but the rogue. Rescued from drowning, he comes nastily and inevitably back to his old, disreputable self. And that pattern of eternal return is true for the privileged as well as the poor. John Harmon can try to play out his preferred fiction of John Rokesmith, the novel's mutual friend. But it simply won't work. His new identity is punctured as disguise and he must return to being John Harmon, the son and heir of all the Mounds, if he is to have any place in the novel's final distribution of prizes. (And, of course, paradigmatically, Pip, despite starting so much further ahead than Oliver, can never fulfill those expectations Oliver is born to.) Riah, then, as an archetypal figure of theatricalized identity, not only the Jew, but Shylock the Jew, models in the most explicit, that is the most theatrical way, the inability of the entire project of as-upon-theatre to initiate for any male "activity more daring, volatile, and free than the constraints and dangers of the world ordinarily allow" (Wilshire 1991: 24). So what made us call Riah's as-upon theatre a break-through?

Trying to think like Dickens, Riah's as-upon theatre is a break-through if one believes (like Dickens) that we can never change roles, only audiences. In other words: if we believe that the best we can settle for is pleasure, not bliss. As-upon theatre insists that, though roles are inescapable, men can have theatre's intersubjective pleasures, including modified applause, without being subject to gratuitous drama's inevitable scrutiny, exposure, and shame. One can act, as upon a theatre, only by thinking about performance. (The talking-cure as home remedy.) On that point, the story-weaver and Riah become as one, and Dickens and Wilshire definitively part company. Wilshire insists the emergent self can only happen within the frame of the watching audience. The self always roots in a public. *Our Mutual Friend*, however, stalwartly searches out not theatre but *camera obscura*, theater's parody, whether one is the solitary character, alone on the roof "passing the . . . scene . . . in review" (IV: ix, 796), or the story-weaver in his chamber, "the relations of the finer threads to the whole pattern . . . always before [his] eyes" (Postscript, 893). The last thing Dickens or the Dickensian wants is an audience that can claim parity. Parity's not even a step from priority. And that's why, of course, Bradley Headstone's undoing starts in front of, and in cooperation with, the audience of his pupils. The poor Schoolmaster lacks a roof of his own. Not to say a loom.

It's worth noting here how the desirable Dickensian camera seems to foreshadow the development of that other *camera*: cinema, performance in the absence of audience – audiences responding to the absence of performance. The *cameral* and film both isolate their target audience into individuals, imposing a semi-ascetic withdrawal from the world, in order to see that world re-represented. the starkest absence – traces on a page, images on celluloid – suggesting the largest presence. But where the cameral, whether chamber or fiction, is the site of the individual Inner Eye, the theatre appeals to and depends on a public and social self. It literally forces its spectators into a community, a community that perforce includes those who perform.

We see clearly now why Dickens turns away from theaters, and why he creates his own peculiar substitute for spectacle. Theaters stage the examined life. They boast the exchange. "I perform, you look. You watch me. I let you watch. You know that I am letting you watch. I know that you know. What I perform, if it were not under the influence of your eye, would be mere doing . . . If you look away, it will be something different; if it were different, you would look away" (Huston 1992: 26).

But Dickens's Postscript – like Riah – proclaims: "I perform. You look but cannot see. You can not watch me. I let you watch only what I project. You know that I am letting you watch. I know that you know. But what I perform is by no means under the influence of your eye. If you look away, you will miss what I am showing and then you will see nothing. So look not for me, but look away at that which is not myself which I choose to display."

Obviously, then, we can't adapt, on anything like its own terms, *Our Mutual Friend*. If to adapt means to submit to our notions and experiences a text, and characters, that offer instead the luminous eccentricity of a special event, an event that grounds and justifies only itself. We can only transgress this text, and texts like it. But before we take up the task of that transgression, our next step, Flashback, needs to explore the complex roots that keep Dickens only as-upon a theatre. We need to explore further and deeper the roots of this anti-performative pattern.

Flashback

The next chapter (3), ". . . to be a Shakespeare," asks why Dickens must reject the theater as a stage for his hero. And the chapter that follows (4), "Exit: 'the sanguine mirage'," explores how Dickens goes about exiting the theater in favor of a far, far better stage. This paraphrase may make it seem that the book is now going to verge suspiciously on that very dull thing, lit. crit. Lest such a misgiving take root, let me affirm here that this book can only imagine two ways to use other books: to laugh with them, or to rewrite them.

I like in Dickens what makes me laugh: his irresistible, indefatigable critique of what James Kincaid has called (in quite other circumstances) "the straightforward life," not simply the straight life but any life which thinks earnest partnering has got to be the only secure basis for happiness. But many more able people than I have taken that critique as their subject.

I focus here, instead, on what I can rewrite to suit myself. Other choices don't seem all that enticing. I don't want to venerate Dickens's, or anybody else's, books. And I certainly think it's a profound waste of good emotion to be angry with them. Books – even great books – are not important enough to be turned into parents.

CHAPTER 3

. . . *to be a Shakespeare*

"it was quite a mercy, ma'am," added Mrs. Nickleby, in a whisper to Mrs. Wititterly, "that my son didn't turn out to be a Shake-speare, and what a dreadful thing that would have been!"

(Nicholas Nickleby xxvii, 353)[1]

Dickens's rejection of theater carries both an intra- and an extra-psychic component – just like everything else. This chapter explores both. It tries to uncover the psychic associations Dickens's traumatized narcissism projected onto acting. And it also tries to recover the meaning (or meanings) contemporary acting was likely to convey to Dickens. Rather too neatly, the chapter separates these two considerations, aligning the first with the first novel, *The Pickwick Papers* (1836–1837), and the second with the third, *Nicholas Nickleby* (1838–1839). But that division is both artificial and misleading. *Nickleby* not only inherits but plunges even further the actor's devaluation begun by the earlier novel. Indeed, if there is one through-line connecting both texts it is this: it is not just an anxious Dickens who finds theater shame-inducing. The theatrical profession itself, to anyone's finding, was already and everywhere seared with shame.

EXCEPT ACTORS SOMETIMES

". . . there are only two styles of portrait painting; the serious and the smirk; and we always use the serious for professional people (except actors sometimes)"

Miss La Creevy, *Nicholas Nickleby* (x, 115)

Dickens's first "villain," Alfred Jingle, is also, paradoxically, his first comic hero.[2] It's no surprise that a deracinated, plebeian Dickens should start out siding with an impecunious, on-the-make Jingle against the fatuous, bourgeois dilettanti of the Pickwick Club. What does surprise is that about a quarter of the way through, the novel suddenly and unexpectedly switches loyalties. Pickwick transforms from comic butt to sentimental hero. And Jingle himself disappears, until the closing numbers of the plot. There he unexpectedly reappears, also entirely recast, as the pathetic, feeble, charmless object of Pickwick's condescending charity. I want to argue that both Jingle's original ambiguity – at once villain and hero – and his sudden eclipse root in his profession. He is a stroller, an itinerant actor. And his villainy as well as his not inconsiderable, and distinctly sexual, comic charm derive from his performative skills. Actors, Dickens starts off insisting, are, if not mad, then sooner rather than later bad, and always dangerous to know. Understanding why he should feel that to be so is the next step in grasping why the Dickens theatre must be always and only as-upon.

Pickwick and Jingle pair off almost from the novel's start as something like the two halves of a classic clown act. Pickwick performs as *auguste*, the white-faced clown, the "epitome of culture" who "behaves elegantly and authoritatively" (Bouissac 1981: 164). Against him, Jingle plays *faire-vouloir*, the ugly clown always wearing a "suit either too large or too small . . . and eccentric in other respects" (p. 165), who "lightheartedly violates" the cultural regime *auguste* maintains. In this pairing, *auguste* Pickwick seems to represent the dead-end of what J. G. A. Pocock (1985) has called the ideology of "commercial humanism," the counter-civic, bourgeois ideal of eighteenth-century mercantile life. The Merchant's Tale that succeeded the Knight's Tale.

Commercial Humanism promised to compensate the refined and polished representative of commercial society "by an indefinite and perhaps infinite enrichment of his personality, the product of the multiplying relationships, with both things and persons, in which he became progressively involved" by traveling around on business or meeting foreign businessmen (Pocock 1985: 49). Self-enriching travel is, of course, exactly the initial agenda of the Pickwick Club: with its "lively sense of the inestimable benefits which must inevitably result" to an individual "from extending his travels, and consequently enlarging his sphere of observation, to the advancement of knowledge, and the diffusion of learning" (i, 1). And even after his many defeats and humiliations that ideology continues to echo in Mr. Pickwick's final apology for the "pursuit of novelty" that drove his earlier travels. They were directed, he claims, in the best commercial humanist tradition, "to the enlargement of my mind, and the improvement of my understanding" (lvii, 796–797).

Of course, a culturally, and economically, impoverished Jingle lacks access to Pocock's reading of Commerce. To the stroller Pickwickian

Commercial Humanism seems merely a sort of archaic grandiosity, a stolidly complacent insensitivity. And therefore the ugly clown repeatedly insists on trumping the white clown, imposing on this representative of outworn elitist culture, culture's contrary, *nature*, vividly displayed in what Steven Marcus calls Jingle's "qualities of free inventiveness, of active, spontaneous creativity" (Marcus 1965: 192). Qualities that are clearly marked as theatrical. Qualities which clearly echo his similarly marginated and talented creator.

But then, as we read along, all of a sudden, we're not supposed to mock Pickwick any more. We can laugh, gently, at him, but we must also begin to see him as a hero of principle, even to admire him as a lovably impetuous angel in gaiters. The butt of the novel's original satire has become the code by which the remainder of the book abjures us, if we can, to live. And if we can't live by it, then we should at least feel for it an unremitting nostalgia. And Jingle, in the process, deteriorates into an emasculated, mealy mouthed nonentity.

To a great extent this transformation happens because the novel begins to see that Jingle's deflating energies are not really up to subverting the real threat emerging against the Dickensian imagination: Law, a power that menaces not merely Pickwick but Dickens's own freedom to create: his texts, his career, himself. Dodson and Fogg, who run the breach of promise plot, appear, embodying a new kind of "hegemonic masculinity," the organized male socioeconomic structure which in any society dominates all women and most men (Carrigan, Connell, Lee 1987: 90–91). Early on, while the Rochester soldiery can leave Pickwick feeling "ashamed" (ii, 44), they amuse Jingle. These foppish soldiers are merely Napoleonic leftovers, comic extras out of opera bouffe. Their day closed at the Congress of Vienna. But with Dodson and Fogg, the novel witnesses a new and timely menace, the early nineteenth-century's crucial transfer of loyalties to the ideology of administration: lawyer-land, against which the soldiery – not to mention Jingle – seems as vestigial as the Pickwickians. If Pickwick comes into the novel believing like Edmund Burke that "Manners" . . . are of more importance than laws (quoted by Pocock 1985: 49), he learns from Dodson and Fogg, and the Fleet, the impossibility of resisting the ruthless inefficiencies of those quiche-and sentiment-spurning real men who function as the new "warden[s] of a set order" (Bouissac 1981: 164).

But why should Dodson and Fogg cost the novel Jingle? Why must "Mr Jingle . . . disappear" as Pickwick finds "himself caught in the arms of Sam" (x, 131)? Why does Dickens have to invent this new young man to guide Pickwick through the world? Why not pair Jingle and Pickwick as a sort of proto-Victorian Rogers and Astaire: Pickwick could give Jingle (at least, moral) style, and Jingle could give Pickwick (not literally, of course) sex. But that's exactly why Jingle must go. All along, Jingle, the actor, intrudes, not only wit, but inescapably, the body, the male body, from his initial sexual braggadocio to his pseudo-Ovidian rape of Miss Wardle from the Dell.[3] And Dickens to his shame quickly discovers that the male body, especially the male body confidently exhibited and deployed, is what he both covets and cannot endure.

The first time we see Jingle his body is *escaping* clothing which cannot contain or cover him. And almost the first thing he tells us about himself is that he's Don Giovanni, his servant Job a sadly tattered Leporello: "Conquests! Thousands. Don Bolaro Fizzgig—Grandee—only daughter—Donna Christina—splendid creature—loved me to distraction—jealous father—high-sowled daughter—handsome Englishman [himself]—Donna Christina in despair—prussic acid—stomach pump in my portmanteau—operation performed—old Bolaro in ecstasies—consent to our union—join hands and floods of tears—romantic story—very" (ii, 12). As the dismal Stroller insists, on performers' "bodily energies . . . alone they . . . depend for their subsistence" (iii, 35). A dependence out of which the ensuing plot makes antic hay, as the seductive Jingle cuts his easy swath through the gentry's assembled widows and daughters, threatening both patriarchal Dingley Dell and the homosocial Club.

But the actor's body, Jingle's body, is not just his or any body, it is, paradigmatically, the male body. On the Romantic stage, supremely, the actor is his body, the athlete who speaks. Thus, it is Nicholas Nickleby's "natural physical powers" that make Vincent Crummles certain this completely inexperienced young man can become a successful actor. "There's genteel comedy in your walk and manners, juvenile tragedy in your eyes, and touch-and-go farce in your laugh" (xxii, 283)." "[I]n every other art a man may choose his materials; to make them colossal or not," Thomas Serle testified to the Select Committee on Dramatic Literature in 1832, "but as we have only our natural physical powers to act with, such as they are given to us, we cannot . . . extend them." If his body is "naturally" the actor's instrument, then no matter what the role, he is always and preeminently performing being male.

Serle's uninflected choice of "colossal" shows how universal was this assumption that acting, like painting or sculpture, figured among the pictorial arts. To make the passions readable, performing bodies functioned both within, and as, a sign system, a semaphore corps without the flags – or with flags only in the more patriotic finales. Acting as signal signals itself even in the title of Henry Siddons's important text book, *Practical Illustrations of Rhetorical Gesture and Action* (1822). Here *Illustrations* refers primarily to the plates and explications that fill the book. They show the neophyte what it looks like when professionals stage attitudes (presumably much in demand) like Voluptuous Indolence, Vulgar Arrogance, Sublime Adoration and Rustic Cunning. (Voluptuous Indolence looks especially worth trying, though it seems to require a tree, a basket, and a hat.) But *Illustrations* also refers to the book's entire catalogue of attitudes, expressions, gaits, that is to acting itself, the mastered "gestures" which function for an audience as "rhetorical illustration." The "body serves to express," Siddons insists, "the different situations of the soul" (p. 49). An audience works to decode the performer's body on the basis of this shared, somatic semiosis: "we recognize in these external sensations of the *body*, the modifications which affect the *soul*" (p. 147).

In the late Georgian era – the period of *Pickwick* and *Nickleby* – that body, that sexuality, are not univocally read. Then, as of course now, successful actors were represented "as always-willing sex machines" (Straub 1992: 163). But the actor's body also entered the nineteenth-century marked as "a site of struggle among competing definitions of masculine sexual identity," as Kristina Straub lucidly demonstrates in *Sexual Suspects*, her remarkable study of earlier attitudes toward acting (p. 29). All of these competing definitions – priapic, narcissistic, deviant – refer to a "sexuality that," like Jingle's, is always "excessive and out of control" (p. 26). The late eighteenth century had emphasized the 'effeminate' aspects of acting, delight in display and an overdwelling on emotions. That tendency remained – as indeed it still does today – tarring especially minor theatrical hangers-on. But by the early nineteenth century a contrary "discursive impetus to 'masculinize' the theater" had worked largely "to expel the ambiguities" (p. 48). In fact, Romantic culture was strongly marked "by the increasingly noticeable tendency . . . to construct the theater as a bastion of manliness in an effeminate society" (p. 61). Think, for a glorious instance, of Edmund Kean.

Theatricalized virility pulses through Hazlitt's well-known encomium on Kean's Richard III. The critic literally gushes over the greatest of Romantic actors in his most successful role. Of the famous, and notoriously difficult, wooing scene, Hazlitt insists that Kean knows "Richard should woo not as a lover, but as an actor" (quoted by Donohue 1970:

336). And then Hazlitt – obligingly – defines actor: not just a man, but a superman, one who easily "shew[s] his mental superiority and power to make others the playthings of his will." Clearly, Jingle is no Kean, but just as clearly Kean is Jingle's prototype. At the Rochester Assembly he is playing Kean's big scene in exactly Kean's way, though in a distinctly minor and of course comic key. "I'll dance with the widow," he proclaims (ii, 21). This particular widow's a doctor's, not a prince's, relict. Jingle proceeds nevertheless to perform a virtuoso variation on Kean's Richard wooing Lady Anne. Here's Kean, according to Hazlitt. "Mr. Kean's attitude in leaning against the side of the stage before he comes forward in this scene, was one of the most graceful and striking we remember to have seen. It would have done for Titian to paint." Here's Jingle – not Titian, but a passable pastiche. "And the stranger forthwith crossed the room; and, leaning against a mantel-piece, commenced gazing with an air or respectful and melancholy admiration . . . The stranger progressed rapidly." What Dickens calls the actor's "professional [i.e. theatrical] air" (viii, 105) no one can resist: widow, spinster, critic, clubman, novelist.

Except for *Pickwick* itself. Because it's shortly after this scene that Jingle vanishes suddenly, for (in the Oxford edition) 560 pages. A considerable gap even in a novel the length of *Pickwick*. What's happened?

The short, risky answer: Dickens got back from his honeymoon. The premier theoretician of narcissism, Heinz Kohut, has observed that "certain periods of transition," for example "the time when a marriage partner is chosen," may "constitute emotional situations that reactivate the period of the formation of the self" (1985: 131). At this critical juncture, the "replacement of one long-term representation by another endangers a self whose earlier, nuclear establishment was faulty; and the vicissitudes of early pathology are experienced as repeated by the new situation." Obviously, Dickens's honeymoon comes well after he bunked the Covent Garden audition. But, in analogous ways, I believe, both the audition and the marriage called up anxieties comparable to the more famous and obvious crisis involving the boy Charles's time and shame in the blacking factory. In all these cases, we touch upon a severely burdened narcissism shocked by the difficult-to-refuse demands an insubordinate other makes on a grandiose, insecure self. Thus, newly married, at the moment when Dickens's narcissistic self-dwelling is challenged to focus on the romantically idealized other, he finds a way, in the fiction, to refocus "narcissistic libido upon the narcissistic self" (p. 128).

You may not care for this Kohutian reading (though, if you don't, you're going to be increasingly unhappy with this increasingly Kohutian book), but it is hard to escape the coincidence that just as Dickens started out on his long-postponed, longed-for marriage to Catherine Hogarth, he started to revise his novel in a radically new direction. The new husband-novelist now has his protagonist explore exhaustively the liberating possibilities of breach of promise. He even sends his protagonist Pickwick to prison rather than fulfill a 'promise' to wed, shading the hitherto comic *auguste* into a kind of secular Vicar of Wakefield, until, ultimately, a (deservedly ruined) lady quits all claims to an (impeccably chaste) gentleman. Before the marriage, Jingle's linguistic and priapic energies seemed liberating. As the marriage begins, and the plot continues, the novel begins just as energetically to repress that libido. From now on, homosocial bonding against female appetite insistently will abjure all heterosexual rivalry. Rather than connubial bliss, it's a mutually supportive all-male community the novel works to idealize. Indeed, Dickens appears to uncover in this crisis what will become the increasingly obsessive, virtually defining, project of his career as a novelist: to unwrite in radical fiction the straightforward normalcy his unsatisfactory marriage forced him to live.

In this transformation, the male body routinely betrays the male ego. Thus, repeatedly, Pickwick blunders into erotically pregnant situations, which women variously read as proffer and/or threat, and in which he consistently fails to perform to anyone's satisfaction. But that master situation actually plays itself out in virtually unlimited variation all over the book. The most important among these variations include:

(1) Pickwick, sneaking into a girl's school garden after dark (xvi), is found out as "the man-the man – behind the door!", that "ferocious monster" (p. 223), who must be bound "hand and leg" and locked up "in a closet" (p. 223);

(2) He voyeuristically eyeballs Miss Witherfield at the intimacies of her toilette (xxii), almost fainting "with horror and dismay" but also finding it "quite impossible to resist the urgent desire to see what was going forward" on her side of the bed (p. 309);

(3) As he kisses his hand to a lady in the box opposite the hustings (xiii), the Eatanswill electors cry out: "Oh you wicked old rascal . . . looking arter the girls are you?" "Oh you wenerable sinner." "Putting on his spectacles to look at a married 'ooman' "I see him a winkin' at her, with his wicked old eye". All of these taunts, of

course, "accompanied with invidious comparisons between Mr. Pickwick and an aged ram" (p. 171).

It's not then just Dodson and Fogg's clerks who spot him as "the supposed trifler with female hearts and disturber of female happiness" (xx, 265). As Sam himself moralizes: "Always the vay vith these here old 'uns hows'ever, as is such steady goers to look at" (xviii, 246).

All of these scenes turn on the same dread: public humiliation of the erotically incapable male, libido arrested as shame. This shame the novel insistently roots in a powerful need to humiliate/regulate the man who persists in expressing the apparently indomitable demands of male sexuality. Listen to the Winkles, senior and junior, discussing the younger man's run-away marriage.

" 'You are ashamed of yourself, I hope, sir?' said the old gentleman.
"Still Mr. Winkle said nothing.
" 'Are you ashamed of yourself, sir, or are you not?' " inquired the old gentleman.
" 'No', sir,' replied Mr. Winkle, ... 'I am not ashamed of myself or, of my wife either." (lvi, 793).

Throughout *Pickwick* relations with women bring all sorts of men to similar scenes of shame. Shame even censors those youthful romances with which it compensates itself for the suppression of adult eros. " 'No; it ain't 'dammed'," observed Sam, holding the letter up to the light, 'it's 'shamed,' there's a blot there – ' " (xxxiii, 452). In fact, it *is* shame that prompts Sam's Valentine: "I feel myself ashamed" he begins, composing the elaborate Valentine he prefers to the "normal" card of skewered hearts and scantily clad Cupids for sale in the stationer's window.

Look (if you can) at the frontispiece along with its companion, the facing vignette title page. The frontispiece shows two men easily making a spectacle of their private lives. They look very much as upon a theatre, as lively imps pull back curtains to display a voyeuristic fantasy of untrammeled exhibitionism. But the contrary panel, the vignette, discloses an exhibitionist's nightmare. "The elder Mr. Weller" savagely beats his amatory rival, "the red-nosed" Mr. Stiggins, until he is "half suffocated" "in a horse-trough full of water" (li, 739). One man makes a humiliating spectacle of another, watched by a smiling third, young Sam Weller. We've opened the book on a paradigmatic diptych of shame, a shameful paradigm of Dickens's para-theatre.[4]

The shame in the vignette is shared. Obviously, the suffering Stiggins is being unmanned. But shame invests pain-inflicting Tony Weller also.

It's shame that's driving the husband and father to reclaim his masculinity from the "blind trust" of his second marriage by projecting his own victim's status onto his rival. He is attempting to requalify himself for the ranks of real manhood, imaged and supervised by the comparably big-bellied, heroic general, the Marquis of Granby, surveying the scene from the Inn sign above. All the typical elements of a shame-induced fantasy are present and functioning here. The failed self, hitherto "inferior in competition," converts "lack of absolute control over an archaic environment" into narcissistic inflation through a watched or mirrored grandiosity (Morrison 1989: 12, 102), relying on a combination of anger, rage and contempt. The now impotent victim puts up no resistance, accepting the projected unworthiness entirely into himself. And an on-looking family member consolidates the transformation. Sam, the son, not only witnesses but intensifies his father's scene, fixing the achieved difference between the now successful self and its flawed, despised, dismissed alter ego.

Sam's appearance in both illustrations invites us to construe the frontispiece as a fantasied defense against the vignette, as a way of retrieving pleasure from the labyrinthine scenarios of shame. It is literally fantasied because the frontispiece reveals a moment that isn't in the book. Unlike the vignette, the frontispiece pictures not an episode of plot, but something far more encompassing: not a reading *from*, but the reading *of*, this book. Sam and Pickwick delightedly laugh at a book they share. A book that's got to be *this* book: *Pickwick*, the book they quite literally share between them. What else are they likely to be reading? Is it like Dickens to defer to some other author? The frontispiece, then, fantasizes reading *Pickwick* as a defense against being read into *Pickwick*, a pleasurable possession *of* the story displacing a shameful possession *by* it.

Shame, claims the vignette, is the inevitable motor and outcome to any heterosexual rivalry: that is, *a propos* René Girard, to any form of heterosexual desire. Pleasure, the frontispiece shows, arises only when men, renouncing desire, bond rather than compete. In the vignette, the older Weller, married and remarried, centers at the horse-trough merely the most violent version of heterosexual relationship in a novel in which women regularly, as Doreen Roberts argues, "deceive, bully, trap and terrorize men" (Roberts 1990: 304). In which the sovereign "Dragon (called by courtesy a woman)" is always "uppermost". (ii, 18) Against and in place of the dragon's tale, the frontispiece proposes a pleasurably agamous – they're laughing – male–male union. The younger Weller conveys both Pickwick and himself out of the novel's plotting and into a safe, cozy *homosocial* union, by devoting his life to his master's love. To be delivered from spectators is also to be delivered from heterosexuality; to be freed of plot is to be free for agamy and from theatre, except of course from theatre-as-upon.

The novel does attempt, especially in the early parts, to defuse this sexual circuit of fear and shame by fantasizing a patriarchal counter-circulation of women between benevolent fathers and pliant sons-in-law. Within the make-believe of the interpolated tales, the grandfatherly chair bestows the landlady on the filial Tom Smart. In the main plot, supremely, Dingley Dell's weddings work without any need for a mother of the bride. They represent ways of imagining marriage for "individuals who are ultimately afraid of intimacy with women, terrified as they are of being united with them" (Ross 1986: 53). These fantasies depend on a kind of magic matrimony. A man enters the full power of patriarchy, possession of women and property, production of children, without the use of the phallus. In fact, the novel finally finds a way to fulfill that fantasy in granting Pickwick his last request: "I wish, if my friend Wardle entertains no objection, that his daughter should be married from my house, on the day I take possession of it" (lvii, 796). But throughout the monthly serialization such fantasies tend to pale before the recurring matrimonial paradigm of castrated husbands and devouring wives, like Mrs. Pott and Mrs. Raddle.

Of course, this all sounds familiar to us. We're back where we began, in the previous chapter with Riah and Dolls. The vignette and the frontispiece are the first things we see in this the first of Dickens's novels. And much revised, they're also what we spot thirty years later in the last novel to be finished, *Our Mutual Friend*. The vignette of Stiggins's dunking hints, as a sort of comic embryo, at the full-grown gratuitous drama of Dolls' deadly humiliation. And the juxtaposed frontispiece sets its theatrical imps to pull back the curtains from a cameral space that predicts uncannily Riah's rooftop garden, a cozy as-it-were playing space, in which the self recreates even as it re-creates itself.

Riah's "drama" like Dolls', weighs in, of course, as immensely more consequential than either scene in *Pickwick*. But the narrative logic is the same in both pairs. Pickwick's inner-sanctum stage opens a sort of safety zone into which the novel can move its performers after expelling Jingle from the plot. And the vignette shows the humiliating vortex into which the plot would have thrust Pickwick if the actor had not been expelled. (As it does early in the novel with scenes like Pickwick in the pound.)

Like Pickwick, Riah literally saves himself by retiring from the public to the private stage, while Dolls, like Stiggins, plays out Riah's averted fate. Dolls, like the money-lender, has lost his real identity in his imposed role: he is Mr. Dolls, not Mr. Cleaver, in the same way that Riah has become the Shylock of St. Mary Axe. And his anguished and fatal degradation plays out in public the scapegoated scenario his marginated role demands. And, you can complete this sentence quicker than I can write it: both heroes of virtual theatre are also only – or supremely, according to your point of view – virtual parents. Abstaining from sex, Pickwick and Riah get children – Sam and Jenny Wren, respectively – without having to beget them. The Dickensian miracle of *in verbo* fertilization! But the actual begetters, the comparably alcoholic Messrs. Weller and Dolls, are fit only for shame, surrendering their offspring to parents who seem fit, in large part, because they have stayed chaste.

But in thus connecting heterosexuality to shame and homosocial agamy with self-pleasuring as-upon theatre, I am not *outing* the novel or Dickens. Narcissism is from the start Dickens's essential subject. The imp-curtained frontispiece idealizes that typically Dickensian retreat from the complex challenges of fully adult life: "the Pickwickian ideal is achieved at the cost of a dramatic circumscribing of human sensibility, the avoidance of sexuality and kinship, and the suspension of time and memory" (Rogers 1972: 35). In Dickens's novels, as in most of Dickens's life, the male protagonist's primary object of desire always turns out to be the ego ideal, re-born, Freud argues, out of "the lost infantile sense of primary narcissism, when the infant took itself to be its own ideal" (this is Andrew Morrison, paraphrasing Janine Chasseguet-Smirgel, paraphrasing Freud's "On Narcissism": Morrison 1989: 59). The Dickensian male yearns not for another of either gender but for the self, or rather "for absolute uniqueness and sole importance to someone else . . . for whom the self is uniquely special or who offers no competition or barriers to the self in meeting needs for sustenance" (Morrison 1989: 48). Throughout all the novels, the supreme object of desire remains the self in all of its fantasied perfection. The ideal pairing in *Pickwick* – and Dickens – is neither man and woman, nor man and man, but the self and its servant. Samuel (Pickwick) and Samivel (Weller): a specular romance. A not unexpected or unlikely pairing for a cameral theatre in love with the productions of its own mind.

Resurrecting eros from the tomb of the body, Sam functions not as a stone rolled away but as a kind of man-sized prophylactic, guaranteeing that not a drop of Dickens's most precious psychic commodity, male narcissism, will be spilled or squandered. Sam's a hero because he holds on to gender without in turn being commandeered by sex. He thus turns the novel away from the paths of the Oedipal scenario, the prime matter – as Freud recognized – of the stage. He thereby protects and preserves what Kohut would call archaic self-objects, figures from the earlier, perhaps the earliest stages of the family romance, figures of incest, polymorphous self-pleasure, and especially images of a father who loves uncritically and never threatens. Sam achieves that reversal by re-inventing himself as eternal son to Pickwick's pre-Oedipal father. He sets himself up as a flawless mirror confirming Pickwick's most grandiose sense of self, a mirror perfectly, unswervingly "affectionate, supportive, noncompetitive and facilitating" (Meyers and Schore 1986: 246). Dickens thus resolves what must otherwise become psychic impasse by setting up a sort of phallic arbitrage. Rendering both males simultaneously child and adult gives neither and both "possession" of the phallus. It's the ideal of agamy, a playing at house: Pickwick, master of the house; Sam, father of the family ("Two sturdy little boys" [lvii, 801]). Sam has metamorphosed Pickwick from the butt of Jingle's phallic satire into, not merely a good man, but an "angel," that is a virtual male with no conceivable use for a penis. Together, Sam and Pickwick establish a form of "phallic narcissism" – the situation in which a son who has identified himself early on with a weak father repairs the "shame of being weak" through a fantasied union with an idealized male parent (described in Morrison 1989: 58). An experience with obvious affinities to Dickens's own early life.

Like any good arbitrager (and surely that is an oxymoron) Sam enjoys masculinity, not only for his own use, but in order to get it back into circulation among other men, for Winkle, and, most importantly, for Pickwick. Thus, while Pickwick remains in Bath, the novel, as it were, splits Sam in two, sending him off to minister to the exhibitionist Winkle. Thereafter, as Pickwick and Winkle parallel each other's stories, the novel ensures its apparent compliance with the demands of a hegemonic heterosexuality while at the same time constructing the pairing of its preferred narcissism. The last third of the novel thus perfectly emulates Freud's description of "The Splitting of the Ego in the Process of Defence": "On the one hand, with the help of certain mechanisms he rejects reality and refuses to accept any prohibition; on the other hand, in the same breath he recognizes the danger of reality, takes over the fear of that danger . . . and tries subsequently to divest himself of the fear" (Freud 1940: 275). In the novel's plot, Pickwick rejects the reality of bourgeois sexual hegemony by his reckless behavior before, during and after his imprisonment. At the same time, he does everything possible to establish his charge, Winkle, in a respectable marriage. As Freud comments: this splitting achieves a "very ingenious solution of the difficulty." Indeed. Both sides "obtain their share: the instinct is allowed to retain its satisfaction [narcissism] and proper respect is shown to reality [socially sanctioned heterosexual monogamy]" (p. 278). That is a division that will shape virtually every future Dickens novel.

This ingenious "compromise formation . . . 'salvages sexual pleasure' from those models of 'normal' and normative sexual relations which in Dickens are everywhere 'filled with anxiety and conflict'" (Stoller 1975: 39–40).[5] Sam thus ensures the comic promise implicated not only in the Pickwick icon but in the cult of Dickensian comedy that starts with Pickwick. (It is of course with his comic grotesques that popular culture establishes Dickens's enduring reputation.) He effectively downgrades new-comic romance, the theatre's staple plot for successful management of its Oedipal materials. Romance becomes now merely subplot, the servants' tale. And in its place emerges the prime matter of as-upon theatre, the eccentric solitary's autoerotic triumph (or at least semi-autoerotic: autoerotic with apparatus), a victory Dickens insists we read as at once both aberrant and healthy. Here we hold, I think, something like a key to Dickens's recurring popularity, on the page as well as on the stage. His comedy repeatedly promises, to a Victorian and a post-Victorian audience, stunned by the all-inclusive erotics of patriarchy, that one can indeed enjoy richly his (or her: see Sairey Gamp or Mrs. Jarley) sexuality without ever having to suffer through the events of sex.

But that promise in turn depends upon, and brings us back to, scapegoating the actor. Jingle reappears in the novel because Pickwick's renewed goodness must be witnessed as omnipotent and justified by that now jailed, and apparently ruined, "insatiable sex-machine." The broken actor is now spared nothing in the novel's prodigious arsenal of humiliations, repeatedly drawn out to be exhibited as shabby, sparkless, obedient, lachrymose. And he is made to concede the justice of his fall: "serve him right-all over-drop the curtain" (xlii, 598). He's even got to boast that it's only Pickwick's renewed benevolence that has "made a man of me" (liii, 744) – apparently, another and even less expected benefit of Sam the arbitrager's circulating phallus. Solo, Jingle can only repent; he can not reform (p. 746). Like Pickwick, he has become a sort of managed dependent of his former servant, Job. But this "worthy couple" (p. 746) is clearly an odd couple, parodying the novel's agamous, idealized central pair.

The players' union is, the novel strongly implies, homoerotic, drawing on the deviance always hovering about discourse of the actor. Job, we are told, is "attached to [Jingle], and all that," an "all that" about which the novel is clearly "contemptuous." "No man," it warns, "should have more than two attachments – the first to number one, and the second to the ladies" (p. 743). (But "to the ladies" doesn't read here as "to the women." It's an attachment only in the Pickwickian sense: clearly rhetorical at best, something like "Gentlemen, I give you – 'The Ladies!'." Narcissistic "number one's" the only one that really counts in *Pickwick*.) Jingle thus finishes where Pickwick began, the feminized alternative to a preferred masculinity. *Auguste* and *faire-vouloir* have changed places. It is now the actor who suffers and signifies shame. It's the actor who ends up the new cock-shy, marking the triumph of Dickens's new sexual arrangement, removing forever the threat even his mere presence might convey.

Well, not quite forever, of course. Two novels later and Nicholas Nickleby is not only working in the theatre but is a star. How could such a change come to pass?

Sam affords his master the means for an extraordinary psychic settlement: a way not only not of this world, but also, and more problematically, a way of being out of this, or indeed any, world. It is the escape we saw depicted in the happily retired frontispiece. If we continue to connect the swerve from Jingle to the anxieties of its newly-wed author, then we can say that *Pickwick* finally resolves itself into what Kurt Eissler calls an *autoplastic* text, a fiction which functions – like dreams or fantasies – to resolve through wish fulfillment an author's pressing inner conflict (Eissler 1971: 544). But *Nickleby*'s reversion to the theatrical, following the actor's degradation and exile, suggests that *autoplastic* relief won't, finally, or entirely, suffice to meet all of Dickens's needs.

Nickleby reveals in Dickens a kind of narcissistic remainder, an unspent exhibitionistic deposit, unmodified or unsatisfied by *autoplastic* substitutions. That narcissism is driven by needs "closely interwoven with" but ultimately different from "the drives and their inexorable tensions" (Kohut 1985: 104). These are the needs we loosely and generally call ambition, the need to be looked at and the need to be admired. Those needs even feel different from the needs expressed by the instincts. As Kohut neatly puts it: a man "is *led* by his ideals but *pushed* by his ambitions" (p. 104). And that push generates a stress which may be annealed, but certainly cannot be annulled, by retired association with an idealized other, whether that other is figured as child or as parent. Ambition's requirements can only be satisfied directly, in and through the exhibition of the self. Its discharge demands an admiration warranted by a public performance. And, certainly, with Dickens, the more the need to perform was denied, the harder it seemed to press to create performance wherever and whenever possible, in the domestic, the sociable, the professional and the public arenas alike. Indeed, Dickens may be one of the few people for whom it is not cliché but necessity to call every stage of life some sort of arena. Over and over again his life, and fiction, display a conspicuous shortfall in what Adam Phillips nicely calls "a tolerable relationship to satisfaction," that is: a conviction of "the accuracy," as well as "the possibility of one's desire" (Phillips 1994: 47). Dickens registers just the opposite "conviction": that what he deeply wants is always what undoes him: Catherine, family life, fame, fiction, the glare of the lecture platform.

But in 1837 Dickens was still too young, too aglow with the first flush of success, to know how thoroughly dissatisfied he was quickly destined to become and remain. His task at this early stage was simply to find a form and forum for performance that would simultaneously show the most of, and risk the least to, the hero, and to the psyche that projects that hero. A forum that could realize ambition without risking instinct. Thus, with *Pickwick* an unexpected and overwhelming popular success, Dickens could prolong with gusto Sam's part of the story, a scenario which insisted that the right role was always just waiting there for the growing boy, a story he could tell twice over, in effect, with the overlapping *Oliver Twist*. Indeed, one of the ways in which it is so curiously right that little Oliver speaks English like a gentleman, despite its violation of verisimilitude, is that the gentleman's role is profoundly his despite all those early years of apparent, and grandparental, miscasting. By remaining flawlessly true to his inner recognition of what he is, Oliver ultimately convinces the world, including those who ought to have known from the start, to see exactly who he is. But *Oliver* is only and after all a child's story, a child's fantasy. It reproduces fantasy's terrors and pays richly with them for fantasy's *autoplastic* rewards. Within a very few years, even before 1840, Dickens had clearly come to need the quite contrary relief Eissler calls *alloplastic*: a relief that registers without, not merely within, a way of modifying the other, the social or the real, by making something apparently new. He had begun to require not a fantasy of privileged withdrawal from the world but a public profession, a way of being a man in of the world.

But a profession is exactly what the early nineteenth-century professional theatre cannot provide, to Dickens or anyone else. Here social structure does not just block but boxes Dickens's drive for narcissistic expression.

"Who calls so loud?"
"Who calls so loud?" said Smike.
"Who calls so loud?" repeated Nicholas.
"Who calls so loud?" cried Smike.
Thus they continued to ask each other who called so loud, over and over again . . . (xxv, 329–330)

"Over and over again" because in the theater of the eighteen-thirties an ambitious hero like Nicholas, or a would-be hero like Dickens, can never find a way to answer the "I" he knows himself to be – no matter how many times "Who called so loud" is asked. And even if he could speak that I, he would first, like Romeo, have had to purchase poison.[6]

A SPECTACLE OF THE PLAYER

> In making a spectacle of the player, sexual difference is, in some ways, a less obvious mode of inscribing the power relations of spectacle than the subjection of players on class grounds.
>
> (Straub 1992: 152)

Why does Dickens insist the theater proscenium's a sort of evil eye? After all, didn't even so dour a theorist as Antonin Artaud insist, in the epochal *The Theater and Its Double* (1938), that around itself a renewed theater can "assemble the true spectacle of life" (p. 12)? Yes, indeed he did. But such a renewal depends on the theater's essential emptiness. The book and the page are, when we encounter them, full to the margins, if not already complete then at least already completed. But the bare stage is, as Artaud insists, "no thing" (p. 12), which means it is also the place of "what does not yet exist." That perfect emptiness, as the actors assemble, makes it a unsurpassed matrix of the new, the other, of that which is becoming rather than of that which already has being (p. 13). Such an emptiness is, of course, a mark of the post-repertory playhouse, not or repertory companies like Crummles's, but of theatres where each production begins virtually from scratch, of new companies in long, unlovely rehearsals on bare, dusty boards. Indeed, it's for just that reason that Artaud insists in the famous chapter 6, "No More Masterpieces" (pp. 74–83), that the only path to the reform of the theater, and therefore to the redemption of culture, is by refusing to do old plays, by insisting on making everything new. But for Dickens, as for the nineteenth-century theater he describes, there is never an empty playhouse. His theaters are the preeminent sites of retrofit. We see this as soon as Nickleby steps inside the Portsmouth theater. Even unset and empty, the Crummles's theater is already overstuffed: "bare walls, dusty scenes, mildewed clouds, heavily daubed draperies, and dirty floors . . . ceiling, pit, boxes, gallery, orchestra, fittings, and decorations of every kind" (xxiii,287). And that overstuffing itself reflects an even more significant because ideological plenitude: the dependence of the playhouse on repertoire, the constant interplay of revival, set-piece and plagiarization. "There!," Crummles adjures Nicholas, who has just found himself turned into a playwright, "Just turn that into English, and put your name on the title-page" (p. 296). The stage is a place of constant rather than instant replay, the original recycling center.

Everything in this theatre's infinitely regressive mimesis echoes or copies or approximates something previously staged or waiting in the wings. Mrs. Crummles, "the original Blood Drinker," has taught its contemporary avatar, Henrietta Petowker. But Crummles is being typically excessive when he insists that " 'The Blood Drinker' will die with that girl" (xxv, 318). Miss Ninetta Crummles will doubtless become a Blood Drinker in her turn, and pass on the secrets of the ensanguined imbibition to still later generations of "sylph[s] . . . who [can] stand upon one leg and play the tambourine on the other knee, *like* a sylph." Obviously, such a theater can offer no hope for reforming culture, certainly not a culture comparably crosshatched and contained by genealogies of convention.

Of course, it's a convention to find that: "In *Nicholas*, Dickens celebrates, through parody as well as praise, the magic of the theatre . . . delighting in depictions of actors, actresses, and performances, from the absurdly banal to the humorously serious" (Kaplan 1982: 119). And, to an extent, that's true. Nothing should blind us to the attractive side Dickens found around the theaters. Despite its manifest tawdriness, silliness, and exploitation, the working theater inflicts no more harm than it needs to in order to survive. And the harm it finds it must inflict it gratuitously leavens by unstinting, indeed excessive, generosity. The theatre gives for the sheer sake of the gesture of giving. Of course, what's given is often silly and always merely illusion. But the rush produced by all that excess (in the performers, in their audiences, in us reading) nullifies any danger of infection from all that "False hair, false colour, false calves, false muscles" (xxiv, 302). This kind of fun is not part of the world of true-false about which conventional anti-theatricality makes so much banal fuss. Better still: it inflicts no excess pain. It demonstrates no callous disregard for distress – and that alone makes theatre radically different from every other field the novel scans. When theatre permits harm, the harmed are, generally, collusive in their abuse. Steven Marcus reads the actors as "no less false and betraying than everyone else" (1965: 119). Surely that's too harsh. They may be false and betraying, like virtually everybody else in the pre-Cheeryble half of the book. But they are also significantly *less* false and betraying than virtually everybody else. That is their claim on Nicholas's and the reader's affection. As a result, the theater seems, surprisingly, to house a kind of rough approximation of justice, the quality saliently absent from the legal and political stages of the fiction.

In fact, in the real world theatricality, relatively harmless on stage, becomes actively vicious. Off-stage, in Dickens, we can never tell, not the dancer from the dance, but the performer from the man, or from the child. On all occasions, great and small, virtually everyone in these novels – affectingly and regularly, if not steadily – is displaying ,indeed revelling in, "the histrionic artifice of ordinary life" (Auerbach 1990:114). But *Nickleby's* non-theatre world insistently represents this histrionic explosion as cancerous, dependent on servitude, corrupting sympathy in order to service solecism. Squeers' portrayal of the benevolent schoolmaster. Miss Knag's vaporous exploitation of the milliners. Lillyvick's complacent manipulation of the Kenwigs. All these self-conscious appropriations and approximations of theatre function to debase the already hapless or to deprive the subjugated. And when the powerless themselves perform, they merely collude in their own delusion. Thus Mrs. Kenwigs drives herself and her family to exhaustion, futilely arranging "*programme[s]*" (xiv, 169) to charm the feckless Collector of Water Rents, unwittingly undermining her plan by introducing to him the professional performer, and vamp, Henrietta Petowker.

Dickens introduces here that characteristic syntax of theatricality (that sin tax on theaters) to which he returns throughout his career. Quilp's pint-sized Richard III, domestically tyrannizing his wife and her friends in *the Old Curiosity Shop*. Mrs. Clennam's private chapel of expiation in *Little Dorrit*. The demonic theatre of Satis House set up by *Great Expectation's* revenge-crazed Miss Havisham. Fledgby's jew-baiting, society-squeezing scam in (as we've seen) *Our Mutual Friend*. In these novels as well as in *Nickleby*, playing, in effect, urges rather than bridges the rift bourgeois experience opens between individuals and between classes. And it crams those rifts with chicanery and guile.

But Dickens (at his best) knows that real theaters are not about having truth, but about having fun. (At his best means when he's writing fiction; not at his best means when he's writing everything dully else.) Look at the irresistibly frivolous Lillyvick–Petowker nuptials (xxv), next to which even the Presley–Jackson wedding seems tame. Mr. Crummles determines in advance to be "greatly overcome" when he impersonates the father of the bride. His sheer energy then transmutes that which is "almost equal to the real" (p. 326) into "the completest thing ever witnessed" (p. 327). Even the experienced pew-opener tries to offer him comfort. Part of the sly fun here comes from the unmistakable implication that all real weddings are also intensely theatrical. But, deploying all the energies (and not a few of the costumes) of the Company, the mock-marriage makes us see most real weddings as at best poor theatre, always and sadly amateur. You need practice and training, not sincerity, to make a wedding really work (*vide*: Elizabeth Taylor). Sincere spouses might – probably do – care. They might – probably do – feel. They might even – well, maybe – love. All of which only makes them inevitably selfish and unattractive. But the excessive, theatrical wedding cannily strips all sincere sentiment away from strong libido, disavowing not only other people's needs but one's own. What's left is strong libido as sheer performance. The performer's pleasure derives exclusively from trying out the widest range of affect in a role, in a situation, from exploring one's emotional range: what's most exciting, demanding, exacting, effective, without regard for consequences, pleasant or otherwise. Entirely present to the moment, theatrical libido entirely disavows the notion of the follow-up. From it springs what Adam Phillips calls the "plurality of lives we want" (1994: xxv).

That sort of libido is of course exactly what Nicholas Nickleby continually longs for. He likes fooling with Fanny Squeers. He enjoys flirting with Miss Snevillicci. But the last thing he wants to feel, or to face, is desire. When he encounters its appetitive cravings in poor, plain Fanny Squeers, he behaves with precisely the same cruelty that marks all the other needy people in the novel. What poisons acting, then? Golly, you may well say: what debars such a hero from making a life of the theater, when the theatrical seems to be so much, to be so exactly, what he craves?

Our answer takes us outside the novel. In the early nineteenth-century theatre, the acting "profession" felt like an all but exitless misfunction. Not just to a poor plodder in the provinces. But also to its star: William Charles Macready, Dickens's very close friend, the preeminent classical actor of his day, and, not coincidentally, the dedicatee of *Nicholas Nickleby*. Macready was for Dickens, in many ways, an alter ego. Thus, when Dickens dreamed of reunion with the ghost of his beloved sister-in-law, Mary Hogarth, he saw himself "as real, animated, and full of passion as Macready" (Pilgrim *Letters*: 4, 196). In dreams, passionate Macready may personify everything Dickens envies. But, in life, he embodies everything that Dickens, terrified, denies: the stage, the body, desire itself. He is the Dickens Dickens himself was afraid to act out.

Here is an entry from Macready's journal for the evening of April 29, 1836.

As I came off the stage, ending the third act of *Richard* [the Third], in passing by Bunn's door [Alfred Bunn, the lessee of the theatre] I opened it, and unfortunately he was there. I could not contain myself; I exclaimed: "You damned scoundrel! How dare you use me in this manner?" And going up to him as he sat on the other side of the table, I struck him as he rose a back-handed slap across the face. I did not hear what he said, but I dug my fist into him as effectively as I could; he caught hold of me, and got at one time the little finger of my left hand in his mouth, and bit it. I exclaimed: "You rascal! Would you bite?" He shouted out: "Murder! Murder!" and, after some little time, several persons came into the room. I was then upon the sofa, the struggle having brought us right round the table. Willmott, the prompter, said to me: "Sir, you had better go to your room, you had better go to your room.' I got up accordingly, and walked away." (Macready 1967: 62)

What had poor Bunn done, to provoke such a hammering?

Bunn had insisted that Macready perform only the first three acts of *Richard*, when all that star's best stuff emerged in the meaty final act. But, obviously, there's got to be more to this violence than that single dispute, especially when we read Macready's conclusion to this journal entry: "No one can more severely condemn my precipitation than myself. No enemy can censure me more harshly, no friend lament more deeply my forgetfulness of all I ought to have thought upon. . . Words cannot express the contrition I feel, the shame I endure" (Macready 1967: 63). What drove Macready to that shaming act? The causes are many, and interlocking.

Theatre in Britain had always been morally *infra dig*. But in the nineteenth century it had also become aesthetically suspect. Romanticism, insisting on interiority as the true condition for any authentically human existence, found theatre the enemy's favorite keep. Throughout the century, as Jonas Barish notes, "the artistic conscience, struggling against the grossness of the physical stage, [strove] to free itself from the despotism of the actors" (Barish 1981: 349). The Romantics may have loved and regularly borrowed from the dramatic form but, except for splendid Byron, they wanted to keep it, like so much else they loved, deep in the closet. Thus, the stage had to suffer the alienating scorn of the literati, writers who ought to have been the natural allies of those performing under the aegis of Shakespeare, now not only national poet but also national playwright.[7]

But even more pinching than either religion or Romanticism, for Macready particularly, were the class-biases of the reformed and reforming bourgeoisie. "I had to live to learn that an ignorant officer could refuse the satisfaction of a gentleman on the ground that his appellant was a player, and that, whilst any of the above-named vocations [that is: the law, the church, the army and navy], whatever the private character, might be received at court, the privilege of appearing in the sacred precincts was too exclusive for any, however distinguished, on the stage" (Macready 1967: xv–xvi). This exclusion from royal enclosures rankled Macready all his life. In his first command performance after Victoria's first accession, a *King Lear*, he notes the pleasure with which "I pointed at her the beautiful lines, 'Poor naked wretches!'" (p. 132). (It's lovely, really, imagining Victoria un-amused at being told "Take physic, Pomp; / Expose thyself to feel what wretches feel.") This contempt for what he called "my pariah profession" could invite the Haymarket Theatre's manager, Benjamin Webster, to a court ball, but not the Haymarket's star. It "has given occasion," Macready confessed, "to many moments of depression, many angry swellings of the heart, many painful convictions of the uncertainty of my position" (p. xv).

In such a theatre any actor, no matter how talented, must end up only and inevitably performing his own shame. That shame emerges from a split driven at every level into the Romantic theatre: within the individual player, between ego-ideal and economic power; within the enterprise of theatre, between widely divergent types of intellectual and economic capital; and finally within the scaffold of culture, between the monumental dream of a national drama and the restraining technostructures of monopoly.

Within the player: "I wish I were anything rather than an actor," moans Macready (1967: 42). "I had rather see one of my children dead than on the stage" (p. 151). Acting "is so very unrequiting a profession, that no person who had the power of doing anything better would, unless deluded into it, take it up" (*Report* 1832: 133). We're not talking here about whether the nineteenth-century actor could be termed a gentleman. Not only had David Garrick been buried in Westminster Abbey but so also were Spranger Barry and John Henderson, much lesser luminaries of the late eighteenth-century stage. Actors' social status fluctuated, then as now, with their gifts and with the total achievement of their careers. What undermined and unmanned even an actor like Macready was not his social position but his inability to function within a profession.

His biographers generally treat Macready's shame at acting as idiosyncratic, rooted in the vicissitudes of his particular character and history. His father and mother, successful provincial performers, had begun their eldest son's education at Harrow. Abruptly, however, in the winter of 1809, his father was arrested for debt. (The extraordinary parallels to Dickens continue throughout their lives.) The parents yanked sixteen-year old William Charles from those gentlemanly purlieus and insisted he step into the father's domestic, and professional, roles. And, after that, he was stuck on the stage for the next forty-two years! William Archer, the great late-Victorian theatre-historian, exploits this undeniably "false relation to his life-work" as "the true tragedy of Macready's spirit," turning him – the biography appears in 1890 – into Jekyll-and-Hyde, innate Artist struggling against induced Snob (Archer 1890: 208) – or perhaps innate Snob versus induced Artist.

Of course, Macready's neurotic self-division must figure heavily in any reading of his professional self-laceration. But even as Archer makes this argument he tends to subvert it by detailing the "one unceasing round of annoyances and humiliations" that "must in those days" have been the "life of a 'star'" in a "lax and haphazard generation" of "careless, inefficient and over-worked actors" (1890: 209–210). Yes, over-worked, *if* in work. But work itself was exceedingly rare. Most contemporary observers insisted the entire theatre had fallen into acute dysfunction after Garrick's death. The Parliamentary *Report from the Select Committee on Dramatic Literature* (Summer 1832) begins with the rather lugubrious sentence: "a considerable decline both in the literature of the Stage and the taste of the Public for Theatrical Performance, is generally conceded" (p. 3) But "decline" misleads. In fact, the theatre's problem was that it had remained as it was, while society in general inclined in quite other directions. In the early nineteenth century, theatre constituted one of the few significant exceptions to the ruling pattern of *laissez-faire* expansion. It had remained trapped in the outdated mesh of monopoly.

Whatever else Charles II restored, it did not include the theatre. Before the Restoration, a lively, entrepreneurial theatre had been fostered by competition among several relatively autonomous, share-held London companies. Charles's patents of monopoly (actually duopoly) replaced them in favor of a national theatre that was not at the same time, as it needed to be, a court theatre. (The always impecunious British Crown was not likely, after the Restoration, to lumber itself with the expensive machinery of a state theatre. It remembered Ship Money.) Imperfect competition lumbered with inadequate patronage combined the worst of two systems. The Crown restrained competition but gave the two Theatres Royal no further support or subsidy. Theatrical enterprise committed to the largest scale could rely only on schemes of private capital never adequate to the demands of a "national" theatre. (Sound familiar?)

During the later eighteenth century, the Covent Garden and Drury Lane patent holders repeatedly attempted to solve their difficulties by building larger and still larger theaters, spiraling prices. But that policy only made those new houses increasingly difficult, if not impossible, to fill on any kind of regular basis. (Not to mention the difficulty performers faced in producing vocal effects at less than a shout, or that audiences had with sight lines from any but the most expensive seats.) By the early nineteenth century, theatre-goers might insist, like this letter writer during the Old Price riots of 1809, that "Theaters in a country under a monarchical form of government can never be considered private property, but as a great national concern, as a powerful political engine, as a wheel without which the remainder of the state machinery would be incomplete," heaping industrial metaphor on commercial icon (Baer 1992: 77). But the letter writer was wrong. The theatre in England could not be considered private property. Alas, neither could it be considered public property. Inevitably, its structural ambiguities falsified the practical economics of production. And that falsification in turn soured the theatre's relation to those who attended, and regularly rioted against what they saw, as well as to – our subject – those who performed. Or – more accurately – to those who did not get to perform, since the opportunities were so limited.

Though drama could be staged in specified theatres in the provinces, inside London any drama, tragic or comic, outside the two patent houses could be prosecuted by law. Of course, this prohibition did not stop managers from staging plays, but the patents meant that the other theatres, the so-called minor theatres, were always at best semi-licit. And this illegitimate status made managerial tyranny certain. Any performer employed outside the two patent houses was ipso facto criminal and could therefore have no recourse for redress against entrepreneurial exploitation. That made any ordinary actor's life – in Edward Elton's description – "one of positive endurance and deprivation." The highest salary he could expect in the minor theatres would reach not more than three guineas a week, "and very few receive so much as that, and have to pay their own travelling expenses from town to town, and frequently to provide their own stage dresses; yet it is expected a man receiving that salary shall be able to embody the first characters of Shakespeare" (*Report* 1832: 234). Thus a seasoned performer like William Dowton, sufficiently respectable to be called as witness at the Parliamentary Inquiry, found after thirty-six years at Drury Lane that he now had "no theatre where I can act at present, unless occasionally by breaking the law and acting at a minor theatre" (1832: 89). (Playwrights were equally badly off, in much worse condition than writers for the print media. For the Parliamentary report's evidence on playwrights, see the accounts of Serle, 117; John Poole, 190; Planche, 214; and Kenney, 226.)

Between roughly 1780 and 1850, almost any actor, from the sublime Sarah Siddons to Dickens's "Poor Miss Snevillicci," would have admitted, like Elton: "I have felt myself occasionally degraded by the nature of the performance I have been compelled to take part in" (1832: 233). And these degradations would have covered performances both off and on the stage. Miss Snevellicci is abused by both her condescending fans and the friendly Crummles. She must beg her mendicant way through Portsmouth, soliciting ticket takers for a benefit for which she bears all the risk but from which she can take only one-third of any potential profit. The managerial Crummles put up no money at all, and secure two-thirds of the profit; "her risk, you know," Crummles tells his wife, "and not ours." Little wonder she is "exhausted with the business of the day" (xxiv, 305). Miss Snevellicci is, of course, at the bottom of the bin. But exactly the same sort of thing was being imposed on Mrs. Siddons fifty years earlier, performing illegitimately at Wolverhampton, and therefore forbidden by law to charge admission. The first lady of the English stage was forced to have a "play-bill . . . handed about with '*Nota bene*, no money taken at the door but [one of the performers] has a very excellent tooth-powder at 2*s*. 1*d*. the box" (1832: 12). Wopsle's waterside theatre is, then, neither parody (Carr 1989: 29) nor exception. For all its demeaning vulgarity, it is merely reportage. "I never knew a period," the veteran performer T. P. Cooke insisted in 1832, "in which the profession was at so low an ebb" (p. 147).

So low an ebb, I want to argue, that it really could not claim to be called, in the lexicon of the nineteenth century, a profession at all. And without the shield of professional standing the actor found himself defenseless against not only the fiscal, but more importantly the psychic, vicissitudes of *laissez-faire*.

> "Also professional?" said Mrs. Merdle, looking at Little Dorrit through an eye-glass.
> Fanny answered No. "No," said Mrs. Merdle, dropping her glass. "Has not a professional air. Very pleasant; but not professional."
> (*Little Dorrit* X:xx, 285)

Mrs. Merdle's dismissal implies that it is the dancing Dorrit, Fanny, who is the only professional of the pair. Little Dorrit merely labors. But here Mrs. Merdle has indeed dropped her glass. Fanny, employed as a dancer at a great theatre, is not, can not be, a professional. Tracy Davis has shown in harrowing detail how a dancer's position was, if anything, even worse than an actress's.

> Many dancers made another wage while working in the theatre . . . [But] Dancers' additional costs of tights (8 to 10s. for a pair of worsted, and 30 to 40s. for good silk) and shoes (2s.6d. to 5s. every three or four weeks) substantially consumed any second wage. During periods when daytime rehearsals of a new piece and evening performances of an old piece were called, dancers and choristers who normally worked two jobs lost the day time wage. The lost wages were not made up by the theatre . . . dancers and choristers . . . could be in full-time unpaid employment for eight to ten weeks before each original production. (Davis 1992: 30–31)

(Fanny Dorrit, we know, has no second job in a factory or a shop, but her association with Edmund Sparkler suggests how, like so many young women in positions like hers, she attempted to supplement her meager theatrical wage.) Indeed, Amy understands intuitively what Fanny has missed: that her sister and all her sister's theatrical sisters and brethren have got themselves "on the wrong side of the pattern of the universe" – in a theatre dwindled to a "maze of dust," a "confusion of unaccountable shapes." Back- as well as forestage can be at best – she sees – only "a great empty well" in a universe which *laissez-faire* has patterned into an increasingly exclusive professional grid.

In the nineteenth century the field of power had become, quintessentially, professional. As we saw a while back with Pickwick and the lawyers, "The increase in the number of professionals and the growth of professionalism has been generally accepted by social scientists as a major if not a defining characteristic of industrial societies" (Johnson 1972: 9). That means Vincent Crummles, the amiable manager of the Portsmouth Theatre, entirely misconstrues his own and his family's situation when he boasts to Nicholas Nickleby: "I am in the theatrical profession myself, my wife is in the theatrical profession, my children are in the theatrical profession. I had a dog that lived and died in it from a puppy; and my pony-chaise goes on, in Timour the Tartar" (xxii, 283). In the 1830s, it may still be possible to make distinctions between professional and amateur performers. But it is no longer possible to claim that anyone, even a dog, even a remarkably talented dog, can live and die within "the theatrical profession." Indeed, Miss La Creevy seems to get it just about right when she explains that portrait painters choose between a smirk for ladies and for gentlemen "who don't care so much about looking clever" and a serious attitude "for professional people (except actors sometimes)" (x, 115). Actors are caught, or rather lost in the slippage, between smirk and serious, professional only parenthetically, and even that by exception.

Professions, Steven Brint trenchantly reminds us, label "a piece of sociological material that can be refashioned periodically to suit an evolving social and cultural context" (1984: 8) – not only can be, but, repeatedly, have been. Before the nineteenth century, professional covered the ways in which a gentleman could earn money without compromising his status. It embraced those life and death activities that feudal and post-feudal masters needed handled by almost-equal intimates in ways that reinforced traditional values and arrangements of power: church, bar, medicine, tutoring, architecture and defense. During the nineteenth century, however, pressured by the expansion of capital, the professions expanded to a much larger set of civil categories. An expansion we can trace in the development of the Census throughout the Victorian era. By 1861, "Schoolmasters, teachers, professors" became professionals; twenty years earlier they had been listed merely as "Other Educated Persons." Civil Engineers, 1,166 of them, also became professional in 1861. Land Agents had to wait until 1881. Accountants didn't make it until 1921. And Bankers never have – take that, Mrs. Merdle. (Figures derived from Reader 1966: 147–153.)

In the sense of the Victorian census, professions had come to refer to all and any of the self-valorizing, self-governing occupations, in which the producers define the consumer's needs and also the manner in which those needs are met (Johnson 1972: 45). Professions proved vital to industrialization; their infrastructures provided the only stable base on which rapidly expanding, inherently volatile *laissez-faire* development could reliably count. In the sociologist Terence Johnson's scheme, they match neither *patronage*: oligarchic, corporate, communal, "the consumer defines his own needs and the manner in which they are to be met," nor *mediation*, as in financier capitalism, the welfare state, or medieval Christianity, situations in which "a third party mediates in the relationship between producer and consumer, defining both the needs and the manner in which the needs are met" (1972: 46). (An obvious example of the latter, closer to home, is the contemporary American University in which the Administration mediates between an only apparently professional professariat and the fee-paying students or the subsidy-providing legislature. Faculties become truly professional only if they control the Endowment.)

Even this abbreviated analysis of the intrinsic connection between bourgeois professionalism and industrial capitalism suggests two overlapping ways to explain why acting, specifically Romantic acting, fails to qualify for professional status. Evan Watkins argues that from the nineteenth century on, "The authority of the professional . . . lay in the mastery, the capacity to act on . . . 'disorder' . . . to provide the kinds of 'answers' . . . indispensable to clients" (1989: 101). They become indispensable, certainly, to a world that seems increasingly irrational, abnormal and perverse, an apparently amoral world constantly in crisis. To adapt Henri Lefebvre (1991: 9), professionals work "as power's proxy." They subordinate individuals to a centralized power by "advancing" knowledge, thereby ordering incipient chaos and annealing its concomitant anxiety. (In our day, clearly, the therapist thus represents the quintessential professional.) But Romantic acting modeled the failure to cope. Othello, Richard the Third, Macbeth – the triumvirate of great roles by which the Romantic First Player was judged: all replicate the exceptional individual's failure to surmount not only the shape of destiny but, more crucially, the demonic force of his own self-destructive desires. Quite different Romantic leading men, Macready and Kean, underwent passions quite differently: as Leigh Hunt argues: Kean "more terribly," Macready "with delicacy" (quoted by Archer 1890: 192–193). But *undergo* passion is what both had to do. The Romantic actor thus performed professionalism's other. He embodied power's dread: the "fragmentation, separation and disintegration" of both self and society (Lefebvre 1991: 9)

And what he underwent briefly onstage by proxy, the Romantic actor endured permanently offstage.(Here's the second and more important of my two explanations.) In character, the actor was publicly victimized by passion. In person, he endured a parallel economic exploitation. The actor was educated above the level of craftsman but deprived by the patent structure of control over his own performance. That control was held by the House Manager (as we saw with Bunn and Macready). The player thus embodied bourgeois culture's (to borrow the title of a Dickens story) *dark twin at the window*: un-economic, powerless and therefore paradigmatically unprofessional, middle-class man. And of course that is exactly the sticking point of Nicholas Nickleby's self-condemning outburst at Portsmouth. "Oh! that I should have been fooling here!" (xxx, 398). Impoverished, he mock-duels powerlessly with sham gents on the stage, while his sister is almost destroyed in London by real and rich villains, the authentic Maiden set upon by the genuine Savage. And it is likewise the point of Crummles's curiously un-motivated return to the novel, after an absence of literally hundreds of pages. He pops up to emigrate, just as Nicholas, erstwhile actor and now merchant, begins to realize his potential as economic man, and there-fore lover. In "positively his last appearance on this Stage" (xlviii, 625), Crummles models the complete failure of that professional enterprise and theatrical dynasty of which he entered boasting, and which briefly snagged Nicholas.

This parlous fiscal condition doesn't mark merely marginal theatre types like the Crummles family. Crummles doesn't fail commercially because he acts badly but because he acts at all. Look at Macready. In 1847, ten years after *Nickleby*, the preeminent tragedian of his day was planning to move to America and settle in Cambridge MA because he couldn't make an adequate living acting in Britain. Nor could anyone, it would seem: "London, May 3. . . . Letter from King, of the Dublin theatre, informing me that the theatre is smashed and Calcraft [J.W. Calcraft, manager of the Theatre Royal, Dublin] in the Marshalsea for debt. I should feel deep concern for him if I had not concern for myself in the loss of *L.* 150 he has unwarrantably detained – belonging to me! My old luck!" (Macready 1967: 241).

But the point here is: it isn't luck. Nor is it Micawberish individual improvidence. No one works harder or more ingeniously than Vincent Crummles. Except perhaps his daughter, the Phenomenon. Falling back on luck suggests how opaque even the most astute of actors finds the deep structure of his own situation. This opacity echoes in the Parliamentary hearings' constant, curious insistence that the changed hour of the middle class dinner explains the drop in theater attendance. Something indeed had changed, and changed profoundly, in the way in which the middle class behaved, but that change was to be found not in the dinner hour, but in the hours spent on Exchange. And this brings us to the third of our splits: within the scaffold of culture.

The general incapacity to plumb that larger cultural change ruined not only actors but just about everyone who worked for and within the patent system – including its managers. Thus, "from the rebuilding of Covent Garden theater in 1809 to 1821, [the proprietors] did not clear a shilling by the regular drama." The only profits in those years came from doing Christmas pantomimes. And after 1821, "even pantomimes have failed," Francis Place reported, "and there has been no income beyond expenditure" (1832: 206). By 1832 the debt on Covent Garden theater had amounted to a staggering £256,496 (1832: Appendix 15). Yet – and here is the most surprising, really the most shocking aspect of this crisis: despite the incontrovertible evidence that the patent system kept the proprietors poor, not only did these entrepreneurs cling to its defense but so did the great actors themselves like Macready and Kean, and even Charles Mathews, the eminent comedian from whose comic "At Home"'s the young Dickens "borrowed" so much.

Mathews had been thirty-seven years on the stage at the time of the Parliamentary Commission. He was half-proprietor of the Adelphi, perhaps the outstanding 'minor' theater at the time. Yet he stood staunchly with the monopolists, his rivals, claiming that opening the patent would "brutalize the regular drama" (Report 1832: 166). This is one of those occasions of folly that demonstrate so powerfully how fruitless theory is likely to be, any sort of theory, when it comes to organizing a coherent map of capitalism. As Dickens repeatedly insisted, the real problem with capitalism is not that it works so effectively in concentrating power but that it is generally so appallingly inefficient and therefore uncurably ruthless. Almost any episode within capitalism's screwball trajectory is more likely to turn out incoherent rather than homogeneous, fissiparous not teleological. We need only point, following Eric Hobsbawm, to "the fashion for piratical 'take-overs' of business corporations and other financial speculations which swept the financial districts of ultra-free-market states like the USA and Britain in the 1980s, and which virtually broke all links between the pursuit of profit and the economy as a system of production" (Hobsbawm 1994: 342). Or merely recall Alan Greenspan's inimitable, and unsettling, phrase, "irrational exuberance," to make clear that the only difference in the long run between capitalism and chaos is that chaos doesn't even enrich the few. Miracle. Bubble. Panic. Crash. Capitalism's old un-sweet song.

And, of course, this tendency toward chaos becomes even more marked, in the case of the patent theatres, through the clearly demonstrated proclivity of all monopolies to wax unprofitable. In Albert Hirschman's inimitable phrasing: the "limited type" of monopoly, the type that corresponds to the duopoly of Covent Garden and Drury Lane, always marks "the oppression of the weak by the incompetent, and an exploitation of the poor by the lazy . . . durable and stifling as it is both unambitious and inescapable" (Hirschman 1970: 59).

The actual theater proprietors and their lessees turned out with appalling regularity to be nothing less than villains. Indeed, as the patent houses became unprofitable, they attracted the nineteenth-century equivalent of hostile takeovers, "so many adventurers and speculators without fortune" (1832: 90). "[M]oney making men," the writer Thomas Moncrieff characterized them, with "no regard for the drama further than as a means of profit to themselves," who saw nothing odd in doing "*A New Way to Pay Old Debts* as a first piece, and then Othello as a farce, and both . . . represented in a most disgraceful manner" (1832: 176). In fact, by the 1830s, shares in both Covent Garden and Drury Lane had become in effect little more than junk bonds. With reason did Macready call his nemesis, Bunn, that "beast."

But with impervious tenacity everyone involved in the patent theatres, managers, actors, literati, clung to the contradiction that impoverished them. Such tenacity suggests that we are confronting here not simply another scenario of economic delinquency but, more powerfully, a paradigmatic instance of ideology. What cultural model, we must then ask, could be so glamorous, so compelling that it could bind, and blind, the theatre establishment for so long to the machinery of its own evisceration? What unwilled unseeing, for example, allowed Macready to accept a gift of plate from the Covent Garden actors with a speech that concluded: "One of my motives has been the wish to . . . establish an asylum for . . . my brothers and sisters who profess [acting], where they might be secure of equitable treatment, friendly consideration, and, most of all . . . respect" (Macready 1967: 121). And yet to write six days later "of the extravagant expectations of the actors, who expected to share with me in the chance of their salaries, and also to divide any surplus! I see the impracticability of the attempt to raise them from the condition of serfs; they have not the nobleness to be really free" (p. 121). He can not see or feel or even sense the inconsistency between insisting that "as a director I must be a despot" (p. 120) and at the same time lamenting that he is himself "manacled in every way as, literally, the servant – instead of the tenant – of the proprietors" (p. 136).

Macready and the theatre he epitomized were blinded not by the monopoly itself – they saw its flaws all too painfully – but by the idea behind the monopoly: the monumental chimera of a national drama performed in a national theater. As Macready phrased it in his farewell to the stage: the attempt "to establish a theater, in regard to decorum and taste, worthy of our country, and to have in it the plays of our divine Shakespeare fitly illustrated," a task he believed to be the unfulfilled "duty" of those who owned and managed the patent theaters (1967: 293).

The idea of a British national theatre developed through the eighteenth century, centered, as Michael Dobson has shown, on the apotheosis of Shakespeare as the national poet. It roots in what Henri Lefebvre calls the *monumental*, the key value of European culture from the fifteenth to the nineteenth centuries (Lefebvre 1974: 146). Clearly, the social and aesthetic system that shapes Bernini's colonnade to St. Peter's or the garden front at Versailles also produces elephantine Covent Garden and gargantuan Drury Lane. The two great theaters not only look like St. Paul's or Blenheim, they represent the same sort of structured space. Typically, monumental space opposes the grandest possible polarities to generate at the same time overwhelming scale and an illusion of weightlessness: in the bubbled thrust of the dome, in the airy uplift of the painted ceiling, and – not least – in the grandly illuminated illusionism of the stage. These uplifting spaces in turn display clearly intelligible "signs and surfaces which claim to express collective will and collective thought," brilliantly concealing beneath their glamorous surface both "the will to power and the arbitrariness of power" (Lefebvre 1991: 143). They insist that the yoke of the state is easy and the burden of community light. Within their overarching order any individual can, and should, find his or her ideal possibility, uplifted, inspired, addressed. As a key component of the monumental, the national theatre thus claims to order a populace into a people, a people who find its destiny and happiness in yielding to the claims of a nation: a renewed Globe for an expanded and refulgent Albion.

But, as with so much of the *ancien régime*, monumental theatre generated its own overbuilt undoing. Monumentality demanded the national

drama centralize performance in great metropolitan houses, mounting
in repertory a different play every night for (roughly) the same audience.
That meant enormous work forces both on and off the stage. By the
early nineteenth century both Drury Lane and Covent Garden were
employing larger staffs than a typical Manchester cotton factory. And
by the 1830s each of the two theaters could hold nightly audiences of
about 3,000. Ironically, however, as the theaters enlarged, it became
harder to hear and even to see the actors. And so to meet expenses
managers began to supplant drama with spectacle (1832: 121). Ultimately, the legitimate drama found itself depending on something akin to
circus to keep itself alive. "Did the lions draw money," the treasurer of
Drury Lane was asked by the Parliamentary Committee. "The lions
certainly paid their expenses," he answered modestly (1832: 75). In the
name of drama, the drama was annulled. "Within the last few years
have you found spectacle fill your theater better than the legitimate
drama? – Yes, novelty; the old drama certainly is not very attractive"
(1832: 74). The galleries came to call the shots, literally crowding out the
very upper and middle class audience to whom this national drama
might be thought most likely to appeal. "I do not go to those theatres,"
George IV told William Dowton, "because they are so large; I am not
comfortable" (1832: 92). And the middle-class Francis Place insisted: "I
never paid, and I never will pay 7s. to go to boxes; many whom I am
acquainted with have staid away for the same reasons, as well as from
their not being able either to see or hear" (1832: 206).

Thus, while the market for fiction was galvanized by *laissez-faire*
competition, the monopolized theater turned back the tides of capital:
sail persisting into an age of steam. Still responsive to the liturgical
rhythms of an older Church-State year, the theaters continued to close
not only on the Wednesdays and Fridays of Lent, and for all of Passion
Week, but also on the anniversary of the execution of Charles I. Like
Lot's obdurate wife, they looked futilely back to a vanished era of
expanding, interlocked national and royal power. Their real parallels
were not with the multitude of independent cotton spinneries and iron
works currently transforming the landscape, but with the chartered
overseas trading companies, like the South Sea and the East India,
which derived their permanence and their (apparent) security by statute
and official sanction. The chartered companies had, of course, become
not only obsolete but scandalous as capitalism moved from its mercantile to its manufacturing phase. But the theatres royal remained trapped
in the calcified venture-economics of the Restoration.

They remained trapped because the fiction of what they were supposed to produce continued more attractive than their obvious failure to
deliver real satisfaction to anyone on other side of the proscenium. That
fiction sprouted from the common conviction that a national drama,
unlike the boulevard theaters of private spectacle, meant a "common
exhibition" (Charles Churchill, *The Rosciad*, 1761), a performance in
which the audience not only had an interest but a right. Commercial
theaters belong to their owners, but national theaters belong – or claim
to belong – to everyone. They profess to exhibit common civic structures and common moral values to an audience which in common, if
unequally, share the national inheritance. In London, paradoxically,
even when that relationship was most contested, it was also most
endorsed.

In the patent theaters, audience and stage were almost equally visible
throughout the performance. Dialogue not only passed between the
actors but back and forth across the pit, from spectators to stage and
from performers back to audience. Scenes like Wopsle's harried Hamlet
in *Great Expectations*, where the audience makes almost as much noise as
the performers, do not mark only the minor, illegitimate theaters.
Comparable tauntings were a regular feature of the two Theatres Royal
from the eighteenth through the first third of the nineteenth century.
But these disturbers of the theatrical peace were, by and large, not
punished, even in the worst of the theatre riots, the famous Old Price
riots of 1809. During the Riots juries regularly declared that free speech
was the founding condition of the stage, not only free speech from the
stage but a free speech to the stage. "On the one hand . . . ownership of a
building or patent did not confer on the proprietors either the right to
set prices or proscribe behaviour; on the other hand, once having paid
admission, individuals were free to choose the appropriate form of
response" (Baer 1992: 74).[8] These unruly audiences were pressing not
for, but against, innovation, not for smaller, commercial houses but for
the reinstatement of the old price, and all the old arrangements. Indeed,
we can speculate that it was precisely because the fabric was being
steadily stripped from every side of the traditional social environment
that the London audiences clung so fiercely to the covering fiction of a
national stage. A national theatre, they insisted, gave them as much
right as the monarch to command performance.

The monopolized theatre's failure to protect those rights was paid for
in the actors' shame. Just as he was degraded in the Green Room by the
conditions of his employment, he was insulted on stage by the conditions

of his display. Regularly, from the late eighteenth century on, increasingly dissatisfied spectators disrupted performances and harried actors, turning them into the scapegoats of a monumental failure. The spectators' rage seemed to them not mob violence but the civic expression of their "right to inflict or not to inflict pain on the actor's body" (Straub 1992: 169). "Actors who refused to submit were frequently beaten up off the stage as well as pelted by trash while on" (p. 169). And even so eminent a figure as Garrick was at times called upon by the gallery to "kneel and apologize for a real or imagined offense" – a ritual humiliation just like Jingle's at the end of *Pickwick*. Against those demands the actor had no recourse, just as he had no recourse against managerial tyranny. In a national theatre, he was a public servant. And the service he offered was his own humiliation to balance the shortcomings of the institution that so terribly misused him, and so consistently misled his audience. How right, then, Mrs. Nickleby was to think it a dreadful thing for her son to have been born a Shakespeare.

Macready's attack on Bunn thus parallels the Old Price riots, and both of them parallel the struggles of the Crummles company. They're all three inadequate responses to a flaccid system's incapacity to deliver to any of its clients the theatre they desired. With this crucial difference. The plebeian rioters got the price hike and the structural changes reversed. Crummles, however, had to emigrate. And poor Macready wound up paying Bunn £150 damages. He might try to cry out to audiences as well as to the manager: "You damned scoundrel[s]! How dare you use me in this manner?" But his frustrated roar would have made as little difference with audiences as with the manager. In the theatre Dickens confronts, even a Macready has only two choices: starvation or humiliation. In effect, no choice, just shame either way.

Of course, after the monopoly's 1843 repeal, the social and psychic standing of actors changed rapidly. By the 1861 census, acting had become an official profession. There were then 1,563 of them. By 1882, *Iolanthe's* Lord Chancellor could blithely sing of "other professions in which men engage / . . . The Army, the Navy, the Church, and the Stage." And about the same time the first theatrical knights are dubbed. But while the patents of monopoly sustained the monumental chimera, exaltation and repression could afford little maneuvering room for mere professionalism.

And that is why Nicholas Nickleby, and his creator, refuse the refuge of theatre, as audition (creator), as profession (character). They elect instead Hirschman's alternative option. Rather than voice, they choose, or at least they think they can choose, to exit – stage and shame alike. Which leads us nicely into the next chapter: "Exit: 'the sanguine mirage'."

CHAPTER 4

Exit: "the sanguine mirage"

that glorious vision of doing good, which is so often the sanguine
mirage of so many good minds
A Tale Of Two Cities (II:xxiv, 272)[1]

The previous chapter concluded with the notion that Nicholas
Nickleby, and his creator, could successfully exit theatre, all that damnable "fooling here!" (xxxx, 398). Such an exit would evade the shame
Dickens and his contemporaries associate with unmanaged public exhibition without having to forgo the admiration and esteem the hero, like
his author, so obviously and desperately craves. But an option to Exit
makes sense only if it faces with some symmetry a counter-option
marked Entry, in this case entry to a non-theatrical world where
ambition has a reasonable chance to satisfy the entrant's grandiose
psychic demands. A world, then, that heartily cheers the immature, the
agamous, the episodic, the mimetic: that hails a hero who, forsaking all
others, forgets who he's been, to forge himself into whoever at the
moment he wishes to become. A world sufficiently broad-minded not
merely to accept but to acclaim Narcissus, supreme connoisseur of the
self.[2]

Narcissus haunts the second half of *After Dickens*. But my Narcissus
loves his I with a difference, the difference elaborated by his most
empathic post-Freudian defender, Heinz Kohut, the father of "Self
Psychology."[3] Kohut follows psychoanalytic convention in marking a
crucial split between object love and narcissism, the libidinal cathexis of
the self. But he also breaks with that tradition, refusing its impulse to
downgrade narcissism into a jejune sort of psychic second best. That
belittling Kohut credits to Western civilization's obsessive, intrusive
stress on altruism, keeping the other: brother, neighbor, guest, as the self
(Kohut 1985: 98). Freed from altruism's overdetermining mandates,
Kohutian narcissism emerges as "neither pathological nor obnoxious."
Rather, integrated into a mature personality, it functions as "the touch-
stone of a person's individuality and identity" (p. 109). It focuses and
even protects the ego. For Kohut, it's narcissism which generates the
"healthy enjoyment of our own activities and successes" that keeps us

productive, and, just as important, it's narcissism also that produces the "adaptively useful sense of disappointment . . . over our failures and shortcomings" (p. 107), which tells us when it's smart to quit.

Narcissism drives Dickens's freakish, anti-referential, and entirely inimitable prose. Narcissism empowers the comic eccentricity which makes his minor characters more memorable than his major, and which accounts for so much of Dickens's enduring hold on his readers. And of course it's narcissism that generates agamy: which we can now more clearly define as preferring the self to the other, with good reason.

We can even go so far as to claim that protecting narcissism is what Sydney Carton is actually though covertly proclaiming as the "far far better thing that I do now" – covertly because narcissistic agamy is truly the love that dare not, in altruistic society, speak its name. In exactly the same way, it's narcissism that makes Carton's prototype Dick Swiveller the real hero of *The Old Curiosity Shop*. His name says it all, if you're willing to be vulgar. Which also means, of course, that Little Nell is merely the novel's victim. Indeed, we can and should read *Old Curiosity Shop* as a novel that takes, with enormous and profound ingenuity, the protection of narcissism as its privileged subject. Nell, with no sense of self, has no choice but to fade away and die, lost in a world of beloved objects, the shop of curiosities, becoming at the end on her tomb the last and most beautiful of those curious objects. But mendicant, appetitive Swiveller, all self, saves not only himself, but Nell's double, the Marchioness whom he reinvents as Sophronia Sphynx, to preserve her mystery. Which must be why, by the way, in a famous Dickensian puzzle, Dickens refused to claim that the Marchoness was Sally Brass's child by Quilp. The Marchioness is Athena to Swiveller's sublimely, comically narcissistic Zeus. She survives where Nell doesn't because she is nobody's daughter or granddaughter, only and supremely a very funny Idea.

But we can't stop here. Kohut takes his defense of narcissism much further than a merely salubrious defense of self-esteem. He insists that beyond this elementary form an amplified narcissism can generate a range of more highly specialized, and acclaimed, qualities of the self. Like Freud, he recognizes in narcissism the mainspring of humor. But then, going well beyond Freud, he also credits narcissism with spurring creativity, empathy, transcendence and wisdom (1985: 111). All these desirable, perhaps even heroic, features spring from narcissism's formidable powers of idealization and internalization. The narcissist retains in a remarkably unmodified way the "original bliss, power, perfection, and goodness . . . projected" by the infant "on the parent figure" (p. 101). If disturbed or denied, that original idealism becomes introjected into the self and its grandiose projects: terribly, as the totalitarian projects of grand or petty tyrants – Quilp; less troubling, as a dry, obsessive utopianism, as in the road to Martha Stewart Living, or, so much more banal, Le Corbusier (where there are not even treats to eat). Transformed and encouraged, however, narcissism refuses to resign itself to loss, to the ordinary give-and-take of object relations, that is: to life, and love, as we know it. Unselfishly, even generously, narcissism strives instead to re-create perfection, or something as close as possible to perfection, in both the productions, and the style, of the self. This heroic narcissism becomes the characterizing mark not of the self-centered and the vain, but of the artist, the scientist, the (Kohutian) therapist and, most paradoxical of all, the saint.

That transformation, perhaps even better that transfiguration, of elementary into amplified narcissism requires, in Kohut's phrase, "a maximal relinquishment of narcissistic delusions" about the "physical, intellectual and emotional powers" of the self (1985: 122,121). The heroic narcissist – artist, scientist, therapist, saint – "matures" by transferring the possibility of perfection from the self to the object for which the self selflessly cares: the work of art, the experiment, the cure, the kingdom. But here Kohut begin to trace a path that Dickens fears, indeed loathes, to tread. At heart Dickens *is* Philoktetes, as Edmund Wilson all those years ago insisted: the spurned, abandoned, wounded hero who defines himself as, above all things, wounded; the hero who cannot tell any story except about himself, who won't let any other story be told, except the story of his wounding and its shame. He can invent and enjoy Swiveller but only as a figure of lower-caste fun, explicitly not the author's alter ego. Dick Swiveller, Sir, is no Nicholas Nickleby.

Exactly because he cannot follow the "higher" narcissistic path of relinquishment and self-transcendence, Dickens goes about building novels that emerge as what Freud would call a *defense*. (And right at the start let me make it quite clear how glad I am that he did. I have no interest in writing about the higher sorts of good, about, say, George Eliot. If you want to hear morning prayer in a workhouse – I say – go to a workhouse.) This fictional *defense* is what we earlier identified as the *cameral*. It's a defense of self-centered exceptionalism against conventional masculinity. A *defense* against conventional demands for "normal" sexual and social maturity. Against "reasonable" demands of the other on the self: be they moral, or altruistic, or legal. A *defense*, even, of elementary, self-centered narcissism against its amplified, self-transcending transformation. If you want to see how that transformation would read, turn to *In Memoriam*, or, better still, indeed best yet, *The Idylls of the King*. But since our subject is Dickens not Tennyson, we'll stick with the *defense* maintained, and return to *Nickleby*. It is with *Nickleby* that Dickens's fiction finds its essential form: "as upon a theatre," the cameral novel which does not conduce to convention's idea of maturity but instead defends the traumatized self against the world's claims.

And I'm sufficiently non-narcissistic myself to admit here that I am returning to very much the same argument that, fifty years ago, Dorothy Van Ghent memorably called the "View from Todger's," the routine transformation of spirit into matter, and vice versa. Van Ghent located this inversion in Dickens's attentiveness to a world that has lost coherence, of nature somehow gone wrong. I am arguing for a somewhat different cause, for a willed and chosen withdrawal from, and subsequent subversion of, any sort of natural or social order which might claim the power or right to impose itself on the supremely, agonizingly, narcissistic self.[4]

THE BOY IN THE GLASS BOOTH

> Whoever does not exit is a candidate for voice . . . But the direction of the relationship is turned round: with a given potential for articulation, the actual level of voice feeds on *in*elastic demand, or on the lack of opportunity for exit.
>
> (Hirschman 1970: 34)

The Dickens novel finds its form at exactly the mid-point of *Nicholas Nickleby*, in the movement from the mirrored space of the hostile London coffee house to the glassed-in writing room where the Cheeryble twins provide Nicholas an enduring shelter. The glass-enclosed coffee room represents a lower-middle-class, that is a Dickensian, fantasy of male hegemonic being. Because they are doubled, the facing glasses suspend the ordinary dynamic of visual process: recension, diminution, incompletion, distance. Instead, the twinned mirrors "multiply" and "enhance" their proper subjects, aristocrats like Hawk and Verisopht (xxxii, 411).

In their surface sheen, all that you are is shown: you are, literally, all show. What elsewhere might induce shame, or at least reserve – like a cad's exploitative erotic conquests – these glasses recycle as boast and brag: hegemonic narcissism without compunction and trouble-free.

Such glass has no way to image the incomplete. Lack, disguise, even reticence, Nickleby's repertoire of specialties, they cannot begin to register.

Nicholas makes no impression in this aristocratic glass because he's someone waiting still to happen. He needs the serial, linear space of growth and development, of *bildungsromanen*, posited fragilely on that most middle-class of hopes: that the best is yet to come. Aristocrats, of course, know in their bones that the best has been: they're living well on inexhaustible, ancestral interest. And proletarians know that the best has nothing to do with them in any case. They suffer neither hope nor nostalgia. But Nicholas suffers acutely from both, which is why we find him stationed solidly on the wrong side of quite another sort of glass than those high-toned mirrors, the "one thin sheet of brittle glass" with which the chapter opens, the shop windows' "iron wall" that defines an apparently unbridgeable divide between haves and have-nots (p. 409). Without property and status, he is, in effect, the proto-Victorian original for a very modern type: early invisible man. Compulsively, fruitlessly, he begs Sir Mulberry, "Will you tell me who you are?" (p. 417) Nonchalantly the baronet refuses to treat this would-be hero as anything like a social equal: "an errand-boy for aught I know" – indeed, as anything like a human presence, continuing instead to lounge in the opposite booth "as if he were wholly ignorant of the presence of any living person" (p. 416).

Nicholas can't make an impression in this space in large part because he has stationed himself beyond a barrier even harder to scale than that of class, harder because he preserves it himself, indeed preserves it as himself. A merciless economics may make him a scarcely visible man, but his even more relentlessly elementary narcissism has made him an utterly invisible boy. Oliver Twist's bigger brother, Nickleby knows himself, and longs to be known, supremely, merely, and only as a son. Physically mature, he nevertheless remains, and wishes to remain, what the novel's title first names him: a Younger. To Hawk, then, he defines himself as "the son of a country gentleman," Hawk's equal he claims "in birth and education" (which shows bravado, but is patently untrue) and then he trails off into the lame: "and your superior I trust in everything besides" (p. 417). That "son" and "trust" betray him. He can't name the empty "everything else besides," he can't even sketch what it might contain, because he can't imagine himself a man, let alone a gentleman. He wants recognition in this smoke-filled womb of privilege, but not really as a man of the world preening with his kin, only as the cherished and worthy protégé of a loving and omnipotent protector.

But in a world of men, the permanent lad continually rediscovers that he can only lay claim to rage, unquenchable, virtually ungovernable rage, shame's fist. That's the actual, sorry substance of Nicholas's "everything besides" which swells into his culminating assault on Hawk. Like his cameral near contemporary the Lady of Shalott, Nicholas has reached a breaking-point, when living off shadows can no longer suffice, the point when the mirrors must go smash. Both the quarrel and the chapter conclude with an unspecified "loud cry, the smashing of some heavy body, and the breaking of glass – " (p. 418), a break-up in which I hear (with Kohut) the "traumatic rejection of an environment that will not respond empathically to the [hero's] rekindled narcissistic needs" (Kohut 1985: 152).

From the start of his story, Nicholas is (like Dickens) revenge-prone, always ready "to respond to a potentially shame-provoking situation by the employment of a simple remedy: the active (often anticipatory) inflicting on others of those narcissistic injuries which he is most afraid of suffering himself" (Kohut 1972: 144). Narcissism regularly connects to rage, Kohut argues. Indeed, he defines rage quite specifically as enfeebled narcissism's aggressive reaction to threats to its uncompromising insistence on limitless power and knowledge. On the one hand, an archaic grandiosity insists the narcissist be exhibited and admired. On the other hand, the traumatic rejection of that grandiosity rebounds to anchor within the psyche as shame, a shame which insists exhibitionism be stymied and frustrated. These are, of course, exactly the terms with which we have just been reading the coffee-room sequence. But *Nickleby* figures these contrary impulses even more pointedly in" the complex contrast between Nicholas's two early surrogate "fathers': the benevolent father Crummles and the sadistic father Squeers.[5]

From the first glimpse we get of his boys happily practicing their sword play under Crummle's encouraging direction, we begin to see how the Crummles Company works to benevolently revise Dotheboys Hall. Crummles, patriarch of the happy theatrical family, a family that is a theatre, does everything he can to encourage the much-rejected Nicholas to perform. Squeers, malevolently refusing to recognize boys as sons, does everything he can to hide away, to dispossess, to humiliate the apprentice whom he masters. The two patriarchs and their contrasted worlds project Nicholas's intense inward struggle between those see-sawing impulses: shame perpetually frustrating grandiosity; grandiosity constantly struggling to evade shame's powerful prohibition. And that intolerable struggle generates in turn a deep-seated, all-pervasive rage, the hybrid of shame and grandiosity, a rage which the young Dickensian protagonist eventually must direct out from the self against the world.

Throughout the novel's first half, Nicholas struggles against expressing that rage, struggles, not quite manfully, but certainly best-boyfully. Repeatedly, he forces it down or he projects it out onto others. When he does allow it expression, he denies or evades recognizing it for what it is. Instead of rage he calls it revenge (his word is *avenge*): justifiably righting the wrongs others have done or are doing, especially wrongs against others than himself, against his cousin, for example, or his sister. But like his archaic need to exhibit himself, the need to prove himself by inflicting pain anchors deeply in the unrelenting threat of his imminent psychic collapse and dissolution. That's why in a rare candid moment, Nicholas warns Squeers not to "raise the devil within me" (xiii, 155). He can openly acknowledge that devil his own but he cannot admit that the devil is his self.

Just look at what happens at Dotheboys (Part VIII). Clearly, Nicholas suffers his confinement there as a narcissistic trauma. Though he feels sorry for the boys, he in fact does little or nothing for them, skillfully excusing himself for cooperating with the system. Nicholas Nickleby is no Oskar Schindler. He's not even a Pied Piper who, having beaten Squeers, chooses to lead the boys out of bondage. In the end, he's perfectly content to save only himself, not even bothering to rescue the prime victim, Smike. Whatever pity he may feel for Smike and the others, the "state of feeling" that really lays him low roots in his recollection "that, being there as an assistant, he actually seemed . . . to be the aider and abettor of a system which filled him with honest disgust and indignation." As a result, "he loathed himself" (pp. 95–96). This is not the loathing of a self-confident, self-assured man, unexpectedly thrown into an ugly position. It's exactly the reverse. That self-loathing re-activates a continuous and defining failure in essential self-esteem. Thus, when he attacks Squeers, he warns: "I have a long series of insults to avenge" (p. 155). But these are not insults to Smike or anyone else. Those only *aggravate* his *indignation*. The indignation festers in his own indignity, the insults to the self, insults going back well before Squeers.

Beating up Squeers, Nicholas both gives way to and fights against the hidden accuracy of his apprenticeship to the master-monster, that other grandiose pretender who uses violence to squash any slight to his implausible pretensions. Their fierce and violent confrontation shows how much closer akin they are than either can bear to admit.

Squeers . . . struck him a blow across the face with his instrument of torture, which raised a bar of livid flesh as it was inflicted. Smarting with the agony of the blow, and concentrating into that one moment all his feelings of rage, scorn, and indignation, Nicholas sprang upon him, wrested the weapon from his hand, and pinning him by the throat, beat the ruffian till he roared for mercy. (p. 155)

Mercy which, of course, such rage cannot sanction. Obviously, Nicholas, stronger, younger, bigger than Squeers, could control him as easily as he later does Lenville. What is he – about two feet taller? Nicholas doesn't need to do things like throwing "in the full torrent of his violence . . . all his remaining strength into half-a-dozen finishing cuts" (p. 155). Except that kind of violence is exactly what we see that he does, most deeply, need. And if we don't know that by the end of the Yorkshire sequence, we surely recognize it when it reappears in the coffee-room. Nickleby's encounter with Hawk is marked by exactly the same rage, exactly the same sadistic need to satisfy violently a narcissism violently beleaguered. "Nicholas gained the heavy handle, and with it laid open one side of his antagonist's face from the eye to the lip" (xxxii, 417–418). If Nicholas can't find himself reflected in that flattering glass, no one else shall either.

And it is at that point that Nicholas, fleeing blindly, miraculously "happens" upon a new way, a way out of rage, a way out of frustration, a way to be recognized. Dazed, able to "see or hear no more," he "turn[s] down a bye-street" (p. 418), a reclusive sanctuary from the "spoiled," "crabbed" wilderness of "the whole wide world" (xxxv, 448–450). And there, almost immediately, it happens again: the first Cheeryble draws him into yet another "bye-street" (p. 450). Nicholas is no longer operating amidst the passages of any mainstream. He has, in this doubled bend, abandoned the difficult Oedipal paths of self-making, of *bildungsroman*, for the comforting self-affirmations of the pre-Oedipal. And from the moment those bye-ways claim him, he can relax successfully into the role he, and all subsequent Dickens heroes, long for, the petted and pitied boy-child: "before he had been closeted with the two brothers ten minutes, he could only wave his hand at every fresh expression of kindness and sympathy, and sob like a little child" (p. 454).

We can see all this, literally, in the glass brightly. Up until the Cheerybles appear, glass functions as the novel's sign and instrument of alterity and exclusion. Lack is certainly what the luxurious coffee-room mirrors mean for Nicholas. And the far less grand window-glass of commerce depends on a comparable exploitation of lack: the tantalizing come-on to commercial spectacle. Indeed, that's just the sort of glass in which Nicholas first encounters the Cheerybles: the Registry window where jobs are tantalizingly offered in print, only to be denied in fact. "Nicholas, carrying his eye along the window-panes from left to right in search of some capital-text placard, which should be applicable to his own case, caught sight of this old gentleman's figure, and instinctively withdrew his eyes from the window, to observe the same more closely" (p. 448). Everything speaks here of a sameness both bogus and empty, a world of work-a-day ennui: same masters, same mistresses, same servants, same estates, same opportunities (pp. 447–448): a single, rueful, endlessly repeated lie. That's why, I think, Nicholas *instinctively withdraws*, as though he knows that this kind of glass is not the correct material for aligning himself with the new force he requires.

And he's right, of course. Almost the first thing his new benefactors do is establish Nicholas – not along the frame – but within a glass house, the curious "counting-house like a large glass case" (xxxv, 451-ff) in which he is set to work. There, in a space scrupulously ordered, fetishistically pure, prodigiously, even obsessively, "free from dust and blemish," Nicholas and Tim Linkinwater meticulously maintain the Cheerybles' perfect books. That new glass space is then a preeminently Dickensian space, a space of and for writing, a space of speckless, shameless, entirely cameral performance.

The material that sustains this "open display" (xxxvi, 470) will become after about 1845 the new glass of the engineers. It will emerge as the prototypical nineteenth-century structural material, simultaneously strong and delicate, valued equally for its ability to let in (light and warmth) and to keep out (dirt and cold), literally the crowning glory of those strikingly contemporary spaces: the train shed, the covered market and, crown of crowns, the great exhibition hall. But still heavily taxed in the 1830s, Nickleby glass is a luxury item, the material of Paxton's Great Conservatory at Ducal Chatsworth, being built at exactly the time the novel appears (Kohlmaier 1986: 47), but not yet of the mass-spectacle Great Exhibition (1850). Nicholas's "glass-case" (p. 451), then, like "a real glass-house, fitted with the choicest curiosities" (xxxvii, 469), is a jeweler's, or some other sort of luxury vendor's, fantasy show box. Built Large.

A priori, such a space guarantees the worth and value of what it displays. Could anything be less like a theater, and still convincingly sustain exhibition? On stage the actor is always at work, proving, demonstrating, performing his value, and subject always to the censure (but only sometimes the applause) of a jealous, withholding, judging audience. However, to be set out in a perfect glass case, guaranteed by the presenter, ensures that one is already choice, unimpeachable, rare. No question of shame here; the setting warrants entire adequacy. And nix to any cavilling pretense at *nil admirari*. If you don't like what's displayed in such a vitrine, it's you, not the object, that's clearly at fault. The exhibitor *must do*, more or less; but the exhibited has only, merely and supremely, *to be*.[6]

The invisible man has metamorphosed into the best boy in the glass booth, coddled, indulged, protected, sheltered, supported, braced. Nicholas and his author have located the key features of a new paradigm for display. It's new for Nicholas, new for Dickens, and new for culture. It's the paradigm of the barely nascent regime of mechanical reproduction, the anti-original, mass-circulation age of, among other things, cheap parts publication for fiction. The age which its godfather Walter Benjamin describes as apperceptive, self-absorbed, incidental, absent-minded, everything, that is, that can resist, refuse or subvert an earlier (Oedipal) regime of the concentrated, the pursuing, the achieving (Benjamin 1969: 239). Sadly, at this point, we can't do much more than gesture toward the connection, though it would be a pity to pass it by without also suggesting how apt the age of mechanical reproduction seems for the successful pursuit of agamy, whose untrammeled narcissism seems to generate exactly those qualities that mark for Benjamin the coming, that is, the present age, the age in which the invisible man yields to the all-too-visible boy.

To protect the boy in the glass booth, the novel falls back on what we saw working so well in *Pickwick*: the soldering of a hybrid hero, a marginal but active young man, with a furiously benevolent pre-Oedipal parent. With this combo the self unexpectedly encounters – rather than, say, makes, achieves, attains – identity. One minute Nicholas is "picturing to himself . . . all kinds of possibilities" (p. 447), none of which includes anything like the Cheerybles. And then suddenly, with an incidental glance, he is taken swiftly up by Charles Cheeryble, who immediately can't wait – "Don't say another word. Not another word . . . We mustn't lose a minute" (p. 451) – to pour out for the unprepared ephebe some of "the plums from Fortune's choicest pudding" (p. 453). Looking to be a menial, Nicholas finds himself unexpectedly adopted as heir and son. Never did a Ganymede less to lure or recompense his enraptured Jove, or Joves.

But why twins? Why won't just one motherly old father do? After all, it worked so well before, that being loved unreservedly by a wealthy older man. But the brothers' predecessors in the preOedipal, Mr. Pickwick and, Oliver's grandfather, Mr. Brownlow were in pretty nearly equal parts loving and fallible. Pickwick, paradoxically, was too good to keep himself or Sam for long out of quod. And Brownlow had that irritating habit of finding young Oliver only to lose him again. These two early tries at parental substitution suggest the problem may lay in the prodigious amount of idealization required to inflate and sustain an unfailingly munificent and benevolent parent, an idealizing power the narcissistically traumatized prodigy – Oliver *par excellence* – can scarcely manage. And certainly society and its structures, to which the pre-Oedipal figure must be securely opposed, have no stake in idealizing on the ephebe's behalf. In *Oliver* Mr. Brownlow is always being dragged down by his conventional upper-class partner, the aptly named Grim-wig. And there's nothing Pickwick can do about Dodson and Fogg, but mope. What's needed, then, is some source outside both the protagonist's self, and the society he opposes, which can first put up and then guarantee the idealistic capital, at it were, on which the hero and this hyperinflated imago must both depend.

The particular magic of twins converts mere likeness into identity, and thus, by extension, promises coherence to even a deeply traumatized figure like Nicholas, so damaged he needs not merely love but magic. The Kohutian analyst Doris Brothers argues that twinning embraces "a longing for closeness with . . . a selfobject" who "embodies . . . hidden aspects of the self," affirmative aspects that permit the individual "to *restore* a sense of cohesive selfhood following shattering trauma" (Brothers 1985: 195, 206). In Kohut's own terms, it confirms "the feeling that one is a human being among other human beings" (Kohut 1984: 200).

A better twist on the issue of twinning, however, might follow up the autobiographical implications of the Cheeryble intervention: their mandate that Nicholas keep books. We could then read this cardinal sequence as Dickens recasting the magical intervention that saved or rather made his life. The twins turn their protégé to scribbling just as that other proto-lovable pair, Chapman and Hall, out of the blue, magically made the young Dickens into the author of *Pickwick*.[7] What Nicholas is about to move toward, then, becomes what Dickens himself has just come through: the unimpeachable justification of the eternal son's enduring narcissistic trust that suitable fathers will discover and conserve him.

Writing, Nicholas's writing, Dickens's writing, redeems the botched Covent Garden audition. Both author and protagonist have put professional theater firmly behind them, while from the new vocation to write have already appeared immediate and fantastic rewards that even the stage could never provide. Rather sweetly in fact, a little later on, Dickens even forgets that Nicholas doesn't also write fiction and has his hero passionately defend writers from thieving adaptors (xlviii, 632–634). A conflation easily excused when we realize not only how completely Dickens identifies himself with Nicholas's redemption through scribbling but how much like fiction Nicholas's writing really is, at least like fiction as it came to, and from, Dickens. For both author and alter ego writing requires neither training nor knowledge (xxxvii, 471). It is entirely, crucially unprofessional, i.e. you don't go to school or train as apprentice or pass an exam to be allowed to do it; indeed, schools, training and exams can't make any difference in how well you do it. This kind of writing develops from the writer's character and personality, not his station, or his stationing. It recognizes innate quality over and against credentials. And, for both Nicholas and Dickens, as soon as it is tried, it is mastered. Within two weeks Nicholas's writing skills equal those of the old master Linkinwater. Simultaneously laborious and fantastic, then, this writing epitomizes the *cameral*, an insulated, eccentric, idiosyncratic performance of the deeply talented self which can fulfill every grandiose, narcissistic fantasy and at the same time form a perfect defense against all forms of scrutiny. In comparison to its as-it-were performance, any professional theatre will always come in at best a sorry second. (Of course, these are early days, when writing seemed to open up suddenly and unexpectedly the shining path. Later writing was to become for Dickens something closer to sheer torture.)

But it's also crucial that the benefactors register as twins because their doubling displaces the previous pairing that wouldn't behold Nicholas with loving adoration: the coffee room's hegemonic glasses. The Cheerybles are strikingly like those mirrors. At their base of operations, "Everything gave back, besides, some reflection of the kindly spirit of the brothers" (xxxvii, 470). Reflection, plenitude (*everything*), amplitude (*besides*): we've met these qualities before, of course. The twins' "kindly spirit," then, does for Nicholas exactly what the mirrors did for Hawk and Verisopht, exactly what the mirrors wouldn't do for the "errand boy." They banish all threat of lack from whatever is caught up within their so perfect field of "reflection."

But those other, earlier mirrors were in effect spectacularly the

reverse of "kindly." They demanded an incessant preening that turned
on a stifled awareness of lack. Their restrictive, specular surfaces
shadowed darker pentimenti which they demanded the self-adjusting
hegemons match, or to try to match. The twins, however, produce, a
mutual admiration society. Each finds in the other a perfect fullness, but
a fullness which is at the same time the antithesis to otherness. The
Cheeryble reflected becomes the Cheeryble reflector in an endless and
perfect circuit of inextinguishable self-affirmation. They are, indeed, a
kind of mad dream of self, without at the same time seeming to have any
nasty taint of ego.

This means that the twins are inherently a performance: a self
projected and viewed outside itself. And that performance is also, dare I
say it, another version of *cameral*. The Cheerybles structure in and out of
themselves a kind of mobile as-upon theater. Each guarantees to the
other the perfect audience, the audience that carries no hint of otherness
or critique. They thus express, once more, and supremely, the Dickensian dream of theatricality: a performance structure in which there is
no outside, in which all is inside, where what works as outside is really
only the inside out. That's – as we've seen – the performance ideal for
which the Dickensian protagonist has been longing and searching from
the start: a performance in which he too could become "the very type
and model" of himself (p. 453), where a perfect sameness would stretch
unmenaced between self and ego ideal. Longing and searching, because
that perfect fit is nowhere attainable in any sort of actual theater. But
lodged within the Cheerybles' perfect circuit, the Dickens hero can at
last "see" himself and be seen as that flawless self he needs, but which,
on his own, he feels too shamed to imagine himself to be. The Cheerybles' as-it-were theater thus founds and guarantees the model Dickensian display. "There an't such a young man as this in all London . . .
not one. Don't tell me! The City can't produce his equal. I challenge the
City to do it!" (xxxvii, 472). Production has moved from the City's stages
to the Cheerybles' bye-way.

Cameral privacy, and cameral fiction, ensure what it seems neither
over- nor understatement to call Dickens's immaturity project, the
as-upon-a-theater that cultivates, consolidates and conserves elementary narcissism. Conventional maturity demands the subjection, indeed
what feels like the subjugation, of the protagonist to the wish (desire) of
the Other(s). Heroic narcissism demands the dyer's hand: the subjugation of the self to the needs of the sublime Cause. But insistently
immature agamy guarantees the unquestioned, threat-surviving su-

premacy of the narcissistic Wish. The Cheeryble bye-way marks the spot where Nicholas and Dickens can boast together: this is it, this is "Where We Stopped Growing."

INTERLUDE: REFLECTIONS ON A NORMAL DEVIANCE

This Cheeryble "bye-way" means among other things that the world can never win when you play "hide and seek" against it. "A wonderful fact to reflect upon, that every human creature is constituted to be that profound secret and mystery to every other" (*A Tale*, I:iii, 44). The cameral novel, weaving indecipherable riddles, promises to keep both characters and novelist "secret and myster[ious]" from any form of scrutiny, internal or external. It permits our (limited) inspection of character and setting but baffles our entry. It encourages our admiration but it repeatedly insists we *wonder* from outside at the "profound mystery and secrecy" of the subjects displayed. *A Tale of Two Cities* warns that even in the most ordinary sort of town "every one of those darkly clustered houses encloses its own secret . . . every room in every one of them encloses its own secret . . . every beating heart in the hundreds of thousands of breasts there, is, in some of its imaginings, a secret to the heart nearest it" (p. 44). And against all those secrets not only the narrator but the rest of us must "st[and] in ignorance on the shore." The cameral firmly stations us as readers outside, watching, observing, admiring, and guessing, at best.

Another way to describe this guessing-game would be to claim that Dickens's novels, in Michael Riffaterre's terms, *repress* rather than *refer*. The *referring* text "makes sense only inasmuch as its signs . . . stand for things, or rather, for other signs that we are trained to remember in connection with the signifiers" (Riffaterre 1991: 30). But the *repressing* text depends on assertions that can "not be verified," that refuse to submit to our scrutiny, in either sense of the term, our seeing or our judging. Of course, as Riffaterre rightly insists, some sort of reference is necessary for any sort of reading to happen. But *repressive* writing displaces signs' "habitual referents with new ones that are complementary of, or contrary to, these habitual referents" (p. 30), denying our customary associations, our *memory* of life as it is or should be lived now. The cameral of course turns out to be repression at its prime. Writing from the bye-way turns away from the discipline of the "real." It prefers the enclosed, protected glasshouse where our fantasies require no verification but the mirrors we ourselves set up for adoring confirmation.

As style this sort of repression unleashes in Dickens an inexhaustibly fecund energy: his inimitable way with words (exactly parallel to Manet's comparably inimitable way with paint). But this reliance on repression also means (among many other things) that Orwell gets it dead wrong when he claims that "When Dickens has once described something you see it for the rest of your life" (Orwell 1954: 90). It seems pretty obvious to me that this is exactly what *doesn't* happen to you when you read Dickens. Of course, Dickens writes memorably. But the whole point of the "View from Todger's" is that nothing stays still long enough to be seen. When a description is indelible, it's usually the description of a fog, or a welter, or of mud, of something that can only be grasped by piling metaphor on metaphor, not by pointing, or showing. After all, what's the most often quoted passage in Dickens? Surely, the "best of times, worst of times" opening to *A Tale*, the whole point of which is to make merciless fun of everybody else's attempt to say anything accurate about any subject at all.

Dickens's vertiginously pyrotechnical prose is thrilling exactly because it regularly and systematically *confuses* "our conventional expectations." James Kincaid gets the effect precisely when he claims that Dickens's language *turns* us "in too many directions at once, by giving a clear signal that then vanishes, by offering a confounding variety of interpretive possibilities" (Kincaid 1987: 96). Thus, as in Manet, "the visible" as visible "comes to *be* the illegible" (Clark 1985: 48–49). Or in Kincaid's somewhat more terse formulation: "There is no 'it' to get." Well, of course, there is an "it" – of some sort. But it's an it you can't get at or to, or in. It's always on another side, a side to which you can relate as beholder, silenced, admiring, irrelevant, but not as audience, threatening, interrogating, demanding. It is an it that is simply out of this world. You're as likely to get at or in it as you are to get at, or in, Carroll's looking-glass world.

Of course, as Peter Brooks has shown, all plot is foreplay, a continuous, pleasurable postponement of the climax that must inevitably bring things to an end. But Dickens's plots, strung out month by month in the seemingly endless postponement of parts publication, are much more profoundly opposed to revelation of any kind. The cameral, in effect, does not want to know what happened if knowing means something like truth, truth in an economy of reference and utility, truth that insists growing up means putting away the things of a child, that a boy's cozy bye-way is merely a dead end. No, keeping to the truth, Dickens's novels repeatedly insist, can and will do only enormous harm. Truth refers. It is the stuff of eternal vigilance, that which calls itself liberty but which, in Dickens's view, can only in its turn repress. Thus, trying to get at the truth of the Jarndyce, or indeed the truth of any, case in Chancery, consumes all who enter the court. They choose the better part who, retiring to the bye-way of Bleak House, surrender all interest in discovery. Similarly, getting at the truth of the bank robbery ruins the Gradgrinds. And when he returns to see the truth of his benevolent intervention, Magwitch winds up destroying himself and his project. Little Dorrit is much wiser. She burns the Clennam will, so that the ugly truth of Arthur's actual parentage will never come out and disturb their final happiness. It would have been a far, far better thing to leave Dr. Manette's memoirs buried in the Bastille. When his true history is revealed, he finds himself the unwitting threat to his daughter's and granddaughter's life. Concede your curiosity about what *really* happened, Dickens repeatedly admonishes: the viewfinder, inevitably, will see himself undone.

Obviously, to read Dickens in this way departs from those highly influential analyses that, implementing Foucault, ally omniscient Victorian narrators with other key nineteenth-century surveyors like the prison warden and the factory inspector. Nevertheless, I believe, as is by now perhaps overabundantly clear, that the prospect of this all-permeating inspection horrifies shame-plagued Dickens. He aligns himself instead from the earliest novels with scrutiny's victims. This puts me much closer to an earlier and no longer fashionable set of readings like early, and even middle, J. Hillis Miller (even Miller himself doesn't seem much to like these readings any more). They locate at Dickens's "center" passages like the one quoted from *A Tale of Two Cities*, which recognize "the inalienable secrecy and otherness of every human being." For Miller, at least at one time, and certainly for me now, Dickens repeatedly repudiates "the idea that another person can be a kind of transparent alter ego whom I can know and possess without the intervention of any shadow of mystery or strangeness" (Hillis Miller 1958: 243).

Of course, it becomes easier, and perhaps even more persuasive, for me to assert the possibility of an anti-panoptical Dickens as we move further and further from the eighties' affair with Foucault. We can now accommodate the undoubted power of Foucault's historical scrutiny but at the same time ask for more nuanced and less categorical readings of the nineteenth century than his ferocious insistence on discipline at one time seemed so excitingly to reveal. It's also useful to stress in this context the parallel value of resituating Dickens outside the category of realism into which so many readers would lump the whole of nine-teenth-century fiction. Clearly, writers who emerge at the end of the 1850s do lay claim in different ways to an omniscience that is part of the Victorian sense of oversight. I'm thinking of novelists like the two Georges, Eliot and Meredith. But Dickens, I would insist, belongs to an earlier, romance tradition, which inherits its forms and objectives from the late eighteenth century. Here I would urge that we take much more seriously Terry Lovell's remarkable, and curiously undervalued, *Con-suming Fiction* (1987). Lovell makes an extremely persuasive case for a new history of the novel centered on its stimulation of the 'debased' forms of fantasy and escape. If the panopticon was being built by mass society, the disparaged, feminized form of the novel represents one of the ways the spied-upon tried, at least in imagination, to escape that over-view. Following Rosemary Jackson, Lovell names a kind of "counter-pan-theon" who remain loyal to the fantastic and skeptical of the realistic canons of character and coherence. That group includes Sade, Godwin, Mary Shelley, Emily Brontë, Dostoyevsky, Kafka, Pynchon *and* Dickens (Lovell 1987: 62), figures insistently not at home in the society that surrounds them, and a group, I am happy to say, that is regularly, if not entirely, agamous.[8]

Dickens's agamous, narcissistic, aberrant immaturity enterprise writes adult fulfillment as either the continuation of, or the return to, wrongfully interrupted, childish bliss. This decisive stress on childhood doesn't merely sanction, it sanctifies the protagonist's abdication from all the socialized desiderata of maturity: the mutual, the dual, the interchangeable and the genital. It's what Agnes Wickfield is always pointing upward to. Downward points only to the greasy genital horror of Heep! Thus, when Dickens's immature heroes marry happily, they happily marry their Little Mothers (*Little Dorrit*) or a Doll from the Doll's House (*Our Mutual Friend*). Dora turns out to be a predictably bad wife for David Copperfield not because she's a child but because she *also* behaves like a child in a world where being a child is the husband's prerogative. *Bleak House*'s Howard Skimpole is doubly damned for playing the child: but he is wicked because he is only playing at immaturity. (Those three adult daughters came from somewhere.) His behavior represents the equivalent of saying, during the game, that it's only a game. In fact, Skimpole's largely in the novel to point by contrast to the real child, the deeply immature, would-be hero of the novel, John Jarndyce, whose true best friend must inevitably be named, of course,

*Boy*thorne. Dickens doesn't fail, as so many anti-aberrant critics argue, because he can't write convincingly adult, erotically mature men and women. He writes them: Clara Copperfield and Mr. Murdstone, Em'ly and Steerforth. He just doesn't admire them. They feature at best in the subplot.

That's why I find myself murmuring against Foucauldian readings like this one, brilliant as it no doubt is: "A Victorian novel such as *Bleak House* speaks not merely for the hearth, . . . but from the hearth as well, implicitly grounding its critical perspective on the world within a domesticity that is more or less protected against mundane contamination" (D. A. Miller 1988:82). I don't find the domestic hearth furnishing the "critical perspective grounding" Dickens's "protected domesticity," if that hearth enshrines values to which we generally attach words like conventional, Victorian, bourgeois. Of course, if Kincaid's recent work is correct, then we've got to realize that *child-loving* Victorians didn't on the whole group round the hearth either. Or that they hyperbolized it, another way of getting at the same thing. But so far, we still seem to agree to mean by Victorian the repressive rather than the polymorphously and unselfconsciously, and indeed the radiantly, aberrant. By such standards Dickens simply and certainly lacks what the telegenic Right would consider Good Family Values.

Insofar as Dickens imagines that "mundane contamination" can be "protected against," such protection comes from energies in "deliberate flight from any economy of reference" (Kucich 1985: 170), flight into the aberrant bye-ways of the rigorously immature. Of course, his characters often long and work fiercely for domesticity, as does Davy toiling like Bunyan's Christian toward the empyrean release of Betsy Trotwood's cliffside cottage. But that longing itself represents a flight from failed domesticity, a rejection of the routinely brutalizing experiences of conventional family life, family life organized around and by church and state. Dickens can't see parents as merely good or bad. He's compelled to organize them in categories that correspond more closely to terms like ineffectual and monstrous. He can depict "normal" families. But fairly reliably they turn out to be socially contrived facades, like the mother-run Bagnets or the daughter-dropping Meagles, comic and sometimes horrendous parodies of the domestic status quo. More typically, his "normal" families incline to the unhappy, the cold and/or the cruel: the Dombeys, the Dorrits, the Steerforths, the Harmons, the Jellybys. His rare happy families are generally incompetent (the Micawbers), fragile (the Peggotys) or both (the Plornishes). And those happy families also tend to be, a perhaps worse problem, lower class. Dickens may be aberrant but that doesn't mean he is not also a lower-middle-class snob; even more terrifying, and obdurate, he's a British lower-middle-class snob.

Of course, many favored characters, especially at the beginning of his career, do manage to uncover a secure domestic address. But that address becomes less secure as his career continues. And after the mid-1840s it is rarely biologically based or genealogically organized. Nor is it usually a single family dwelling. Beginning perhaps with Scrooge and the Cratchits, happy Dickensian private arrangements tend to be oddly public and to depend on (what I for one shudder to call) alternative life styles: pick-up affairs, add-a-relation contrivances, the "family" as *bricolage* composed from the debris of collapsed "normal" lives. Bleak House, paradigmatically.

But even stranger places, like Quarantine in Marseilles, can do quite easily for happy sociability. Quarantine certainly turns out to have been more comfortable than any of *Little Dorrit*'s other truly domestic arrangements: the Clennams' family home (the home as Conventicle); the Gowans' grace-and-favor apartment (where all the talk is of family); the Merdles' family mansion; the Dorrits' family cell; even the Meagles' villa which they find literally uninhabitable. (Of course, the food in Quarantine is French, which says a lot in British fiction.) Fiercely anti-Catholic Dickens can even imagine the frost-bound monastery of the Great Saint Bernard a warmer and more gracious haven than any British home. And that is because in Dickens almost every family dwelling turns out to be some version of Bleeding Heart Yard. Of course, his heroes and heroines know the value of a room of one's own. But they generally prefer to find that room in someone else's house. Instinctively, Dickens sides with the renter rather than the *rentier*. It's little wonder, then, that he favors instead the temporary, the fugitive, even the borrowed space.

Or even better, the public space. As the 1840s move toward the 1860s the Dickens novel seems more and more bent on ending up outside shelter. (In parallel to agamous Emily Brontë's moors and Lewis Carroll's Christchurch meadows?) During those years Dickens himself is breaking through the domestic baffles, ruining and then discarding his marriage, reclaiming agamy from the conventional conformities of his youth. At the same time his characters increasingly find their likeliest end-stop outdoors, apart from any sort of conventional Victorian hearth-place. Thus the famous conclusion to *Little Dorrit*: the newly-weds emerge from the church to live the remainder of their lives, apparently, on the streets, perpetually jostled by "the noisy, and the froward, and the vain." Or the original, and for me only persuasive, ending to *Great Expectations*: perpetual bachelor Pip encounters degraded, damaged Estella lounging in an open carriage outside a shop. The first pair is happily because unconventionally married; the second pair is unhappily apart, but both pairs wind up physically, emotionally and socially outside, because outside seems to an aberrant Dickens the only address at which one can lead one's own rather than someone else's idea of a life – whoever that someone might be: John Jarndyce, Mr. Dorrit, Mrs. Clennam, Miss Havisham, Magwitch. By the end of the 1850s the Dickensian protagonist can attain the bliss he grasps for himself only by scandalously cutting across convention's bias, by refusing to submit to being history's subject, insisting instead that he can subject history itself to him.

That's why, in the novel that culminates this movement, Dickens can imagine no better, nor more bizarre, final target than the scaffold. When Sydney Carton, Dickens's *beau idéal*, steps boldly off that tumbril, the narcissistic hero completes the trajectory Nicholas Nickleby began with the shattering of the glass. Nickleby's happenstance bye-way turns out to lead to the guillotine. The Cheerybles' sheltering glasshouse gives way to the brazen exposure of the scaffold. Yet Carton enacts on that scaffold not shame but the most archaic, the most grandiose of all narcissistic fantasies. He performs Evremonde, not Carton, as Christ, the savior who surfs time and transcends history. And in that performance he achieves a psychic inflation he could accomplish neither by imitating the real Evremonde, the deracinated Soho hubby, nor by being himself, the lawyer's skivvy. In that scene, that moment, that far far too famous speech, we locate the best (not of times but) of Dickensian performances, as-upon-theatre's agamous, aberrant smash.

MOUNTING THE SCAFFOLD

Sometime after 1857, Dickens suddenly, unexpectedly, found a law he could break. He started his complex "affair" with Ellen Ternan, and began to plan the semi-autobiographical *A Tale of Two Cities*. In that novel of revolution, self-immolation and triumph, the scofflaw-hero Sydney Carton succeeds as the fantasy double to his inventor's private situation: "While creating [Carton, Dickens] imagined himself as himself and as playing Carton's role" (Kaplan 1988: 417). Of course, Carton remains a distinctly Dickensian, that is non-phallic, erotic hero. And this time round the motherly father, Manette (Man, with a feminine diminutive), becomes the defeated husband's pal, not the hero-lover's support system. Nevertheless, Sydney Carton helps make it clear why Oscar Wilde in Reading Gaol asked to read Dickens.

Doubtless, Wilde's Algy would confirm Carton as a more advanced Bunburyist than either himself or earnest Jack, as perhaps the most audacious Bunburyist in all of nineteenth-century British literature. It's one thing to be Jack in town and Ernest in the country, quite another to be Carton in London, Evremonde in Paris, and Christ on the scaffold. And not just on the scaffold but on the stage and on film *ad saeculum saeculorum*. Carton's adaptors routinely turn out to be as deluded by his bunburying as the crowds surging round the Place de la Concorde who think he's Evremonde. Repeatedly, in film and on stage, he re-presents himself as good, worthy, self-sacrificing, gallant. Think of Ronald Colman (1937), or Dirk Bogarde (1957). But Dickens saw Sydney Carton as something far, far better than merely very good. Dickens saw Carton as entirely, and perfectly, frivolous, the matchless fulfillment of the original choice to stick by the byc-way.

Juxtaposing Nickleby to Carton, we thus see Benjaminian apperception ripen into its new, improved, late-model version: Derridean frivolity. Benjamin and Derrida may seem at first an odd couple. But apperception turns out to be something like French frivolity's German, and Germanic cousin. Both continue into a secular, material world the earlier, theological, very British, and deeply proletarian aspirations of Antinomianism, the belief in an individual salvation outside of, beyond, above the mandates of law. Apperception names how you start refusing the regime of effort, hard work, self help and service. And frivolity is what you've provided for yourself after you're done.

It's no surprise that an academy wholeheartedly devoted to the need to discipline and punish has paid little attention to Derrida's *The Archeology of the Frivolous* (1973). Brief, witty, often dense, it responds to the long, tedious and always dense *Essay on the Origin of Human Knowledge* (1756) of the eighteenth-century philosopher, Etienne de Condillac. Condillac argues for a return from the abstractions of post-Cartesian metaphysics to a philosophical discourse of severe empirico-logical economy and vigor. Those rejected abstractions depend heavily upon what Condillac's world called *frivolous*, arguments that use futile, unhelpful or even just useless terms. The frivolous thus "consists in being satisfied with tokens," or with – as Derrida puts it – "the signifier which, no longer signifying, is no longer a signifier. The empty, void, friable, useless signifier" (Derrida 1973: 118). In the age of internet, we doubtless find ourselves sympathetic to Condillac's arguments against "speaking to speak, without object or end, with nothing to say" (p. 122). But Derrida hears in this dismissal a "philosophy of need," which "organizes all its discourse with a view to the decision: between the useful and the futile" (p. 119). The useful clearly privileges the signified over the signifier, the referent over the sign.

Oriented toward theater, I also hear echoing in Condillac's notion of a "serving discourse" the discourse of melodrama, as Peter Brooks presents melodrama in his foundational study, *The Melodramatic Imagination* (1985). Both Condillac's utility and Brooks' melodrama share an obsession with epistemological economy and clarification: "a desire to make starkly articulate" (Brooks 1985: 4). Simultaneously moralistic and anti-metaphysical, melodrama strives like utility "to find, to articulate, to demonstrate, to 'prove' the existence of a moral universe, which, though put into question . . . does exist and can be made to assert its presence and its categorical force among men" (p. 239). Conflating terms, we can imagine melodrama happily taking as its socially redemptive task the nasty business of trimming away the frivolous. It steadily reduces to the point of nonexistence any and all "Excess of the signifier in relation to the signifiable," until a "socially [not individually] defined," usable, controlled meaning emerges and is stabilized (Brooks 1985: 67), a semantic and social order that language can neither spawn nor disturb.

But deeply suspicious of precisely that bourgeois culture of service and utility, the frivolous cautiously conserves its own, incessantly jeopardized, power to maintain itself nimbly beyond the claim-jumping usurpations of reference. Derrida insists on the signifier's autonomous priority. Words accumulate meanings; meanings do not accumulate words. This fundamental priority undergirds the signifier's fundamental otherness from the signified. And that otherness, "its folding back on itself in its closed and nonrepresentative identity" (Derrida 1973: 128), opens the way not only to the desuetude Condillac deplores, but to the originality, the "trailblazing" (*frayage*) that allows genius to add "to language by deviating from 'current usage' in order to be original." It is that deviation, the swerve toward autonomy and invention and away from utility and convention, that constitutes the frivolous for Derrida, and that constitutes, for Dickens, Sydney Carton.

A Tale of Two Cities depends on a single grand chiasmus, a cross-over figure that at the same time both represents and accomplishes agamy's driving goal: substitution of the self for the other, with a coordinate replacement of genital libido by narcissism. The novel sets a hard-working, heroic husband from melodrama, the aristocratic Darnay called Evremonde (or is it Evremonde called Darnay: let the substitutions begin!) against a failed, marginated figure of the frivolous, Sydney Carton, "sensible of the blight upon him" (II: v,122). By the end of this novel of revolution, not only has Carton replaced Darnay in the plot but so has virtually every place and value in the text been similarly exchanged. Nowhere is Dickens more ingenious, more duplicitous, more thoroughly or delightfully de-moralizing.

After all that "best of times, worst of times" build-up, the Revolution winds down into stasis. Its violence merely replaces one oppression with another. Finally, there's little to choose between Monsieur le Marquis and Madame Defarge. (Her aristocratic *De* says it all.) Resurrection men are grave-robbers. Brothers are spies. And recalled to Life means being perpetually entrapped by lunacy. But frivolous self-marginalization, through duplicity, seduction and manipulation, recreates all the lives it touches. The mob thinks it's killing Evremonde-Darnay when it's actually apotheosizing Carton. But that apotheosis also turns death into eternal life, and life into a kind of living death. Frivolity has saved the day that melodrama badly squanders. Carton emerges not merely a hero, but virtually a Messiah: "I am The Resurrection and the Life." And the last we see of poor well-meaning Darnay, he's a neutered, drugged, duped and nattering heap. Nothing fails like goodness; nothing succeeds like apperceptive, frivolous failure.

Darnay, to give him credit, does aspire to frivolity. He's constantly trying to rename himself: a sure sign. And he does attempt to break with the confines of history. Throughout the novel he struggles against representatives of both *ancien* and *nouveau régimes,* in France and in England, to renounce the claims of the historical on his identity, insisting on his right and ability to invent his own significance. But what Darnay cannot renounce is the discourse of need. He feels compelled to return to the maelstrom of the Revolution when the family's former retainer Gabelle appeals to "his justice, honour, and good name" (II: xxiv, 272). No matter what he calls himself, Darnay cannot read that self or allow it to be read outside the chain of signifiers that constitute the conventional moral order, the order of maturity in which the Other's wish makes a non-negotiable claim on the self's agenda. Not surprisingly, Dickens inverts conventional wisdom to suggest that such dependence on the conventional is actually a subtle form of vanity, the vice that melodrama regularly requires its audience to accept as virtue. Darnay expects to "be gratefully acknowledged in France" for his benevolence, "and he even saw himself in the illusion with some influence to guide this raging Revolution." For Dickens such *amour-propre* will always mistakenly try to satisfy one's own narcissistic needs by fulfilling other people's demands. The novel dismissively images this error as a "Loadstone Rock," "that glorious vision of doing good which is so often the sanguine mirage of so many good minds."

That notion of a "sanguine mirage" catches something of Dickens's sense of the fruitless, bloody Revolution. It also suggests what by the late 1850s has become for Dickens the fundamental difference between marriage, a keystone of melodrama, and drive, at least as drive is constructed by the frivolous. Marriage like the Revolution furnishes an over-optimistic vision of human potential that inevitably traps and betrays "so many good minds." At least, for Dickens, it entraps those good minds that marry mid-fiction. Dickens's novels can only fantasize courtship. They cannot image an enduringly successful marriage. His plots present weddings in the traditional New Comedy mode as the prize at the end of the party. But for those non-comic or non-villainous characters who marry *during* the narrative, marriage is invariably realized as disappointment and loss. Love can be bestowed on us apperceptively. Marriage takes concentration to endure and flourish. That's in part why Dickens finds it antipathetic. Like Darnay, his imagination longs restlessly for stimulus and change, and for unearned rewards. Dickens has to criminalize the romantic courtship of Pet Meagles by Henry Gowan. Gowan, the novel's only candidate for the role of romantic hero, inevitably, and more or less inexplicably, turns out to be in league with the novel's wife-murdering villain, and indeed behaves vilely to his own wife-victim. Just as his predecessor as romantic hero, Steerforth, destroys Little Em'ly, without hope or redemption. Indeed, as David, in a more bittersweet vein, destroys the object of his romantic crush, Dora Spenlow. The marriage plot in Dickens invariably is just that a plot, carried out by the likes of the cruel and the cold, like Murdstone or Dombey, when it is not being instigated by simple-minded bores, like Edmund Sparkler.

But beyond the inevitable tedium of fidelity, melodramatic eros raises even starker specters. Prizing innocence and what *A Tale* calls "real service" (III: xiv, 392), melodrama reads desire, with Condillac, and indeed with Locke, as a trace inscribed on the subject's chaste, inviolate slate. Thus eros in melodramatic scenarios tends to mean not desiring but being desired. It unfolds not from a gap within, or a need fundamental to, a character but from a rupture in time or space that invades the closed realm of the subject. For Dickens this means that such conventional passions must be experienced as external, unwanted and unwonted, excessive and inexplicable. Where others find Cupid, he sees cupidity. That's why, from the start of *A Tale*, Darnay seems a shade criminal. And it's his erotic interest in the heroine that immediately involves her family in scandal, and ultimately prods her poor victim of a father back into madness, "as if the golden arm uplifted" outside their door had "struck him a poisoned blow" (II: xviii, 223). Of course, Darnay makes a prodigious effort to separate from his past. Nevertheless, his love can't help but manifest itself as another instance of the murderous Evremonde lust, the original source of Manette's abduction into insanity.

Melodrama would finally displace such suffering with redemption and apotheosis. The villains would be unmasked, and the happy family, reunited after its unearned suffering, would settle into the just peace of bucolic Soho. But *A Tale* frivolously refuses any such remission. Our final glimpse of the Manette menage shows them stopped in the family carriage at the customs barrier, a carriage that's become a metonym for lunacy: the occupant-inmates "helpless, inarticulately murmuring, wandering . . . in a swoon" (III: xiii, 385). Before her marriage, Manette had warned his daughter that if she were not to wed she would be "Struck aside from the natural order of things" (II: xvii, 217). But, as it turns out, marriage engulfs Lucie not in anything natural or ordered, or not natural and ordered for very long, but in the maelstrom of the Terror. That's not coincidence or bad luck; it's frivolity's sense of melodrama's fundamental mis-calculus. Men like Darnay, men who marry, and like it, and keep at it, mature men, are the same kind of men who try to reverse revolutions. They are the would-be heroes who insist on being recognized as naturally good and who above all else believe in and commit themselves to performing service, to experiencing the "golden arm."

The "golden arm" is that extraordinarily complex, mysterious sign outside the Manettes' door.

In a building at the back, attainable by a court-yard where a plane-tree rustled its green leaves, church-organs claimed to be made, and silver to be chased, and likewise gold to be beaten by some mysterious giant who had a golden arm starting out of the wall of the front hall – as if he had beaten himself precious, and menaced a similar conversion to all visitors. Very little of these trades . . . was ever heard or seen. (II: vi, 123)

The gold associates the arm's promise with Lucie's. Her golden hair becomes the thread she constantly weaves, binding her loved ones into the Soho pastoral, the clear counterpoint to the shroud-making circle knitting around Madame Defarge. The arm outside Lucie's door, beating itself precious, thus promises what the guillotine denies, a redemptive suffering, the good pain which turns terror into justification. That transformation, of course, represents melodrama's key claim for serious attention: the insistence that the individually willed, or at least willingly accepted, suffering of "lurid and grandiose events" will ultimately transform weak individuals into "hyperbolic figures" who undo structural subjugation in an ultimate "victory over repression" (Brooks 1985: 4). To set melodrama in operation one freely embraces as the "natural order of things" the paramount claims of need and service. In return, the melodramatic scenario will "mobilize [the subject], moralize it, subject it to the law, fix it in an order" (Derrida 1973: 134.)

That's what the golden arm beating itself precious promises. But how reliable is such a sign? Is it, in fact, a sign at all? How can it be, if it is, as the passage insists, somehow also the actual arm itself "starting out of the wall?" And aren't signs which make us feel they are the real thing, and not iconic, not signs but those cozening cousins of the sign, mirages? After all, we never do see the giant or his beaten gold, or indeed any of those other artists or the enriching, uplifting goods promised by and in this melodramatic space, the church-organs, the chased silver. The giant arm only "claims," only "purports," to operate *chez Manette*. Always just "starting out," it never seems to get round to the actual transmutation. In fact, not only do we never locate this court-yard's treasures and treasure-makers, we find nothing real or palpable there, only endlessly imprecise "Echoes." That means we are, for sure, for this text, in the realm of melodrama, the domain where actual signifiers disappear into the uplifting swoop of a grand, transformative signified. The golden thread, then, like the melodrama that spins it, isn't posting a sign so much as it's casting a lure.

Its melodramatic promise actually masks, the golden arm suggests, a deadly *menace*, the "poisoned blow" that ultimately falls on the Manettes with the consummation of the marriage. Taken in by the uplifting promise of redemption through pain, the melodramatized subjects in fact get only pain – no gain – reeling beneath the burnished, polished blows that incessantly and inevitably follow from their entrapment. As Manette suffers when he high-mindedly protests against the Marquis on behalf of the peasant sister and brother. As Lucie suffers when she dutifully follows her husband to France. As Darnay suffers, and causes all the members of his family to suffer, when he heeds Gabelle's plea. The golden arm turns out to be Soho's version of Lodestone Rock, another "glorious vision of doing good which is so often the sanguine mirage of so many good minds."

Frivolity insists it has the know-how to elude that entrapment: it displaces the Other's cupidity in favor of the self's obsessive, narcissistic fascination with itself, centered on the frivolous subject's ability to fold back on itself, both semantically and erotically, for both meaning and fulfillment. The opposite of "service," frivolity thus becomes a term for "need left to itself, need without object, without desire's direction . . . the seeming repetition of desire without any object or of a floating desire" (Derrida 1973: 130). We see this at once in the debut of the novel's frivolous hero. Carton not only interrupts but ruptures entirely the chain of historical signification, substituting himself for Darnay in the novel's first trial, "the upshot of which was to smash this witness like a crockery vessel," and to set Darnay free (II: iii, 104) – something earnest Darnay can never quite manage for himself. Carton maneuvers that replacement so easily in large part because he has no established, public self to jeopardize by advertising this "floating" identity. Carton performs Darnay convincingly exactly because he is so utterly lacking in conviction as Carton. Insistently apperceptive, he holds on to nothing, achieves nothing, for himself. Like Darnay the frivolous hero also has his mirage. In fact, it's precisely the same phantasm: "a mirage of honourable ambition, self-denial, and perseverance" (II: v, 121). But for Carton there's no Lodestone Rock. This vision makes no claim on responsive action from him. It is, simply, always, acknowledged as mirage. Frivolous, apperceptive, Carton knows in his bones he's "incapable of his own help and his own happiness" (p. 122).

Carton's incapacity requires some way to stage himself as-upon-a theatre. And here we return to the high-toned glass that so thoroughly stymied Nickleby's attempts to preen himself into gentility. Nickleby's failure rooted in his refusal of what we began this book by calling *mimesis*. He insisted he actually was what he set out to perform and not, as he needed to, its self-invented copy. Carton knows better, or at least he does better. He looks out for and locates exactly the sort of empathic mirrors which allow him to luxuriate in his narcissistic fantasies without risking any sort of check or submission to regulation. That glass he finds in Lucie and her marriage.

Darnay and Lucie furnish all unawares a kind of proto-scaffold to

Carton on which he can erect the idealized self without any of the risk or responsibilities of attachment. Full of the most inventive guile, he gradually seduces Lucie's imagination until on the eve of her marriage, he lodges himself securely in her heart, without any obligation to satisfy other parts of her anatomy. She is persuaded to keep his image in her "pure and innocent breast" – the terror at any kind of carnal contact is palpable – a secret even from "the dearest one ever to be known by you" (II: xiii, 182). Carton thus turns Lucie's breast into a version of Riah's stereoptical roof: "hold me in your mind, at some quiet times, as ardent and sincere in this one thing" (p. 183). By the end of his little scene with another man's fiancée, he has made certain that "when the little picture of a happy father's face looks upon" her, she will necessarily "think now and then that there is a man who would give his life to keep a life you love beside you." And that man is not that little child's father. Like all the major males after Pickwick whom Dickens chooses to endorse, Carton is nimbly adroit at avoiding phallic performance.

Of course, all these earlier substitutions merely foreshadow Carton's master-stroke of mimetic replacement at the novel's end, the ultimate frivolous gesture of the entire Dickens corpus. Deploying the sentimental discourse of need and service against itself, Carton simultaneously masks and achieves his sublimely selfish end. Wrapped in the pious language of the Gospel, "I am the Resurrection and the Life," Carton manages to usurp not only Darnay's death but – and here is Carton's real point – his life, not to mention His Life. That transmutation is so bold, it escapes the bounds of plot. It is supremely *episodic*: the past slips harmlessly away leaving the agamous hero completely free mimetically to perform the role he has chosen to be. For that reason, it has in effect to register itself outside the story in a kind of conditional supplement. "If he had given an utterance to his [thoughts], and they were prophetic, they would have been these" (III: xv, 424). Carton finally inscribes himself in the Manette–Darnay *ménage ad saeculum saeculorum*.

Darnay's child will now bear Carton's name. And this appropriated child will in turn make illustrious not his biological, bill-paying father but the eternally absent Carton. Carton who even in death will make a permanent third between husband and wife: "each was not more honoured and held sacred in the other's soul, than I was in the souls of both." His frivolous invention, what he calls "my story," subsumes the entire world of history and of the family. In a radical inversion of the giant's golden arm, the naturally generated, historically guaranteed signified is erased entirely by the self-imposed, narcissistic signifier, the sign that Lucie and her family must always see. The sign that conventional adaptors love to embrace.

But Carton's triumph takes him also literally out of this world, and out of this novel. His story can only happen in an imaginary future, after the plot closes down. In the novel's final pages Dickens powerfully imagines a bliss beyond the cameral. Indeed, the cameral declines into the carceral, all those prisons which regularly swallow up Darnay and Manette, those decent, ordinary, marrying and inseminating and sharing men. Carton, however, is the hero who makes himself free of the prisons, and free from the cameral, to enact his fantasy on the most public sort of stage. But he is himself a kind of "sanguine mirage." He raises expectations, episodic, mimetic, agamous expectations, which he shows us no way to fulfill. Appearing to exit, Carton has in fact nowhere to go. Heroes from glasshouses shouldn't mount scaffolds. If you want to exit history, he – or Dickens – seems to say, then, like the Lady of Shalott, you'll have to pay for that exit with your life. Despite his grandiose rhetoric, Carton pays for his frivolity with his death. And he dies in a novel for which prayer is lower-class flopping and religion mostly a bad joke.

Even Carton, then, even our adorable, cagey, unscrupulous Sydney, can not escape the choices that bind that key seer of the nineteenth century, the Ancient Mariner: Death or Life-in-Death. Boldly, Carton pseudo-triumphs in Death. Every other male after *Nickleby*, every one who matters to Dickens, settles more or less for Life-in-Death. And even Sydney's path of frivolous glory really has nowhere to go. It literally does not signify: that is its boast. And therefore it has nowhere to lead. Something that becomes unavoidably clear when we see that Dickens's remaining fiction cannot follow even Carton's sanguine mirage. Eugene Wrayburn perhaps comes closest and look what happens to him. Surviving decapitation looks like the only thing worse than dying of it. No, Carton does not open a breach remotely comparable to Nickleby's. There's no new way from which he permits us to bid the cameral a lasting and grateful goodbye, to step from it into a world where we might manage on our own. *A Tale of Two Cities* is, we remember, a novel about a revolution doomed from the start to fail. And what follows Carton's ambiguous exit? That unrelievedly bleak trio. *Great Expectations*. The novel that thoroughly unwrites *Nickleby's* fictions of benefaction, bitterly exposing the lie on which it was premised: that sometimes someone might do for a stranger a piece of disinterested good. Then the savage *Our Mutual Friend*. Finally, the fratricidal fragment *The Mystery of*

Edwin Drood. Rage not only recalled, but renewed. Close down the bye-way. Bar the glass house. *Huis Clos.*

Which dismal reflection leads us to look back at the stretch between *Nickleby* and *A Tale*, the stretch over which we blithely skipped earlier in this chapter, and to explore what happens in that gulf by a much darker light than the frivolous seemed to promise. If we jump from Nicholas to Carton, Dickens seems to trace a way out of both world and performance to achieve that as-upon-theatre where the self triumphantly fulfills its aberrant, unequaled promise. But when we look back over that stretch of time and books, overshadowed by the guillotine's inevitability, we find we've suddenly changed our tone, and, as Cole Porter memorably has it, "how strange / the change / from major to minor."

THE HIGH COST OF DEFENSE

After the novels of the mid-1840s, what we might consider Dickens's best plots tend not to happen. Of course, plots abound in Dickens, like grace in Bunyan. But behind what does happen – increasingly, misery – there lurks a ghostly or skeletal buried plot (all those wills, all the uncanny coincidence), novels aborted before they can properly begin. Dickens is now routinely spurning, maiming, starving and killing off later versions of those very boys and young men whose lives and adventures had formed the narcissistic spine of the earlier novels: Weller and Nickleby and Nubbles give way to Paul Dombey, Steerforth, Jo, Richard Carstone, Tom Gradgrind. Even David Copperfield never quite gets the life he seemed promised, though he does much better than his contemporaries. And this diminution of the young, would-be hero repeatedly blights, in turn, the promise of those who want to love them. Within a decade of finishing *Nickleby* it seems ghost stories have become just about the only stories Dickens is able or at least willing to tell.

The programmatically optimistic *Christmas Books*, for example, repeatedly rely on the stories of ghosts. The Ghost's Walk in *Bleak House* doesn't merely predict the fall of the Dedlocks, it speaks of an entire world literally stalked by the phantom Chancery case. In *Little Dorrit*, Hamlet-like Clennam is haunted by the ghost of a father who insists Do Not Forget. Pip goes to school to the ghostly Miss Havisham, only to be the better entrapped when the revenant of his real benefactor Magwitch takes up lodging with him. This is not the broadly diffused late-Romantic nostalgia for the vanished, ecstatic, Wordsworthian past. It's Freud's melancholy, not mourning – grief for what didn't happen, not for what did. We keep returning to a paralyzed past not because it was pleasant but because it never had the chance to become the present, and so continually swallows up all chance of a future.

This lost story becomes, especially after *Copperfield*, the story of the lost best boy, or, better, the once and future boy, the boy who doesn't get the glass house, or doesn't get it in time, never finding what Fortune has hidden expressly for him to enjoy. Life-in-Death. Now the pre-Oedipal father fails to materialize when needed, as the Cheerybles did for Nicholas, and Scrooge for Tiny Tim, or even Cap'n Cuttle for Walter Gay. His place gets usurped by the cruel father (Gradgrind) or step-father (Murdstone) or horrific-criminal adoptive father (Magwitch).[9] Best boys a-plenty continue to wait, fully worthy to receive Cheeryble-like plums: Copperfield himself, Richard Carstone and Jo, Clennam, and quintessentially, of course, Pip. And then there are those other boys who could be best-boys if only someone sufficiently sage and powerful could get to them in time: Tom the Whelp Gradgrind, and Tip Dorrit, and Charley Hexam. But for each of them, though generally in quite different ways, that promise of plums, and therefore the boys' inherent promise, goes unrecognized, unfulfilled.

Instead, these middle novels kill off boys to let very good girls bloom. The scapegrace scamp has become the scapegoat. Steerforth and Carstone are, of course, explicitly erotized. But even when these middle-period ephebes play no erotic role, they fall into harm's way apparently simply because they are phallic. Characterization – male characterization – becomes conflated with castration, and boys seem cut off before their prime explicitly to prevent them from growing into fully phallic men, into other Steerforths. Where the earlier fiction invests its energies in saving figures like young Oliver, Paul Dombey can now only die, and Jo can only be destroyed. But, Charly, the girl with the boy's name, Jo's skivvy double, not only thrives, but seems in thriving to fill the place Jo empties. The hobbledehoy Nickleby can break through his brash naiveté and conclude happily married, philoprogenitive, heroic; but Richard Carstone can only decline, sucked dry by the vampirish Vholes.

Indeed, it is almost as though Dickens himself throughout this period plays Vholes toward all his dependent young men. Vholes destroys his particular victim Richard for the sake of Household Words, "making hay of the grass which is flesh, for his three daughters. And his father . . . dependent on him in the vale of Taunton" (*Bleak House* xxxix, 603). Dickens's analog *daughters* are, of course, not his own by the flesh but the heroines of his pen, Florence, Sissy, Esther, Amy. And *father* here seems to point toward their "fathers," those aging or aged Patriarchs who cozily settle not only with, but on, their infinitely supportive little women: the Messrs. Dombey, Wickfield, Jarndyce, Gradgrind, Dorrit, etc. To support those establishments, Dickens, dismayingly like Vholes, drains from his young men, his "disowned counterparts" (Phillips 1994: 22), their hopes, their chances, their lives, reinvesting those energies in the preferred female figures, or in boys who like behaving like good girls, David Copperfield, Prince Turveydrop. It's not just Dombey & Son that turns out to be a daughter after all. This pattern, the dying lad sacrificed to batten the thriving lass, recurs throughout the middle period. But, paradoxically, sacrificing the boy for the girl also turns out, usually, to diminish, if not decimate, the girl's chances too. Thus, Prince's weakness returns Caddy Jellyby to the drudge's life she tried to escape when she fled her mother's house. David's psychic frailties blight delightful, spontaneous Dora. And Richard's collapse ruins Ada. Only Amy Dorrit and Esther Summerson really escape similar fates, in large part because at the appropriate moment they spurn a young man's suit, John Chivery's to Amy and Guppy's to Esther, preserving themselves for the prematurely aged suitors, Clennam and Jarndyce, already and obviously dead below the belt.

Indeed, J. Hillis Miller's eloquent evocation of the *shadowed* life in *Little Dorrit* extends, I think, to virtually all the best-boy fiction in the second half of Dickens's career: "to be 'shadowed' by some sadness or blindness or delusion or deliberate choice of the worse rather than the better course is the universal condition of all the dwellers in this prison of a lower world" (Hillis Miller 1958: 230). Those last words, "prison of a lower world," invoke (I suspect deliberately) *Little Dorrit*'s unforgettable catachresis of Keats' Autumn Ode: "far aslant across the city strike the long bright rays . . . bars of the prison of this lower world." And they suggest that we might take as specimen text for this underworld of lost and haunting stories the bitterly sad conclusion of the Preface to *Little Dorrit*, perhaps the most poignant text in Dickens's fiction about remembering, repeating and *not* working-through:

whosoever goes into Marshalsea Place, turning out of Angel Court, leading to Bermondsey, will find his feet on the very paving-stones of the extinct Marshalsea Jail; will see its narrow yard to the right and to the left, very little altered if at all, except that the walls were lowered when the place got free; will look upon rooms in which the debtors lived; and will stand among the crowding ghosts of many miserable years. (p. 36)

The past functions here as a kind of buried plot returning as a specter that no one can escape. All change is superficial. The past generates an apparently unassuagable melancholy, grief for a lost chance which, when contemplated, shows itself almost unbearably ghastly. The narrative cannot remember, recognize and then go forward. Instead, it is compelled constantly to return grief-stricken to the events, the situations, the personages of that past, lost, devastated story, a parody of the return to childhood that promised so much when the Cheerybles introduced it.

These later novels thus tend to read like séances. All kinds of presences surround the actual characters, begging to communicate, to get in touch, to be recognized, to make a claim on the viable characters who themselves frequently feel incomplete without that contact. Not only figures and patterns but also objects from the past keep materializing to trace their obscure messages on oblivious, fugitive heirs. Wills. Letters. Gestures. Files. Clocks. Clennam père's King Hamlet-like insistence on Do Not Forget is just a very poor joke. How could anyone forget anything in this haunted world where the most ordinary artifact is likely to turn out a vestige. But, as in séances, the promise of contact is bogus. The specters can do no good. Contacting them makes no difference. Or it makes things much worse.

In novel after novel, *revenants* from that once-upon-a-time, incubus-like, fasten on other, innocent figures in the present who become condemned to repeat what otherwise can not enter into becoming. So the dashing Hawdon seems reincarnated in the completely unrelated figure of Richard Carstone. Hawdon's ruin of his own, his beloved's and their child's lives echoes in Carstone's comparably dashing, comparably ruined, comparably ruinous career. Arthur Clennam's loss of the young Flora Casby echoes twenty years later in his mirroring failure to carry off Pet Meagles, though this time no one actually opposes him. Just the reverse. And, in the most memorable instance, both Miss Havisham and Abel Magwitch obsessively recreate their own blighted lives by battening on the orphans they purchase. These figures signal an overwhelming nostalgia for the scenarios of ordinary happiness. But at the same time they warn how utterly without glamour ordinary happiness is. And thereby enforce the burial of their potential plots.

Why can there be no release from these deep-seated patterns of grief? Because to achieve such a release, Dickens's oh-so-promising male protagonists would have to learn to manage, rather than defend themselves from, the harrowing demands of shame and of rage. They would have to refer rather than repress, that is: surrender grandiosity and settle instead for ordinary lives and ordinary consolations, surrendering their archaic selves to the subduing claims of maturity. In Kohut's terms, they would have to discipline elementary into amplified narcissism, *overcoming* their fantasies of *unmodified grandeur, accepting* instead *limitations* on the self and an *idealization* of the quotidian task. In other words, Dickens's heroes would have had to start *growing* again. Then the buried story could return as the supreme, early fantasy: the smooth integration of the superior hero into the repressive dynamic of the family romance, that *bildungsroman Nickleby* promises to become but isn't. The un-dead plot would retrieve what Nicholas refused (or found refused), the alloplastic story of thriving male ambition rewarded by a recognized place in the bourgeois order. An other way of saying all this is that Dickens would have had to become a realistic novelist.

But ordinary happiness is for Dickens literally unimaginable. Or perhaps it is more to the point to say that Dickens can only imagine ordinary happiness as comic, even farcical. David and Dora really making a go of their common little menage? That's no more plausible than Dickens and Catherine doing the same. Hawdon, Honoria and little Esther together at last and happy forever? Arthur Clennam married to Flora Casby, inheriting both his family's counting house and her family's slum rentals. Pip getting Estella, and Estella not being entirely foul about it? Those stories never even have a chance. Instead, narcissism spurs aggression; the frivolous becomes indistinguishable from the ferocious.[10]

After 1850 there's virtually a murder per plot. Does Dickens now write *roman policier* for the sake of the police, we wonder, or for the sake of the crime? His wrath may be palliated, sometimes, yes, but it is too fundamental, too constitutive, ever to be slaked. Discovering writing's as-upon stage has done virtually nothing to relieve Dickens's own narcissistic burden. Whose life is angrier than Dickens's? Who is more intemperate? Who crueller? "A misplaced and mismarried man," he described himself in the late 1850s. "Always as it were, playing hide and seek with the world and never finding what Fortune seems to have hidden when he was born" (Kaplan 1988: 376). But what more could anyone have asked from the world or Fortune than what Dickens had by that point gained? Was there no limit to that sense of grandiosity? Obviously, the pattern story for all of those older men who literally possess younger women is his Faustian relation to Ellen Ternan. And the rest of the biography is likewise full of this anger and frustration combining to produce outrageous treatment of his wife, his children, his publishers, his friends. Nothing he invents can assuage anxieties so fundamental.

It's this repressive, defensive, cruel narcissism that turns even the empathetic adaptor, enthusiastic for agamy like Swiveller's, toward a systematic transgression of Swiveller's heirs. Defense for fiction, as well as for superpowers, not only has its costs, but seems to end up costing more than it's worth.

CODA

Which brings us to Adaptation, the final third of our triad and the *practical* part of this book. What should we see – rather, what should we want to see – when we put Dickens on the stage (or on film)? Should we see Carton's tale through Lucie's deluded eyes, as do most adaptations of *A Tale*? Or don't we want to reveal and revel in the frivolous at work? And if that's what we would do with the *Tale*, how should we treat all the other novels, the novels of the buried plot? Should we with them mourn what can not be realized, what cannot be recovered? Or should that recovery be exactly what it is we set out to stage? Should we improve, complete, update the immature to make it pass muster as maturity, normalizing what refuses and rejects our scrutiny. Or should we start off impervious to immaturity's painful self-justifications and prepare the stage instead for agamy's genuine liberation?

Of course, you already know the answer.

III

Resolution

Homages in lieu of a manifesto. Georges Balanchine used to insist that it made no sense for his dancers to do the same thing the music was doing. Why should choreography double composition? Perhaps you never can tell the dancer from the dance, but certainly you should be able to tell the dancer from the score. Alfred Hitchcock used to direct his actors to perform love scenes as though they were plotting murder, and to plot murder as if they were making love. Hitchcock and Balanchine seem to me to know everything there is to know about adaptation.

Part III foregrounds Grotowski. The next chapter (5) describes a Grotowskian adaptation of *Little Dorrit*, ultimately guiding you through the performance as it was originally staged. That's followed by a much shorter, final chapter (6) offering a self-help guide toward starting up your own adaptation. After that, of course, you're After Dickens on your own.

What can come from this juxtaposition of Dickens and Grotowski? One answer would be: a safer exit from Dickensian shame than any tumbril might provide. Another answer, actually another way to put the same answer, would be what Stefan Brecht writing on Grotowski defines as *"real information,"* that is: what "might have been, could not be, might be, or cannot become" (S. Brecht 1970: 189). Real information about the Dickensian sources. About their evasions, their cultural decorums, their self- and consumer-imposed censorships. About what they must evade and erase, what they might have been but could not become. And, at the same time, real information about the audience. About us, about what we "might have been, could not be, might be, or cannot become." *Real information* thus turns out to be another name – though one not quite so good for *bliss*.

CHAPTER 5

How To Do It

Originally, this was where I took on the paradigmatic, conventional adaptations I'd like to displace, productions like the RSC's *Nicholas Nickleby* and Christine Edzard's *Little Dorrit*. That face-off started as an autonomous chapter. And then it retreated to an Appendix. And now, as you see, it's disappeared entirely. I've found I can't make rejection and resistance sound anything but sour. And this is a book that at least aims to provide, as I've just said, bliss.

The stage is in love with the timely. It knows "the readiness is all," and, consequently, it not only suspects but loathes the timeless. Ignore whatever claims to be spirits, it warns us, sublime or other. Above all pay no attention to ghosts, even dear, familial, predecessor ghosts, when live friends and lovers, and blooming cherry orchards, call for attentive cultivation. The stage is about Cordelia's dead body, or Iphigenia's, or even Hamlet's, and that nothing can excuse, or explain, or compensate for those bodies' loss.

Dickens, as we've seen, writes against the body, and against the stage. He is, famously, smitten with Cordelia's dying. Little Nell (his *first* Cordelia; Amy Dorrit being the last) he tenderly, lingeringly transforms into an embalmed fetish, the site of pilgrimage and distended, lachrymose cherishing. Indeed, nowhere, no way can Dickens find good use for bodies. He writes to overcome, to transcend, to idealize the shameful necessities and feared inadequacies of the flesh. How fascinated he is, however, by dust, by ash and slime, the stuff of decay, which is, he insists, all that composes the world outside the cameral.

If, producing Dickensian adaptation, we cooperate with Dickensian etherealization, the stage is undone. We subvert the particular ways in which theatre witnesses human experience. Instead, don't we want, and need, to stage the body's righteous protest against Dickens's intolerable derogation? And the shape for that protest I suggest we take from

Grotowski's "Poor Theatre," the theatre that insistently focuses, and finds no other spectacle equal to, the parade of the performer's body.

A Quick Confession: the "Argument" that follows does not describe what we set out to do when we began to adapt *Little Dorrit*. It merely suggests what, after we were finished, we understood ourselves to have done.

THE ARGUMENT

OPHELIA: Belike this show imports the argument of the play.

$\qquad\qquad\qquad\qquad\qquad\qquad\qquad\qquad\qquad$ (III.2.140)

We called our adaptation of *Little Dorrit* by Dickens's original title, *Nobody's Fault*. (So, later, did Christine Edzard, for half of her *Little Dorrit* film.) To some degree, going back to the cancelled original was a boast. But in no way did it mark an attempt to recuperate anyone's notion of lost Dickensian intentions. Just the reverse. Thus, when I asked, shortly before we opened, if any one in the cast thought the audience might have trouble following their performance, one of them cheerfully answered: "only if they've read the novel." And that was a boast too.

Little Dorrit is an adaptation; a way, as Jonathan Arac has shown, to read *Hamlet*. But Hamlet is himself an adaptor. He adapts *The Murder of Gonzago* into that production of *The Mousetrap* with which he catches the conscience of the king, an adaptation on which he spends a considerable amount of time and thought. And, it turns out, the more we can learn about adaptation from *Hamlet*, the better we understand not only what's at stake in Dickens's own adaptation, but also in our own latecoming attempts to adapt the adaptor.

Both novel and play share a fundamental "situation, that of a man caught between his dead father and his morally compromised mother," a father whose Do Not Forget urges the son "to get on with things" (Arac 1988: 318). Clennam seeks to find a secret wrong to rectify, "Driven by guilt over a wrong of which he is unconscious, like Hamlet." At the same time, also like Hamlet, he falls prey to an impotent self-denial, figured in the trope of Nobody. *Little Dorrit*, it should be pointed out, if only in passing, also adapts *King Lear*, as The Dorrits: A Carceral Family Romance. But that's a point Arac is not interested in arguing, sensing perhaps that, as with everything else that has to do with Cordelia or Amy, it will doubtless come to Nothing. And it certainly did nothing for my actors, since the Dorrit family plot spurred no interest at all in any of them.

What has to increase our interest here is the fact that *Hamlet* offers not one but two adaptations: more precisely, it stages one adaptation and promises another. At the play's dramatic center there's *The Mousetrap*. At its conclusion there's the adaptation of *Hamlet* that Horatio offers to stage for Fortinbras: "give order that these bodies / High on a stage be placed to the view, / And let me speak to th'yet unknowing world / How these things came about" (V.2.379–382). The *Hamlet* we see thus ends with the *Hamlet* we don't see, just about to start up. Unless of course the *Hamlet* we don't see simply repeats the *Hamlet* we've seen. But that seems unlikely. Hamlet and Horatio think in quite different ways about adaptation. In fact they, happily, offer us two quite different models of adaptation to work with.

Horatio promises Fortinbras political theatre. We know it's about politics because it's about choices that backfire and policies that don't work. All those "carnal, bloody and unnatural acts" shouldn't have, needn't have happened. They amount mostly to "*accidental* judgments, *casual* slaughters" (V.2.384 – my italics). There are, of course, "cunning" and "forced deaths" (385) in both. But Horatio wants to show us that those deaths came about fundamentally through error: "purposes mistook / Fall'n on the inventors' heads" (ll.386–387). Horatio sees *Hamlet* as ripe with the materials with which a clever, minatory *aide de camp* can brief a commanding general about to become head of state: Operation Elsinore. That makes his *Hamlet* political not only in its content but in its form, not about some *them*, but pressingly about this *us*. This action has got to be staged, and soon, "lest more mischance / On plots and errors happen' (ll.396–397).

And that's also what makes Horatio's *Hamlet* tragic, at least according to the psychoanalyst Bennett Simon. Simon insists that tragedy is about the competing claims of self and community. "The tragic hero," he says, "is carrying a burden for all of upholding and fulfilling an ideal in order to preserve a larger entity" (Simon 1988: 257). But Simon's sense of "burden" is exactly what doesn't make something tragic for Heinz Kohut. Kohut concedes that a "code-transgressing deed" may indeed be needed to set in motion a plot's "pattern of guilt and retribution." For Kohut, however, the real thrust of tragedy roots in "the hero's narcissistic triumph" (Kohut 1985: 38). And here, I think, he speaks for Hamlet himself, as hero and as adaptor.

Let's face it: Hamlet would be mortified – were he not already dead – at the sense Horatio intends to make of him. Tragic Man (Kohut's, not to mention Hamlet's, sorts of argument cannot forgo capitals), for

Kohut, for Hamlet, has nothing, or very little, to do with guilt. We can put that better perhaps the other way: for both of them, Guilty Man is the reverse of Tragic Hero. Guilty Man is the Claudius of the closet scene, all drives and structural conflicts. Guilty Man "wants to achieve redemption and reform himself and society" (Kohut 1985: 49), even as he does little to reform society, and nothing to reform himself. "My stronger guilt defeats strong intent," acknowledges the incestuous-fratricidal-regicide king. And yet, in almost the same breath, there follows: "Help, angels! Make assay" (III.3.40). This is the man of work and pleasure, obsessed with the first, guilty about the second, formed from ego-superego conflict. Guilty, he's also, by definition, moral, driven by the fiction of a happy ending, if only a projected happiness like the restored state Horatio and Fortinbras begin conspiring to construct out of rotten Denmark. Of course, Guilty Man can be, often, Comic Man, though he rarely sees himself as funny. More usually, he's Historical Man. What Fortinbras has already become; *vide* the conquest of Poland. Or what Horatio is likely to be, if he manages to get Fortinbras to make him Prime Minister. Foolish, Guilty Man turns out to be Polonius. Neither foolish nor historical, he's the Duke in *Measure for Measure*. But Guilty Man is never, in Hamlet's view (or Kohut's), Hamlet.

Hamlet-Kohut's Tragic Man feels no guilt at all. And he certainly doesn't want to have any truck with angels. When Horatio speaks that famous, unspeakably maudlin, parting line, we know for sure Hamlet has died in vain. He's about to be canonized, diminished from narcissistic hero to plaster saint, he who would more likely see and treat those "flights of angels" as so many versions of Rosencrantz and Guildenstern. Hamlet knows about guilt but what he knows is that guilt means others: the audience, those "guilty creatures sitting at a play" (II.2.590), his uncle, his mother, their co-opted courtiers. Virtually everyone, in fact, except his above all else supremely innocent self: "I, the son of a dear father murdered" (l.584).

This sort of Tragic Man can and does feel badly about himself. He also, of course, feels very badly for himself. However, what he feels isn't guilt but (our old sweet song) shame, humiliation at having let himself down, at having lowered his dignity to behave like the lesser version of a mere player, "a rogue and peasant slave" (ll.569–572). This Tragic Man is actually "independent of fear and guilt, of expiation and reform" (Kohut 1985: 49). He is driven by neither pleasure nor morality but by ambition and rage, the fuel of a supremely grandiose self. And that means, inevitably, that he has no interest in community. Hamlet can't bear even the custom, let alone the crimes, of the country, though he is "native here / And to the manner born" (I.4.14–15). Denmark's rotten. That's all there is to say about Denmark. Let's get back to the University, where we are the star.

In sum, Hamlet can't imagine thinking like, or acting like, Fortinbras. He works only to establish the triumph of the self. It doesn't matter who gets crushed in the process of establishing that self: *vide* Ophelia. Always right and always wronged, Tragic Man beavers away at making himself the main attraction, even at somebody else's funeral. "I loved Ophelia. Forty thousand brothers / Could not with all their quantity of love / Make up my sum" (V.1.272–274). Such a cynosure surely has clear right to adapt everything he looks upon for his own use.

Side by side, these adaptors, and their adaptations, look like this:

> Horatio inserts himself and his audience within the frame of adaptation. Hamlet refuses every relationship as a threat of subordination, and therefore stations himself outside the frame, observing, commenting, judging, refusing inclusion or interaction. Instead of himself he *inserts* "some dozen or sixteen lines" of his own setting down (II.2.541), and thereby makes *The Murder of Gonzago* image the world as he alone knows it to be.
> Moralizing Horatio adapts to warn against repetition. Don't let this happen again, he begs. Tragic, narcissistic Hamlet adapts in order to repeat, and thereby trap the guilty other within that repetition.
> Interested in guilt, Horatio looks toward history, accidental, casual, mistaken. Tragic Hamlet looks to fate; it saves blaming himself.
> Horatio roots the story in the community; Hamlet in the family. Of course, he can't imagine why the Player should weep about Hecuba. "What's Hecuba to him, or he to Hecuba" (l.559). The only story that matters is the story of the family, one's own family.

All of which probably makes it quite clear why Dickens sides with Hamlet. (In case you do too, you might want to look again at the extraordinary Horatian adaptation of *Hamlet*, John Frankenheimer's 1962 film, *The Manchurian Candidate*, set in New York and Washington in the aftermath of the Korean War, with Angela Lansbury as the most Medean of Gertrudes, and the Ghost as a highly skilled team of Chinese Communist brainwashers. To give you some idea: Frank Sinatra is the remarkably persuasive Horatio, and, of course, the film's romantic, and dramatic, hero. It's certainly a lot more interesting, and entertaining, a *Hamlet* than Kenneth Branagh's turgid homage to Tolstoi.)

Like Hamlet, Dickens insists that the only story worth telling is the family's story, in all its irredeemable pathos: mother, father, daughter, son, wronged precisely as mother, father, daughter, son, the story that can't be altered or swerved from (Fate), the story that can only be read in the one way (Recognition). "The readiness is all" (V.2.220) precisely because it is unthinkable to imagine the self as other than it is. Indeed, readiness (Hamlet) and redemption (Horatio) begin to pull apart as opposites. Adaptations like Hamlet's get all the political, historical, moral baggage out of the way, get rid of Horatio's mights, to replace them with Hamlet's musts. And what Hamlet's particular story *must* say is what Dickens insistently rewrites: you can't be a son and survive as a self. It doesn't matter if the father is good (old Hamlet) or bad (Claudius), no son can survive any father's demands, any mother's falsity. Just look at Polonius and Laertes. Laertes has got to escape to France to get away from his father's self-righteous overdetermination. And when he returns home, he returns, inevitably, to a grave. And don't, by the way, bother to look at Ophelia, because there is no way the son can enter heterosexuality without loss of psychic integrity. But if a son can't himself parent or survive being parented, he can, if he's tragic, die and, if sufficiently narcissistic, triumph.[1]

This *Hamlet*, Hamlet's *Hamlet*, is also Clennam's, the story he makes his own. Of course, it's not Shakespeare's Hamlet, or rather it isn't Shakespeare's *Hamlet*, since Shakespeare gives up both Hamlet's and Horatio's versions. Nor is it Dickens's *Hamlet*, or, more correctly, it isn't Dickens's only *Hamlet*. Dickens gives us Hamlet's *Hamlet* in *Little Dorrit*. Five years later – after Ellen Ternan changes his life – he can give us something much closer to, if not identical with, Horatio's *Hamlet*. In *Great Expectations*, Pip not only reads accident and mistake in virtually every catastrophe but manages even to find himself guilty. Pip as Hamlet likes, at least respects, Jaggers-Claudius, forgives the false mother, Miss Havisham, reconciles with the revenant father, Magwitch, and even survives the duel with his double, Orlick-Laertes. Satis House may start off as Elsinore, but it's an Elsinore minimally carceral and ultimately dissolved (in either ending), in large part because Pip finds out that accepting sonship gives the self a firmer ground than anything it can invent on its own. In fact, in this *Hamlet* trying to invent your self turns you into the ridiculously bad version of Hamlet that a mortified Pip goes to watch Wemmick play. *Great Expectations* just can't take Hamlet's *Hamlet* seriously. But seriously, dead serious, is exactly how Clennam takes, and makes, the *Hamlet* he adapts.

Clennam adapts for himself exactly the same narcissistic agenda that drives Hamlet, the best boy denied the superior place and life he was owed. There's the identical addiction to repetition and uncompromising alienation from a public order that is irredeemably, grotesquely corrupt. The same insistence on his own utter shame and complete innocence. On the real guilt of almost all others. On the impossibility of any compromise with the structures of this world. On the centrality of the tragic family. (Not satisfied with his own unspeakable relations, he dips into *Lear* to find another set, the Dorrits, nearly as bad.) On the absolutism of his self-idealization. On the superiority of his motives. On the horror of sexuality, and the repugnance of all erotic experience. On the superiority of death and admiration to mere life and relationship. Of course, Clennam is Hamlet grown middle-aged and grave. But that gravity also recuperates the stage tradition. Following Garrick, nineteenth-century theatre insistently played Hamlet as a gravely middle-aged Prince of Denmark, the accent on Prince, with all the formal rigor of the *ancien régime*.

Like Hamlet, Clennam dominates his story and his world through a strategy of *over-acceptance*. The term is Keith Johnstone's, to describe the behavior of certain exceptional characters who accept not only "all offers made . . . something no 'normal' person would do," but who also "accept offers which weren't really intended" (Johnstone 1979: 99). On this over-accepter both sorts of offer, the real and the imagined, "produce the maximum possible effect" (p. 102). You may well object: but Clennam does nothing but (what Johnstone calls) *block*, at least in the first third of the novel, refusing every sort of offer made to him no matter what the source. Yes, but what Arthur blocks are all the distracting, tempting offers that might generate integration into old or new plots: old from his mother and from Affery; new from Mr. Meagles and Pet. Gluttonously, he clings instead to that firm and extravagant overacceptance of the only role he is prepared to play: the innocent victim; more specifically, the scapegoat.

Clennam launches into some version of this masochistic litany to anyone he can momentarily restrain as auditor:

Trained by main force; broken, not bent; heavily ironed with an object on which I was never consulted and which was never mine; shipped away to the other end of the world before I was of age, and exiled there until my father's death there, a year ago; always grinding in a mill I always hated; what is to be expected from *me* in middle age? (I:ii, 59)[2].

Like Hamlet, self-scapegoated Arthur can not ever ferret out sufficient pain. There is always more to search for, to endure, to languish under, to grow in stature by. Luckily, he functions in a world that operates as a kind of Corbusian machine, a *machine à souffir*. (Which is, of course, not true of *Hamlet*, where everybody, for altruistic or self-interested motives, would like to help Hamlet stop suffering, except for Hamlet, and, of necessity, his father.) More than any other quality, it's that unbounded acceptance of his society's boundless constriction that makes Clennam into Dickens's hero.

It is, of course, a cliché of *Little Dorrit* criticism that everyone finds him or herself finally bound over behind (in the phrase we earlier found so evocative) "bars of the prison of this lower world" (II: xxx, 831). For most characters, family forms the primary and insuperable carceral form. Men and women alike discover themselves imprisoned debtors under the laws of consanguinity, caged by claims upon them from their relations, claims they cannot repay no matter how much they strive. But only Clennam and Amy fully and steadfastly *embrace* this unmitigated incarceration. They pay all and more than all that is demanded, and lots that's undemanded also. Clennam, however, outdoes even Amy at this business of self-undoing. Initially, she functions as his guide, Beatrice to a middle-aged, misled Dante, showing how fruitless blocking can be spun into masterful overacceptance. But, by the end of the novel, when she pleads "take all I have . . . and make it a blessing to me" (II: xxix, 828), she's made to recognize that the pupil has surpassed the mistress. By now the absolute Narcissus, Clennam has manged to reduce himself to an abject hollowness she can now merely echo. While Amy gladly submitted to the burden of others' suffering, Clennam has in effect willed himself ruined. Forced from jail, she faints and thereafter longs inertly for the vanished splendors of its imposed miseries. Without the Marshalsea, its "child" literally loses her place in the plot. But, at exactly the same time Clennam, the Marshalsea's indefatigable suitor, opens extinction into apotheosis by a sustained "act of voluptuous maso-chism" (Innes 1981: 173). Why suffer idle *nostalgie de la boue* when you can make the *boue* a home. "The Marshalsea prisoner, weak but otherwise restored" (II: xxiv, 883).

Announced in *Fidelio*, the restored prisoner embodies the nineteenth-century's *beau idéal* of a tragic hero: the restoring soldier has given way to the prisoner restored. When Fortinbras insists that Hamlet would "have proved most royal," he means Hamlet would have been a great soldier (V.2.397–405). Hence the military funeral and the however-many gun salute. By mid-century heroic action had become virtually inseparable from altruism. The hero is now gentle, rather than noble, and, supremely, "useful" (II: xxxiv, 895), useful to others, that is. His heroic predecessors had needed to be almost grotesquely conceited. This new, bourgeois hero leads "a modest life." Now, it's villainous Rigaud-Blandois who postures with swank and dagger, while Clennam confronts evil not by violence but by submitting to an incarceration he invites and within which he manages to retain his integrity and ideals (not to mention, his nice manners). Imprisonment is of course Dickens's main story. But what started off in *Pickwick* and *Oliver* as comic and sentimental has become by *Little Dorrit* a tragic scenario of heroic action.[3]

What action, you well may wonder. Doesn't Clennam spend the novel alternating between uncaped crusader and impotent mendicant, apparently unable to integrate mettle and altruism, a largely unpersuasive hero, indeed often an unconvincing character? Boldly, he repeatedly launches heroic projects, attempting to correct his family's past abuses, to free the Dorrits, to patent Doyce's invention, projects that generate so much of the novel's memorable satire against contemporary institutions. But, like Hamlet's, all Clennam's projects swiftly and regularly decline into excuses for humiliated self-torment, an oddly excessive castigation since the failure derives not from any particular shortcoming in the idealistic, strenuous hero but from what is apparently an over-determining cultural need to keep him humble, and therefore demonstrably good, to keep him, as he claims, Nobody.

Nobody is the answer. My guess is that Dickens, if not Clennam, is here remembering that moment in *The Odyssey* where Odysseus, to save himself from Polyphemus, puns on the Greek word *outis*, literally no one. (The translation is Robert Fitzgerald's.)

> "Kyklops,
> you ask my honorable name? Remember
> the gift you promised me, and I shall tell you.
> My name is Nobody: mother, father, and friends,
> everyone calls me 'Nobody.'" (IX. 364–368)

The point of the joke, of course, is to force the dull-witted Cyclops to have to yell out, when his friends come asking what's wrong, silly things like this: "Nobody, Nobody's tricked me, Nobody's ruined me!". (p. 411). And so everyone leaves him alone and unassisted. It may seem, at first, that Dickens completely inverts the Homeric source. But does he? Doesn't Clennam, as Nobody, also trick everyone, ruin everyone, mother, beloved, friends? It's this hyper-modest Nobody that allows Clennam to play out the complex stratagems that console and sustain all his Hamlet-like fictions of superiority.[4]

Almost everyone who comments on *Little Dorrit* comments on the Nobody trope. But what seems to pass unnoticed is how Clennam deploys that trope as a last, best way of being heroic. No Dickens hero can triumph through the body. In the body he will be always, finally no more than another, and lacking, man among men. Early novels like *Nickleby* permit the youthful narcissist to refuse corporeal confines by retreating to the omnipotent status of child. Later, when middle-age makes that choice ludicrous, a different strategy is called for. And found. Dickens now empties out the self until it becomes a perfect and absolute void, Nobody, polymorphously available to any use the hero can make of it. Degrading, disempowering, Nobody hollows the hero in the world's eyes, only to enable him, dangerous, manipulative, entirely self-regarding, to escape scrutiny, and bend others to his will. As Nobody Clennam can refuse the mother's demands. As Nobody, he can play with Pet's feelings and her father's hopes. Nobody invites, secures, and betrays Doyce's pitying protection. Nobody forces Little Dorrit to inhibit her own erotic needs, to remain for ever Clennam's child. Nobody centers Clennam as the supreme victim, and at the same time disclaims all responsibility – "Blind leaders of the blind" (II: xxvi, 779) – for the swathe of harm, revenge, self-aggrandizement he leaves behind.

Nobody may recall, at least to the reader of *After Dickens*, Sydney Carton. But an entire *mardi gras* of difference separates Carton's Evremonde-Darnay from Clennam's Nobody, the difference between agamy heroically achieved and narcissism merely stunted, between performance and imposture. Carton feeds his damaged, fragile narcissism at nobody's cost, indeed to everybody's benefit. Everybody he meets is literally bettered by his overweening imposture. Just as everybody Clennam encounters is diminished, impoverished, drained by his unimaginably drab, self-cancelling apotheosis. Carton genuinely and generously enacts a scenario that can accurately call itself Nobody's Fault. But for Clennam everything must always be somebody's fault, somebody else's fault. (He's just like the Terror in that: zealously laboring to empty an already almost vacant prison, the Bastille, in order to turn the whole of a city into a jail, "bars of the prison of this lower world.") Carton willingly pays agamy's price of standing isolated, alone, apart. Clennam insists relentlessly on enjoining on everybody he can collar scenarios of sacrifice and blame. Clennam can't/won't couple to delight, only to deny, decry, discredit. He's in love with an abysmal fiction of implacable debt, the family script of unquenchable atonement, exactly the script Carton sets out to annul. Nobody's fault is everyone's fault, everyone's debt. Carton takes all the burden of debt onto himself. Waning, Carton waxes; waxing Clennam wanes.

Of course, *Little Dorrit* is actually full of alternatives to and criticisms of Clennam's behavior and character. (Elaine Showalter is particularly good at showing how the novel's apparently comic doubles, like Maggy and Mr. F's Aunt, function as criticism of those they accompany [1979].) Pancks shows how to proceed if you want to spring the Dorrits from jail. Ferdinand Barnacle makes it abundantly clear how to affect even this corrupt society. Fanny Dorrit's experienced eye registers exactly how opportunistically intrusive Clennam really is. Affery lets us know when he is being cowardly. Mr. F's Aunt never lets us forget that he is, generally, a fool. Yet, though the novel embeds all of these alternative visions, just as *Hamlet* includes Horatio, Dickens's narrator refuses finally to withdraw his story's wholehearted support from its "tragic" hero.

We may very well prefer to read the novel's concluding scenes like this: "Having destroyed the sexually emasculating 'Mother' and the professionally emasculating 'father,' and having purged the murderous inner shadow, Clennam is free to leave the prison and to go with Little Dorrit into the 'roaring streets' (II: ii, 34)" in an ending "of resigned and mature optimism" (Showalter 1979: 40). But – dismayingly – Arthur actually does none of those things, except of course to go down into the streets with Amy. If anybody does destroy Mrs. Clennam, it's Rigaud, who is then destroyed God knows how. And it's certainly the incomparably able Pancks who exposes Casby. In fact, Clennam does little except, like General MacArthur, fade away "in splendid isolation and disconnection" (Simon 1988: 257). He actually accomplishes only that entire self-immolation which stands in for an ultimate, heroic "unfolding expansion and triumph" (Kohut 1985: 39).

Clennam's real self-chosen task is to make all the others, especially the women but Meagles and Doyce also, come and humbly beg his pardon. They must convict themselves of having failed him, of not having been there in time or sufficiently often, of not loving him well enough. Within the Marshalsea cell they come finally to congregate, stationed like the figures at the foot of the cross, mourning testimony to the ineffable superiority of this suffering soul, "weak" but "restored." He takes as his supreme task to receive from Little Dorrit not the fullness, but the abject surrender, of herself. He makes her literally into the "vanishing point" (II: xxvii, 801) of his life (Welch 1986: 209). And leads her into the whitest of marriages, a marriage in name only. And the name of that union is No-body. I know the text says in an oddly backhand way that they have children, but who believes it? And besides when would they have the time for a family since they're so busy doing all that good off among the "the noisy and the eager, and the arrogant and the froward and the vain" (II: xxxiv, 895).

This ending is indeed optimistic. (It's certainly optimistic if anyone thinks that pair's likely to produce offspring.) But it is the very reverse of mature. To marry Little Dorrit is to (happily) have no home, ever, anywhere, in a novel where home means jail. Instead, Little Dorrit's "vanishing-point" will open into devastation: "beyond [her], there was nothing but mere waste and darkened sky" (p. 802). And so, in the justly famous, extremely moving, final lines, the newly-wed pair literally *vanish* into the bustling London streets: "and as they passed along in sunshine and shade, the noisy and the eager, and the arrogant and the froward and the vain, fretted and chafed, and made their usual uproar" (II: xxxiv, 895). Clennam turns out to be Krook as the hero of romance. He doesn't spontaneously combust. Marrying his jailbird Cinderella, he slowly extinguishes himself in a cinderless *auto da fé*.

Kohut insists that we need tragedy. It "gives the spectator the opportunity to experience, in temporary identification with the tragic hero, the unfolding expansion and triumph of his own nuclear self," in the interminable, lopsided war between the "restrictive . . . inhibiting precepts of civilized society" and the "fragile" ego "fearful of developing our self-expressive initiative and our creativeness" (Kohut 1985: 39). But unalloyed accession to Clennam's demand for heroic status seems to me to exact from us, as it does from Amy, a psychologically and socially insupportable price. Clennam champions the unmodified narcissist's exemplary claim: not that he is more sinned against than sinning, but that he has never sinned at all. To satisfy that claim only the supreme sacrifice will do. Not the willed sacrifice of the self (Carton's), but the total surrender of the Other to atone for the world's hostility to the immaculate Self. "[T]ake all I have," Amy implores, "and make it a blessing to me" (II: xxix, 828).

No. Our adaptation insists, instead, that *Little Dorrit* is indeed Nobody's fault. Our answer to Clennam's bottomless neediness will echo not Amy's but Flintwinch's cynical and all-seeing response to Clennam: "I hope that it is enough that you have ruined yourself," he insists. "Rest contented without more ruin" (II:xxviii, 821). Our Poor Theatre will station Clennam exactly where Flintwinch – and we – need him to be, at the excruciating (as in funny, and as in tortured) intersection of askesis and folly.

Through Grotowski's eyes I came to see that *Little Dorrit* contains as many theatrically viable plays as there are players challenged to stage it. Rather than aspiring to comprehensive coverage – and inevitably failing to provide it – our *Little Dorrit* became a play about Arthur Clennam. But we could just as successfully have made a play about the Dorrits, without Arthur. Or we could have made a play about the Merdles, in which there need have been no mention of the Clennams. There is a superb play in Bleeding Heart Yard by itself. And a very great play indeed in the Meagles and Tattycoram, or in the Gowans and Miss Wade. All of these plays can emerge when the adaptor stops imagining his task as replacement or mimesis.

Instead of trying to imitate the novel, we began by following Grotowski's instruction to search "for the things which can hurt us most deeply." I asked each of the eleven performers to tell me, as they finished each quarter of the novel, which two characters, irrespective of sex, they would hate to play on the stage and why. Their choices centered on Mrs. Clennam and her son, on Rigaud/Blandois, on the Flintwinch pair, and on Flora Finching – all figures whose desires or whose malevolence mystified and even appalled the actors. No one felt interest of any kind in Little Dorrit herself. These perverse choices established for our group the emotional fault-lines of the novel, the points from and along which the most powerful emotions were most likely to erupt for this particular group of performers/readers.

The novel's multiple plots we collapsed into one story, Arthur Clennam's. Its massive cast dwindled to eleven roles, performed by our eleven actors and a broom. (I know the math's off; read on.) The broom was Little Dorrit herself, an idea adapted from Grotowski's staging of the story of Jacob and Rachel in his play *Akropolis*. Our eleven actors included five women and six men. Although we cast roles irrespective of gender – there were, ultimately, three Mrs. Clennams, two female, one male – that particular cast determined who was played and how. With different actors in a different setting even our Clennam play would have been radically different, but nonetheless, I insist, Dickensian. Of course, we were not following the fault-lines of the novel's plot. Amy Dorrit, not Arthur Clennam, occupies the book's center. She usurps it from him in the second monthly part just at the point in its composition that Dickens changed the title from *Nobody's Fault*. In fact, Arthur virtually disappears from Part xi through Part xvi. For the entire third quarter he is little more than the addressee of others' messages. But he was the center of the play my performers needed to do.

The performers costumed themselves entirely from second-hand shops, in bridal and bridesmaid's dresses, morning suits and discarded uniforms. These cast-offs were worn to every rehearsal for two months. By performance time they had been reduced to the faded rags of debtors' fantasy. In this way, we tried to avoid both a mimesis of the past as well as any exploitative allegorization of the present. Whatever our debtors were they were neither recognizably Victorian nor an allegory of the contemporary homeless. The women had a look of so many timeless Miss Havishams, their wedding dresses tattered, soiled, torn. The men in torn morning-suits or ragged tails looked like a wedding party that had just, barely, survived the *Titanic* – or, more *àpropos*, had survived the conventional wedding plot of the standard, canonized novel. Whatever the audience was expecting to find when they saw the name Dickens, what they did find was a first and stark visual warning that here their expectations of discovery, of romance, of bliss, would not be sustained, had already in fact been violated.

They also found Dickens's language. But we had radically restructured and reassigned his text. On stage, his non-comic dialogue is Dickens's weakest element, stagey in the worst ways. But the narrative voice, especially in the novels of the 'fifties and 'sixties, is incomparably evocative. So we drew our dialogue as often as possible from those descriptive passages rather than from the actual speeches assigned to characters. Indeed, very early on, it became clear that *Little Dorrit* contains a remarkable prose, a prose that, broken out from narrative, strongly suggests Whitman. But, of course, the Dickens of *Little Dorrit* is an infernally dark Whitman. And that darkness clarifies what the difference in genres might otherwise obscure: that Whitman and Dickens are the transatlantic versions of each other, the supreme artists of the egoistical sublime. Or perhaps, less exaltedly: that Whitman is Dickens without shame, just as Dickens is Whitman with more than one self to celebrate.

When we did use Dickens's dialogue, we used it recklessly. Routinely, lines migrated from one character to another. *Little Dorrit* responds well to this kind of expropriation. No only does the text routinely double the major (and relatively bland) characters with fictions and fragments of themselves, but the doubles are usually more interesting, livelier, sharper, more driven, and thus more dramatic, than their principals. Thus, when we gave to a character the speech of his or her double, the major figure regularly acquired a force and directness and sharpness he or she does not achieve in the novel, limited as they are there by Dickens's investment in their sanctity.

The performance ended up lasting about seventy-five minutes, without any sort of pause or intermission. Again, following the Poor Theatre's protocol, only small audiences were permitted to attend, generally no more than thirty-five at a time. They were seated never more than a few paces away from the performers who could thus easily make eye, but only eye, contact with them. Grotowski's actors, says Timothy Wiles, "look at us as if they know something about us which we have not yet discovered about ourselves" (Wiles 1980: 155). There was never a moment at which any member of the audience could not feel that he or she was seen, just as he or she was seeing. And the nexus of that seeing was our common connection to the Marshalsea.

The site of the Marshalsea, the narrator insists, will summon up to us "the crowding ghosts of many miserable years (Preface, p. 36). And who would be our mutual – friendly, unfriendly, overfriendly – ghosts, the us who would read a book like *After Dickens*? Our ghosts crowd out from the page – the ghost-writing we have over-accepted, and the ghost-reading: canonical literature, anti-canonical critique. It is those civilized ghosts, false, deceptive, fascinating, that Poor Theatre helps us to call up and to lay to – never more than temporary – rest. Though none of us may be the Marshall himself of the Marshalsea, we most certainly belong to his family-group. We help keep the jail. We depend on the jailer's income, certainly not because we support real prisons with real convicts inside, but because we condemn ourselves to the circumloquacious labyrinths of suffering endorsed. Not that we stage *Hamlet*, and weep. That's mere reflex, not reflection. But because we read Foucault, and believe.

Grotowski insists his productions press their audiences to find the heroes both holy and funny (Wiles 1980: 161). This double vision provided our adaptation a wonderfully tonic, contra-Kohutian, anti-tragic model. We came to see how "parody and ritual [can] mingle intimately," the first not merely *deriding* but also in effect *dynamiting* the latter (Temkine 1972: 116–117). This intermingling of contraries reveals long-suffering apotheosis as, in the long run, at best a fool's gold. And that revelation, in turn, helps us stifle the one reaction Poor Theatre cannot stomach: pity. Pity, as the performer Joseph Chaiken has said, "is a response to that which cannot be changed," but change is the goal of both Grotowski's "work and performance processes" (Kumiega 1985: 97), just as it is, or ought to be, the goal of all genuine critique. Laughter then must subvert pity. Change thereby gets a chance, if we not only see but feel how the protagonist's "outrageous excess" represents his inexcusable, unacceptable internalization of the impulse toward destruction (Grotowski 1968: 23, 42).

From that intersection of askesis and folly, then, our *Nobody's Fault* emerged, modeled, as I hope Polish Grotowski might like, on a somewhat extended version of the once popular Roman Catholic devotion, The Stations of the Cross. They were staged in a markedly carceral, small and low, more Gothic than Revival, stone crypt. Four squat, central columns divided the space into three equal areas: roughly, a nave with aisles to the north and south. To the east, a shallow, raised apse ended in a stone altar surmounted by a stone crucifix. Out of this apse, a small, side door opened into the labyrinthine corridor that led eventually to the building's principal entrance. Through that entry the audience made its way toward the darkened crypt, guided along the corridor by a silent cast member. They found their seats in two facing rows in the crypt's north and south aisles, stools in front, low chairs behind. To the east, the stone apse. To the west, a counter apse, centered on heavy, wooden doors. In this apse we placed a second, slighter, wooden altar. Everything else was cold and bare; the only texture the play of shadow against the stone walls and vaults. A Marshalsea in most ways without, mercifully, the smells.

To start: on the wooden, western altar table Clennam is supine. Outstretched as though racked, precariously balanced, arms and head hanging loose over the forward edge, upper jaw forced back into the skull, eyes roaming from side to side, agape and speechless. The rest of the cast is scattered throughout the darkened space, crouched or huddled in the shadowy corners. Except for Mrs. Clennam. She is played simultaneously by three actors, two women and one man, all imprisoned round a heavy bench in the eastern apse, backed by the stone altar and the stone crucifix. One of the women (Mrs. Clennam/1) is the bridal Mrs. Clennam, veiled, clutching an arm of the bench, trapped forever in the terrible moment of betrayal when she found the "guilty creature" in her newly-wedded husband's arms. The second woman is the mad Mrs. Clennam (Mrs. Clennam/3), the Mrs. Clennam who in the novel's final scenes runs into the London streets, desperate to secure her secret from Rigaud/Blandois's exposure. Ceaselessly she paces back and forth in the little apse, blindly guided by her hands against the blank stone wall, desperate to discover some mode of release. Seated on the bench, heavily draped and hooded in black, the man is the Mrs. Clennam of the wheel chair (Mrs. Clennam/2), the stern and unyielding mother who does "not forget." Midway through the play, the same actor will suddenly appear as Mr. Dorrit, thereafter switching rapidly between the two parental identities, Arthur's denied mother and sought-after father.

Arthur is also tripled. He is Clennam, the man outstretched on the altar. He is also two detached identities, portrayed by two actors, a black and a white man, identically dressed, sinuously bound to each other, speaking lines the novel gives to the mysterious Rigaud/Blandois. We thought of this double-figure as the "Purpose" and "Hope" Arthur insistently rejects in the opening at Marseilles (I:ii). Separated from his imagination, Purpose and Hope transform into the greed and lust that propel Blandois through the novel. Both performers were dance-trained and acrobatic. They prowl, Rigaud-Hope-Greed and Blandois-Purpose-Lust, shadowing Clennam, always at the edge wherever he stands or moves, low, feline, fluid, conspiring: dark and deadly emanations of all that energy he has ruthlessly repressed in pursuit of his own Nobody.

The action that followed from this stating point broke into seventeen, uninterrupted Stations. The original Devotion has fourteen stations, but it stops at the Entombment. We found we needed three more, for Clennam's self-generated apotheosis.

    I Overture: we enter the prison for debt.
   II Clennam decides to return home.
  III Clennam visits the house of his estranged mother.
  IV An afflicted Clennam chooses between two kinds of love.
   V Clennam visits the house of his mother for the second time.
  VI Clennam walks with Little Dorrit on the Iron Bridge.
 VII Clennam enters the Prison.
VIII Clennam encounters the Dorrit family.
  IX Clennam stays too long and is locked into the Prison.
   X Clennam determines to remain immured.
  XI Clennam binds himself to the prison's regime.
 XII Clennam is force-fed.
XIII Clennam is deprived of his dignity.

I: *OVERTURE*

None of the performers moves except for the Rigaud/Blandois pair, circling, crouched below Clennam's wooden altar. They reach out to trace the edges of the table with their grasping hands, kept somehow from rising up to touch and confront him. Suddenly, the Guide, who led the audience in, claps for silence. He intones from a lectern the play's keynote passage from the Preface, indicating to the spectators their location and their role.

I did not know myself, until the sixth day of this present month, when I went to look whether or no any portions of the Marshalsea Prison for debt are yet standing. I found the outer front courtyard metamorphosed into a shop. Then, wandering down a certain "Angel Court, leading to Bermondsey," I came to "Marshalsea Place": the houses in which I recognized, not only as the great block of the former prison, but as preserving the rooms that arose in my mind's eye when I became Little Dorrit's biographer. A little further on I found the older and smaller wall, which used to enclose the pent-up inner prison where nobody was put, except for ceremony.

This guide-book gambit sounds like the conventional Masterpiece theatre format: voice-over of the opening words of a classic text (usually, in film versions at least, with winds sweeping through the leaves of print). But the prose suddenly turns. The audience find themselves, as Dickens predicts, confronted by an entirely different and absolutely heart-crushing environment:

But, whosoever goes into Marshalsea Place, turning out of Angel Court . . . will find his feet on the very paving-stones of the extinct Marshalsea jail; will see its narrow yard to the right and to the left, very little altered if at all, except that the walls were lowered when the place got free; will look upon rooms in which the debtors lived; and will stand among the crowding ghosts of many miserable years.

This stony, subterranean space into which the spectators have let themselves be guided is a jail. Somehow, they have become part of an incarceration. To underscore and fix that realization, the final words of the Preface passage are taken up and echoed by contrapuntal male and female voices, murmured from every corner of the playing space. Female voices: "The crowding ghosts." Male voices: "Many miserable years." The sound rises and then fades. And as the echoes fade away Clennam begins to stir on his sacrificial table.

II: *CLENNAM DECIDES TO RETURN HOME*

The Guide leaves the lectern for an obscure seat among the spectators. Now he is the Mocker, soon to start the crucial "dialectic between mockery and apotheosis" (quoted from Grotowski 1964:121). Throughout the action, especially in the first half, he will hurl at Arthur what were Mr. F's Aunt's jeers and gibes. However, for these opening moments he is silent. He watches with the audience as Arthur painfully inches himself backward off the marble slab, head- and hands-first. When he can press his palms to the stone floor, he back-somersaults to crouch at the bottom of the long empty nave. Rigaud and Blandois freeze. Clennam's return home is about to begin. Anonymously murmured from the corners of the playing space come the ominous lines that in the text lead in to the novel's finale: "far aslant across the city strike the long bright rays, bars of the prison of this lower world" (II: xxx, 831).

Those words re-echo throughout the performance, insistently identifying the playing space as a synecdoche for all the structures of the human situation where Dickens finds inevitable imprisonment. But now, as Clennam inches forward on his belly, the phrases gradually give way to the sad song of the London Sunday, sung from the aisles behind the audience. "Come to Church, Come to Church / They won't come. They won't come" (I: iii, 68). Rigaud and Blandois stand, summoned. They have become the ferrymen who will convey Clennam to his mother. The dismal psalmody drones on. The pair begin to pole the invisible ferry forward. Between them Clennam balances his hands on their shoulders as gliding they propel him into the central playing space.

They "arrive" at the upper end of the nave, the foot of the steps leading to Mrs. Clennam's space. Clennam steps away from them but the ferrymen fawn and beg for payment. Clennam (using language Dickens gives to Tattycoram) rejects their somehow threatening, taunting claims for recompense.

> CLENNAM: Let me pass.
> RIGAUD: Have patience.
> BLANDOIS: You must not mind.
> CLENNAM: Let me pass!

He thrusts them energetically from his path. "Lies! Lies! You come like my own anger. My own malice. My own . . . My own . . . I do not know what you are." They slink back into the nave. Clennam cries out Tattycoram's crowning, narcissistic reproach: "I am ill used, I am ill used" (I: ii, 65). And then he enters his mother's domain. The pair ferry slowly back the opposite way, murmuring their ironic counsel: "Patience. Prudence."

The Mocker calls out from the sidelines: "Arthur visits his afflicted mother for the first time."

III. *CLENNAM VISITS THE HOUSE OF HIS ESTRANGED MOTHER*

Clennam has entered our adaptation as a broken, anti-heroic Odysseus, throwing off purpose and hope, proclaiming from the start that he has no will. He returns not to a faithful wife but an all-too-faithful mother. His preferred Nobody trope we explicitly take back to its source in Western journey narrative, Odysseus's wily escape from Polyphemus's cave. Odysseus calls himself Nobody to hide from the Monster his real identity. For Clennam, Nobody represents a way to conceal from the inquiring Other what Kohut would call the hero's nuclear agenda, the narcissistic trajectory Clennam is determined to achieve despite *monstrous* demands on him for unconcealment and candor.

After being greeted by the grotesquely misshapen servants Flintwinch and Affery, he attempts to impose on his tripled parent the history of guilt he imagines her to bear, trying to force her to accept his version of her life. But her triple voice continually drowns out his claims, literally throwing him over in his demands to be noticed and deferred to, denouncing him with the curse which comes true at the play's conclusion: "Better you had been motherless from your cradle" (I: v, 90). Arthur, excluded, moves back down toward the nave, until he falls back down the apse steps, as though toppling off a much higher precipice. He lies on the stone floor, helpless, twisted, inert.

His mother completes her monumental curse. "Predestined and lost boy – An empty place in his heart – Better you had been motherless from your cradle." And then the Mocker from the sidelines wipes up the Station. "You have a genius for dreaming, Arthur." In the silence that follows, Arthur, broken, crawls to the middle of the nave. The world of the Mother closes in upon itself.

IV. *AN AFFLICTED CLENNAM CHOOSES BETWEEN TWO KINDS OF LOVE*

Forced to accept the defeat of his initial scheme, Arthur "giv[es] up the business" of family and reunion. He takes up instead a new mission, a second "business," one he makes the center of the play's first half: substituting for the failed biological relation of parent and child his own invention and inversion of that bond.

Affery creeps out from the audience where she had hidden during the fierce exchange between parent and child. As the Mocker taunts, she persists in telling Clennam of his "old sweetheart . . . A widow. And if you like to have her, why you can." On that line Flora actually appears, delivered by the sardonic Rigaud-Blandois pair. Flora is now grotesque, an aged, squatting, bird-like revenant. Crouching and cackling like a chicken, she circles round and round Clennam as she unwinds the babble of their failed past romance, trying at the same time to wind him within the long leash she drags from her throat. That leash is held and mercilessly pulled – whenever she awakens – by the even more grotesque figure of Mr. F's Aunt. Flora aggressively tries to make physical contact with Arthur, as she gives the celebrated speech about her marriage and the changes in her life since her widowhood. She licks his hand. She rubs his leg. She grips his trouser with her teeth. Arthur will have nothing to do with her.

Rejecting with horror Flora's all-too-palpable reality, he fastens instead on "discovering" the impalpable Little Dorrit. To Affery he insists that he has spotted a girl "in the dark corner" of his mother's room, "Hidden . . . Noiseless." No such girl has appeared in the scene. But there has been propped against one of the apse pillars an old broom, tied with a wisp of blue veiling. This broom Clennam now begins gradually to invest with character and history. He catechizes the Broom: "Child, what is your name . . . Where do you live?" After a moment, he is answered, the responses whispered in chorus by all the women in the cast, stationed randomly around the edges of the playing space, playing their voices off in echo against the stone walls. But as Clennam begins to hear the Broom's history of life in the Marshalsea, the men's voices weigh in. They counterpoint Little Dorrit's "history" with the play's recurring imprisonment motif: "Far aslant the city / Strike the long bright rays / Bars of the prison / The prison of this lower world." Elated by his "discovery," Arthur tries to make Affery connect Little Dorrit to his mother's own imprisonment. Affery refuses, urging him not to be cowed and to "Stand up against them," his mother and Flintwinch. But Arthur, reinvigorated, takes up the cause as his way to reenter in power the home from which he has been expelled.

V. CLENNAM VISITS THE HOUSE OF HIS MOTHER FOR THE SECOND TIME

Clennam discovers, when he returns to his mother's room for what will be the last time, that he has indeed, and to his shock, effectuated that psychic transfer. This sequence conflates "The dreams of Mrs Flintwinch thicken" (II: x) and "Mistress Affery makes a Conditional Promise, respecting her Dreams" (II: xxiii).

Clennam has purged the past by having himself purged from it. But the situation he encounters turns out to be the exact opposite of what he hoped to achieve by that erasure. Rigaud/Blandois have taken the son's place he had earlier resigned. Clennam now can only insistently, fruitlessly beg his mother to let him assist her in removing the villainous pair. But the re-fortified parent boasts in response to Arthur's complaints: "You separated yourself from my affairs . . . Now he occupies – your place."

Arthur finds himself stalemated. To demonstrate their usurpation of his role, Rigaud/Blandois force Flintwinch to the ground, happily bragging of the murder of Madame Rigaud, "dashing herself to death upon the rocks below" (I: i, 50). With the slightest of gestured commands they make him roll painfully back and forth, faster and faster, along the ground without pause, like a log caught in a terrible, exitless spume. Clennam watches helpless, horrified at his mother's new allies, and at the countercast to his own scenario. He implores: "Mother, look at me! Shall I do nothing to assist you?" But implacably she insists: "I am unchangeable in my decision." And then she dismisses her son, murmuring over and over again, "Let it be / Let it be." For the first time in the play she leaves her (their) space. At the same time, Rigaud and Blandois drag off the now comatose Flintwinch, counterpointing Mrs. Clennam's line with their own mantra: "Up and down. Up and down. Up and down." Clennam is once more left entirely alone and even more completely isolated.

VI. CLENNAM WALKS WITH LITTLE DORRIT ON THE IRON BRIDGE

Self-willed into unwilling solitude, Clennam turns to the Broom which has remained propped at the side of the apse. Tenderly, he whispers to it. "My child, walk a little way with me? By the Iron Bridge. Where there is an escape, . . . From the noises of the street?" (I: ix, 135). He pauses, and then, lifting the broom, takes it as his companion into the empty nave.

This is the crucial mid-play passage. Clennam moves from the genealogical "public" reality of the family house to the (ultimately) preferred fiction of the prison. This prison we mark by his long crossing of a human Iron Bridge, composed by all the members of the cast but Clennam himself. Quietly, as he takes up the Broom, the other performers creep into the central space. He steps back into the nave; they, suddenly, but slowly, rise up in two parallel lines, in postures taken from figures of the Damned in Michelangelo's *Last Judgement*. They stretch themselves into the iron struts of the long bridge. With his "child" Arthur moves toward this bridge. He begins to pass between its members. Seductively they murmur, as he passes, the superb passage in which Clennam describes how he cannot anywhere escape the haunting image of the mysteriously vanished Rigaud. But here that vanished and omnipresent "fellow-creature" is clearly himself.

As though a criminal should be chained in a stationary boat on a deep clear river, condemned, whatever countless leagues of water flowed past him, always to see the body of the fellow-creature he had drowned lying at the bottom, immovable, and unchangeable, except as the eddies made it broad or long, now expanding, now contracting its terrible lineaments, so Arthur – (II: xxiii, 742)

At the same time, in counterpoint to the language of the Iron Bridge Clennam elegiacally delivers to his companion the lines the novel associates with his surrendering Pet Meagles. He describes how "the flowers, pale and unreal in the moonlight, float away upon the river," like "the greater things that once were in our breasts and near our hearts" (I: xxviii, 387). At that moment reality, too, floats from him.

Abruptly, his – and our – reverie shatters. Rigaud and Blandois, break from their places in the bridge. They seize "Little Dorrit." All the others collapse to the ground, rocking in howls of Bedlamite laughter. Rigaud grasps Clennam. Clennam drops the Broom. Rigaud forces Clennam to watch as Blandois tauntingly, grotesquely, graphically rapes the Broom. All Clennam's now discarded libido surges into the action. Rigaud and Blandois are forcing him to witness a grotesque lampoon of what he has displaced from his own nature, the "bursting . . . of the smoldering fire so long pent up" (II: xxx, 842) – the novel's description of Mrs Clennam's desperate flight from her house to the

Marshalsea. Clennam writhes in horror. But he cannot break from Rigaud's grasp. And yet we see that it is in fact the grasped, not the grasper, who is rocking the pair from and towards the violation before them. And then, as suddenly as it began, the rape has ended.

The post-coital Blandois lies gasping on the floor, covering the Broom. A shocked silence follows the demonic laughter. Arthur breaks from Rigaud, not to rescue Little Dorrit, but to hurl himself also to the ground a little distance away, insisting on himself as fellow victim. The rest slink away as they came, each murmuring over and over a broken bit of the long Preface passage, "Whosoever goes into Marshalsea Place . . ."

When they are gone, and he is entirely alone, Clennam, prone, speaks to himself a slightly varied quotation of Dickens's own words recalling the "grief and humiliation" of his own Marshalsea days. "I often forget, forget in my dreams, that I am a man. They have broken my heart." He is completely isolated now in the silenced space, a space entirely of his own invention.

VII. *CLENNAM ENTERS THE PRISON*

Arthur reaches out his arm, to try to comfort himself with Little Dorrit. He discovers that Blandois has stolen away the Broom. Only the veil is left behind. Anguished, Clennam begins fruitlessly to search along the floor never rasing his prone body. "My child? Where are you? Where have they taken you?," he asks over and over again. But there is no answer. Finally, he stops moving.

The Mocker announces: "Arthur comes to the prison for the first time."

VIII. *CLENNAM ENCOUNTERS THE DORRIT FAMILY*

The male Mrs. Clennam enters, transformed into the benevolent patriarch, Mr. Dorrit. He wears an elaborate, shabby, be-frogged, red smoking jacket. When Arthur hears that his greeter's name is also Dorrit, he swoons, to be caught in Mr. Dorrit's supporting embrace.

Comically, Dorrit now reanimates Arthur with speeches borrowed from the doctor and nurse at Little Dorrit's own birth, extolling the quiet of the prison. "The flies trouble you, don't they, my dear? Perhaps they're sent as a consolation, if only we knew it. How are you now, my dear? No better? No, my dear, it isn't to be expected. You'll be worse before you're better, and you know it, don't you?" (I: vi, 101). The actors playing Flintwinch and Affery reappear, now Tip and Fanny. We see from the reconstituted trio of performers that the prison is Mrs. Clennam's house transformed into a setting that will center on the yielding Arthur, and not on the exacting parent. The trio extols at length the "freedom" and "peace" of the prison. But from the aisles voices warningly call out, "The Lock, the Lock" (I: viii, 125).

Suddenly Arthur finds himself centering a *corrida*. The Dorrits are matador and picadors; Arthur, amazed, the bull. We are encountering the first of those pain-filled "genteel fictions" (I: vii, 114) that mask the bitter truths of the Marshalsea. Forced to his hands and knees, Arthur finds himself constrained repeatedly to charge Mr. Dorrit's red smoking-jacket. The action repeats and then repeats again, escalating painfully. Suddenly, Arthur has been stabbed by the hitherto concealed broom, Dorrit's sword. Arthur swoons. Ecstatically he grabs the pole into his groin, enabling his own sacrifice. Entirely felled, he has been made "welcome to the Marshalsea."

IX. CLENNAM STAYS TOO LONG AND IS LOCKED INTO THE PRISON

The prison scenes that follow and which make up the second half of the play conflate Clennam's early elective visits to the Marshalsea with his later self-imposed imprisonment for debt. Earlier the flexible playing space could be any location the action required. Now it narrows to Clennam's stone cell, bare except for a single low stool, a copy of the stools on which half the audience sit.

The Mocker leaves his place among the audience outside the action. He joins Clennam. Now he is the ultimate inside figure, the Turnkey, modeled on Bob, the child Amy Dorrit's friend. But this Turnkey is only the apparent keeper of the prison. It is in fact Clennam who, to accomplish his deepest project of psychic liberation, refuses all physical liberty. Instead, he insists on going through an apparently unnecessary askesis. "I must take," he maintains, "the consequences of what I have done" (I: xxvi, 783).

That repeated insistence concludes a scene that begins with the post-corrida Clennam lying supine, apparently unable to move. Slowly the cast members, the other debtors, gather to lift him to their shoulders and return him to the altar-slab on which he was found at the play's start. At the same time Dorrit clues the audience into the kind of Paschal story within which Clennam is attempting to wrap himself. As the body-bearing procession moves down the nave, Dorrit intones from the lectern: "A reading from the thirtieth chapter of Dickens, his *Little Dorrit*, lines 1 through 6. 'And the last day of the appointed week touched the bars of the Marshalsea gate. Black, all night, since the gates had clashed upon Little Dorrit, its iron stripes were turned by the early-glowing sun into stripes of gold'." But it is Clennam – not "the early glowing sun" – who turns those "iron stripes . . into stripes of gold." He is at once Grotowski's "self-willed martyr" and the perverse parody of his indomitable mother, "using his persecutors to destroy his body in order to purify his spirit" (Innes 1981: 172). Clennam has condemned himself not simply to the prison but, going to the furthest extreme of self-imposed pain, to an unrelenting regime of solitude and starvation.

While he is being carried aloft, Clennam begins to struggle to escape his bearers, as though he has finally realized exactly what it is he is condemning himself to endure. "Is there no escape? None?," he cries out. He begs for a way out, using language from the nightmarish reverie of his enforced stay in the prison Snuggery. The bearers continue to carry him down the nave. And the only answers come from the voices of the Mrs. Clennams. "Let him look at me. / In prison and in bonds here. Reparation. Is there none in this room?" Responding to those speeches, he allows himself to be lowered to the slab, reminded of the model he has taken for himself and of the ensuing necessity to suffer entirely the project of her displacement. He consents to "take the consequences of what I have done."

Bearing candles, Tip and Fanny take their positions at the head and foot of the catafalque, the lugubrious official mourners. And from some invisible source in the surrounding murk floats Little Dorrit's voice, speaking lines transferred now from her father to her suitor. "Changed as he is . . . the old sorrowful feeling of compassion comes upon me sometimes with such strength that I want to put my arms round his neck, tell him how I love him, and cry a little on his breast. I should be glad after that, and proud, and happy . . . Yet in doing so, I struggle with the feeling that I have come to be at a distance from him; and that even in the midst of all, he is deserted and in want of me" (II: iv, 523).

X. *CLENNAM DETERMINES TO REMAIN IMMURED*

Clennam has succeeded in escaping the confines of the body. That success is signalled by the unexpected reappearance of Rigaud and Blandois. They are searching madly through the audience, distraught at his loss. Like blind men they feel their way through the spectators, actually touching the faces and torsos of the audience, all the while repeating their signature "Up and down / Up and down."

This is the only time the spectators are actually submitted to physical contact. That violation of their immunity complicates the response to Clennam. In the first half of the play the Mocker voiced the audience's initial bewilderment and then gradual hostility to the demanding style of the play, especially their hostility to the insistence on self-transgression which Grotowski substitutes for the conventional drama's demand for identification with the characters. As it develops, the play's difficult subject exacerbates their consternation at its difficult form. Forced to confront Clennam's self-imposed, self-brutalizing agony, they become by mid-play pained and bewildered and alienated. That is why the play now forces them into proximity with Clennam's repellent persecutors, forces them to experience a simulacrum of his persecution. This unwilling contact with Rigaud and Blandois re-establishes the necessary tension between horror and sympathy, between admiration at the protagonist's idealism and repulsion at his self-torment, between mockery and apotheosis.

Eventually, Rigaud and Blandois do reach Clennam, feeling their way first up the outlines of the slab. But just as they realize what they have captured, the Turnkey/ex-Mocker begins the next sequence. Rigaud and Blandois are forced to withdraw to the sidelines where they watch Clennam, hungrily.

The Mocker/Turnkey enters the playing space and begins to tempt Clennam: to eat, to move, to leave. The Mocker is now the foolish, kindly Sacristan of so many chancel-centered plays. Clennam refuses every repetition of the suggestion to leave. MOCKER: "Going out now, sir?" CLENNAM: "No, not just now." Eventually the Mocker gives up and leaves Clennam in his chosen solitude.

Now Clennam painfully clambers down from the slab. He falls to his knees and then begins to bend back his head almost until it touches his heels. In this agony, he crawls from point to point along the outlines of his cell, murmuring softly: "My child. My child."

Rigaud and Blandois climb up onto the vacated slab. They whistle to him like birds, trying in vain to attract his attention. Fanny and Tip extinguish their candles and exit, singing brightly: "You are my sunshine, my only sunshine." Gradually, their words fade into a hummed melody, over which we hear, accompanied by the fruitless bird calls, Little Dorrit's own even more distant, still plangent voice. "I have been

afraid that you may think of me in a new light or a new character. Don't
do that. I could not bear it . . . Think of me always without change as
your poor child." (II: iv, 523–524). Her poor child and his echo in fading
counterpoint until Clennam can continue his tortured progress no
further. He collapses at the center of his cell.

XI. *REFUSING SUSTENANCE, CLENNAM BINDS HIMSELF TO THE PRISON REGIME*

Fanny and Tip return, once more happily singing "You Are My
Sunshine." They carry a dog's dish heaped up with grapes. They put the
dish down in front of Clennam. He refuses to notice it. He spurns all
their subsequent attempts to interest him in the food, repeatedly asking
only if Little Dorrit is there. Fanny and Tip express themselves "Aston-
ished" by his behavior. Clennam only replies: "I am as well as I usually
am. I am well enough. I am as well as I want to be."

Fanny and Tip give way to the Turnkey who offers Clennam as a toy
a ball of bright crepe paper. Clennam proceeds to gag and bind himself
with the paper, using his teeth and starting with his feet. He makes the
fragile paper seem the strongest kind of rope. Rigaud and Blandois, as
though mesmerized, find themselves forced to do the same. But they
lack even the paper illusion of fetters; their self-shackling is sheer mime.
Contorting, they fall from the slab and gyrate on the floor in unwilled,
grotesque imitation of Clennam's forceful, controlled self-enclosure.
The watching Turnkey comments in a slight revision of Mrs. Chivery's
comic speech about Young John consoling himself for his beloved Little
Dorrit's refusal of his attentions. "Won't go out, even in the back-yard,
unless there's linen drying; but when there's linen drying then there he'll
sit, hours. Hours he will. Says he feels as if it was groves" (I: xxii,
302–303). Eventually, entirely trussed, Clennam seems to fall into an
exhausted sleep. Rigaud and Blandois discover they are free and resume
their perch on the slab.

Mr. F's Aunt steals in, contemptuously eying her prostrate nemesis.
As the Mocker has become the sympathetic Turnkey, she must re-
emerge to anchor the audience's awareness of Clennam's dark side. She
begins efficiently to try to rip away Clennam's bonds. He awakens. He
struggles to curl into himself, to protect his shackles. But Mr. F's Aunt
persists in stripping away the bands, encouraged by Rigaud and Blandois. All the while she is denouncing him in a speech that begins with
Pancks' abuse of Casby. "Now, you sugary swindler, I mean to have it

out with you. What's your moral game? Benevolence, aint it?" (II: xxxii, 869). The exposé builds to a powerful series of denunciations, until it seamlessly concludes with Flintwinch's castigation of Mrs. Clennam: "You make out that you have been slighted and harmed, but you are yourself all Slight and Spite and Power and Unforgiveness. I see your pride carrying it all through. That may be your religion but it's my gammon" (II: xxx, 851). Arthur calls out for Little Dorrit. He can hear her voice, far off, whispering, but he cannot, yet, make her visible. Mr. F's Aunt leaves only when the crepe-paper streamers hang in tattered remnants from his arms and legs, like the toppled trim of an abandoned may-pole.

XII. *CLENNAM IS FORCE-FED*

Fanny and Tip return to force-feed Clennam, offering him "something green" (II: xxvii, 791), the grapes in the dog's dish not lettuce as in the novel. Teasing, taunting, they slowly, erotically roll the grapes across his hands, press them to his nostrils, force them against his tongue. Finally they manage to stuff one into his mouth. He tries to force himself to swallow. His reflex gags and chokes him. Rigaud and Blandois are delighted. They mime his efforts to swallow, cooing and groaning in parodic ecstasy. Clennam turns away from the grapes in disgust. But he also forces himself to speak thankfully for that which his body forcefully rejects. This scene goes on painfully long. Arthur is left heaving on the floor, spitting out the bits of grape he has only half swallowed, and then gasping for air. He is now broken. Exhausted. Deserted.

Mr. Dorrit reappears, for the first time since the entrance corrida. Suave, kindly, Dorrit places a stool center. Clennam painfully pulls himself into a kneeling position beside it. Clearly, he is near the end of his strength. Dorrit puts his hand to the side of his face. Clennam draws near. They enact a whispered parody of the confessional, Dorrit giving to Clennam the counsel which in the novel he offers his brother Frederick (I: xix, 267). "Oh but you might be, my son, you might be like me, if you chose."

Clennam finds in the proposition of that model the missing clue to the ultimate surrender of will. He hears how he can move on to his final, equivocal freedom. The clue lodges in the gap between victim and martyr. The martyr, the prime instrument of sacred theatre, is (from the Greek) above all else the witness. Theology proclaims the martyr as God's, or orthodoxy's, witness. Psychology less kindly sees him also, and perhaps more importantly, as the first and best witness to himself, proclaiming his elevated state, his election, and at the same time welcoming, prolonging, enjoying all those terrible trials which demonstrate his virtue. Victims require pity. But martyrs know how to center comedy, and thereby to retrieve their bliss from what might otherwise collapse into mere and banal victimization. That's the lesson Clennam has to and does learn from Mr. Dorrit. It's not enough to accept being the target of pain, one must also learn to be the butt of the joke, to turn one's humiliation into a levee.

XIII. *CLENNAM IS STRIPPED OF HIS DIGNITY*

Using Dorrit's own language, Clennam now draws Dorrit's torn red jacket round his shoulders. He forces himself to stand erect, proclaiming, in a speech that derives from the demented Dorrit boast at Mrs. Merdle's Roman dinner, that he is now "the Father of the Marshalsea, if I may establish a claim to so honourable a title." Calling the debtors to him, Clennam crows that (conflating Little Dorrit's life with her father's delusion) he has been "Born Here, Bred here, the child of an unfortunate father" (II: xix, 709).

The debtors – all the other performers – crowd around him. Savagely, they push him to the ground. They kick him back and forth from one to another. They turn him into the ball in a violent, prolonged, lunatic parody of soccer. But Clennam invites their punishing kicks. He makes no effort to escape their pummeling. He gives way entirely to every thrust and push. At every encounter, he cries out Dorrit's boast. "Ladies and gentlemen, God bless you all. I accept the conferred distinction." At the end it is the exhausted tormentors who slink away, leaving the toppled Clennam smiling.

XIV. *CLENNAM REFUSES LITTLE DORRIT'S OFFER OF UNION*

His self-apotheosizing final degradation allows Clennam the ultimate act of renunciation, the recuperation-dismissal of Little Dorrit. At this climactic moment adaptation must ironize the novel's powerful, final evasion of the body's demands: the Arthur–Amy "marriage." It stages what the novel delights to evade.

Clennam's tormentors return to venerate him. In a long line they approach, genuflecting. And as they come near him, they tenderly kiss his bruises. Finally, the last of his worshippers withdraws. Bells ring. All the women in the cast appear in the eastern corner. They are carrying, high above their crouching forms, the veiled Broom, lost and invisible since the rape on the Iron Bridge. Clennam drags himself a few steps toward this procession. Spent, he collapses. Speaking through the women, Little Dorrit begs, "Let me lend you all I have" (II: xxix, 838). But Clennam refuses. He dismisses her, following closely the scenario of ii, 29, "A Plea in the Marshalsea." "You must see me, my child, only as I am. A ruined man far removed from you, whose course is run while yours is but beginning" (p. 829). It is his proudest boast, the achieved goal of his long self-alchemy in the prison's alembic.

Accepting Amy means accepting a consoling role within the banal machinations of bourgeois romance. Clennam wants more, that is: Clennam wants less. He wants Amy, of course. But he wants her not for pleasure but for (his perverse notion of) bliss. Clennam wants a sexual partner no more than Hamlet wants to go to bed with Ophelia. Hamlet makes it quite clear that he wants Ophelia in a nunnery, not in his bed, where he would have to pay attention, at least some attention, to her. Precious attention diverted from himself, and his preferred pursuit of ghosts. Ophelia finds she can't settle for Hamlet's option. Which means that, because she's in Hamlet's play, she goes mad and dies unwed. But Amy is the sublime heroine of metastasized male narcissism. She can marry Clennam just because she can happily consent to be his child, and not "an adult, personal, willful, sexual, sharing and mutually knowing" (Garis 1965: 185). Obligingly she gives him what she has all her life been trained to give her father. What made her attractive to Clennam in the first place (unlike that simpering Pet Meagles who would persist in loving someone not her father's surrogate): her loving adoration, the living confirmation of his supreme isolation, his unexampled affliction, his entire alterity and exemption from the ordinary run of men.

Imposing his apotheosis on Amy, Clennam is able also to impose it on the world which watches these lovers and which wants romance. As Little Dorrit, foiled, is carried off, a round of polite applause breaks out from the surrounding crowd of debtors. They murmur a conflation of the comments on the enriched Dorrit and the impoverished Clennam: "He both spoke and acted very handsome. Very handsome indeed!" (II: xxvii, 790). "Anybody might see: the shadow of the wall is dark upon him" (II: xxxviii, 803).

Rigaud and Blandois now recognize that he has trampled down all the remaining claims upon him for Hope, Desire, Greed, Will. They slink toward the heavy doors that back the altar-slab, enclosing the far end of the playing space. They press themselves against the door panels. They pound against them, desperate to be allowed to escape the implications for themselves, and for the male body, of Clennam's release from "the prison of this lower world."

XV. CLENNAM TRIUMPHS OVER RIGAUD/BLANDOIS

But Rigaud and Blandois now find themselves magnetically dragged back towards Clennam. Hope entirely abandoned, purpose completely denied, the negated self can summon back the separated, repressed elements it requires to complete its fiction. Clennam taunts them: "You want me. Here I am." They try to counter his commands with the insults Miss Wade used on Tattycoram. "Go back to those who did worse than whip you . . . Go back to them . . . Spaniel. Go back." But their taunts are as powerless as their attempts to stay still. Refusing every inch of the way, they feel themselves pulled back along the stone floor until they drag themselves up along his legs and against his torso. Without moving, Clennam has forced them to come to his support in his ultimate triumph. Gradually, the trio transforms from the writhing forms of the Laocoön to a stance echoing Christ, the Virgin and the Baptist at the center of the Sistine *Last Judgement*: Rigaud and Blandois balancing and supporting the heroic and resurrected hero, returned to rule. Clennam cries out, "I have done what it was given me to do" – a version of his mother's blasphemous own Consummatum Est (II: xxx, 849). And in response, from the side, all three of Mrs. Clennam's voices call out for themselves her counterclaim for recognition. "I will be known as I know myself" (p. 845).

XVI. CLENNAM TRIUMPHS OVER HIS FALLEN MOTHER

The doomed mother crawls forward. Her three forms fallen and separate. She attempts to refuse Clennam's powerful demand, pitiably begging "Spare me. Spare me, Arthur." In exculpation she repeats the sad history of her earlier betrayal: "a guilty creature in my place." But Clennam insists (in three voices himself now, sharing out the lines with Rigaud and Blandois): "Restore to me what you have withheld." Clennam can now complete the project that undergirds all of Dickens's fiction: the child's replacement of the imposed, unfeeling, inadequate mother by a benevolent, beneficent and chosen father. Clennam insists that against her will his mother must call out the truth he longs to hear, the truth that will set him free: "Come then, Mother./ Speak then, Mother. Say then. Bring it out." Finally, she can no longer resist speaking that "truth." Screaming it out in searing pain, the three-voiced Mother cries: "I am not your mother." The curse has become blessing. The heavy western doors, closed through the entire performance, now part, slowly and unaided. The space is open to the elements.

XVII. *CLENNAM, ECSTATIC, IS CARRIED FROM THE JAIL*

Rigaud and Blandois fall away. The playing space is filled with fallen forms. We feel the allusion to the finale of *Hamlet*, but this is Hamlet's *Hamlet*, not Horatio's or Shakespeare's. Hamlet/Clennam is towering above the other bodies. He is on the verge of death, in delirium, but he is ready now to take Little Dorrit as his bride.

Mr. Dorrit rises up from the fallen form of Mrs. Clennam/2. He becomes "the sun-burned and jolly father" taken from the novel's Mr. Meagles. Genially, he proffers the Broom. "It's all over, Arthur, my dear fellow. I'm here, my boy, never to part, my dearest Arthur, never any more until the last." Towards this pair Clennam tries to make his way, so unsteady, so weak it doesn't seem possible that he can keep himself erect, let alone move forward. But he is smiling. And as he moves he starts Pet Meagles's exquisite speech when she intercepts Clennam by the river to tell him she has accepted Gowan. "You wonder to see me here by myself. The evening is so lovely. I strolled further than I meant at first. I thought it likely I might meet you." Clennam falters. He falls to his knees. He tries to rise but he can't. He has no strength left.

Mr. Dorrit would move to help him but the Turnkey intervenes. After a moment, Arthur continues speaking from the ground. "You always come this way, do you not?" He inches forward. "It is very grave here but very pleasant at this hour. Passing along the deep shade, out at that arch of light at the other end, we come upon the ferry, and the cottage, by the best approach, I think" (I: xxviii, 382–383). He has reached the Broom. Pulling himself up against it, he manages to stand on his feet. Almost at once he swoons. Mr. Dorrit and the Turnkey catch him. They lift him, still clutching the Broom, into the air high above their heads. Rigid, embracing the pole, he is carried out through the opened western doors. And as he is carried out of the audience's sight, Clennam ecstatically proclaims: "I was never rich before. I was never proud before. I was never happy before. I am rich now in being taken by you. Proud now. Happy now." Little Dorrit's own speech when Clennam finally consents to accept her love (II: xxxiv, 846). The novel's running title for those pages is "ALL LOST, AND ALL GAINED".

Rigaud and Blandois, the two remaining Mrs. Clennams, the only figures left in the playing space, curl up and quietly, human tumble-weed, roll away into the exterior darkness. From the distance comes their last whispered echo of the play's crucial phrases. "Far aslant across the city strike the long bright rays, bars of the prison of this lower world."

There were no curtain calls. The audience, after a few uncertain moments, followed the performers out through the western doors, into a landscape they had not seen when they entered. The actors had disappeared. The spectators were left to find their way back to the point from which they had started.

Raymonde Temkine: "the dramatic text is a question to be answered."

CHAPTER 6

Coda

All during the preceding chapter, I could hear your perhaps not entirely hostile murmur:

interesting yes, inviting even, but Grotowski ran the best trained acting troupe in the western world. His productions took months, in some cases, years to rehearse. And even the adaptation you've just described calls for acrobatic, severely disciplined performers, responding to extraordinary physical, vocal and psychic demands. How can you suggest that the academy follow these models that clearly call for professional or at least quasi-professional commitment?

One response would simply quote Grotowski. This is how, I'm certain, he would answer your objection. "From where can [theatrical] renewal come?" It can come, he says,

From people . . . dissatisfied with conditions in the normal theatre . . . who take it on themselves to create poor theatres with few actors, "chamber ensembles" which they might transform into institutes for the education of actors; or else from amateurs working on the boundaries of the professional theatre and who, on their own, achieve a technical standard which is far superior to that demanded by the prevailing theatre: in short, a few madmen who have nothing to lose and are not afraid of hard work (Grotowski 1968:50).

In the spirit of that *madness* I offer the script that follows, a kind of *chamber* model of the ideas and practices expanded on in the earlier chapters, but easily accessible to anyone interested. It adapts *Our Mutual Friend*, more specifically the Bradley–Lizzie plot from *Our Mutual Friend* which offered so bold a resistance to our scheming earlier in this book. This script derives from the first Santa Cruz adaptation, in 1986. I recreate it here so that I can conclude with the example of a production that was done quickly, and minimally, and successfully. And I also offer it because it completes the argument begun at the start of *After Dickens* with the as-upon-theatre drawn by *Our Mutual Friend*'s powerfully articulated resistance to the stage. And, finally, to be completely candid, I offer it because I have been strongly urged to do so by several of the people who saw it then, and insisted the book had to recover it. And that was too flattering to refuse.

"But," you continue to murmur, "isn't there a trap here, in all this fidelity to Grotowski? Aren't you just replacing one fetishized text, the Dickens novel, with another, *Towards A Poor Theatre?* You're putting down Dickens, only to put on Grotowski." That's a serious objection, even though I am not, of course, putting down Dickens. All of Grotowski's own theatre work does present a kind of sameness – granted: a sublime sameness. *Faustus, Constant Prince, Apocalypsis,* with their shared emphasis on the cardinal elements of the sacred scapegoat, the *via negativa,* and spectatorial catharsis: they can seem very much like versions of the same play. Or, more correctly, the earlier plays can seem like drafts of the one theatre project moving toward its ultimate crystallization in the literally revelatory *Apocalypsis.* It might seem inevitable, then, that if one follows with absolutely fidelity the form of Poor Theatre, one can only wind up staging merely a weak echo of that already brilliantly staged masterplay.

So yes, there's a danger of cloning here. But I don't feel that danger was realized in practice. (I wish! What price cloning if I could have staged anything like the extraordinarily powerful pieces realized by Grotowski and his unmatched acting troupe.) Poor Theatre, in theory and in practice, is essentially intimate. A small number of people perform for a somewhat larger, but still small, number of people something that emerges from their innermost response to what the performers see and feel to be the kernel of the text to be adapted. Starting in this way guarantees that the relation between script and novel is essentially that of a dialogue. At times they are similar but they are never identical. This approach guarantees that the adaptor never writes a script that the actors then learn. Instead, the adaptor and/or director learn from the actors' responses the direction and dynamic the script needs to take. Nothing is staged that the performers don't need. The adaptation thus becomes something like a geiger counter or a seismograph. Its movements trace and record forces observed outside itself, in the collision and confrontation of text and actors. A "Poor" script follows from, it does not shape, the performance, just as it follows from but is not shaped by the book under scrutiny. A Poor Theatre script will, therefore, always and only be what that specific small group makes out of not the text being adapted, but out of itself. So much for cloning.

I had not been to Santa Cruz before we began rehearsing this adaptation of *Our Mutual Friend*. I had no idea what the performance space would offer. We had less than a week to prepare: four (intense) days. Those constraints meant that I had to violate Grotowksi's most basic canon, and arrive with script in hand, well in advance of casting. And that script had to be bonelessly flexible, since I had no idea how large the cast would be until we began rehearsing. Michael Shipley, a professional actor, played Bradley (wonderfully). A few other cast members brought different degrees of experience. Jenny Wren was performed by a remarkable film veteran, Margaret Lyons, and Lizzie by the extraordinary feminist writer-lecturer Regina Barreca. But everyone else was one of Grotowski's amateurs. All of which is simply to say: if we could have the impact we did under those risibly unpromising circumstances, everyone else is virtually bound to succeed, if they want to try.

But the script that follows is not exactly the one we did at Santa Cruz. What follows is really an adaptation of our original adaptation. As how could it not be? I've written this book in the years between that production and this Coda. And I now see it, and Dickens, and Grotowski (perhaps most of all Grotowski) very differently than I did then. But even if I felt and thought exactly the same on all these topics as I did a decade back, I would have had to revise that first script. Only a very dishonest, or vain, adaptation can promise to be an end in itself, and certainly not an end to a book with an argument like this one. Adaptation always postpones the period. It's the literary equivalent of the record which calls out to be broken, or of the chain-letter, except that it carries a very real curse if interrupted. The curse that if we stop adapting we will get ourselves stuck all over again in the myth of the authentic original.

To adapt J. Hillis Miller on narrative, adaptation is "a performative speech act that undoes the done in a new act of enunciation, annunciation, or just nunciation" (Miller 1990: 243). Implicit in that definition is a demand that the undoing never gets done: adaptation's always about always returning to begin again. The undone is always undone again in the ongoing process of undoing. Perpetually *belated* adaptation renounces the pomp of being either first or last. It "can cross out an earlier speech act only by" entering "an endless sequence in which the renunciation can never quite catch up with the obligation," the obligation, that is, to give way and give away. Everything in this book is meant only and at best as a lure, to invite you to do the same but different, just as I do here, to myself.

Those phrases about nunciation and renunciation come from Miller's probing study of personification, *Versions of Pygmalion* (1990). Dickens forms only a passing reference in Miller's complex argument. (Clearly, Miller's done enough for Dickens elsewhere.) But that doesn't mean Pygmalion isn't also Dickens's favorite tale too, especially when he can play both Pygmalion and Galatea at (roughly) the same time as he manages to do in *Copperfield*. Indeed, Pygmalion is particularly relevant to this final section of the book, and to *Our Mutual Friend* itself, because of course the Bradley plot is a Pygmalion story. Lizzie is the Eliza to Headstone's gutter-born, professorial plan to transform her – certainly not into a duchess at an Embassy ball – but at least into a fit wife for a poor schoolmaster. She embodies for him the fundamental assumption of all personification tales: "The shapeless wax is not yet fit for use, but it must be used in order to become useful" (Miller 1990: 8). But this is Pygmalion with, literally, a vengeance. Ironically, Lizzie, like Shaw's Eliza, does get to test the nasty air of the upper strata, but only as the wife of Bradley's rival in educational enterprise, the gent Eugene Wrayburn. Dickens/Bradley's Lizzie marries her Freddy Eynsford-Hill. And that's just as dreadful an outcome (for me) in *Our Mutual Friend* as it is in Shaw's Postscript to the play.

But because Bradley loses Lizzie, because he is, in effect, a counter-Pygmalion, my plot derives not from Pygmalion itself but from what Dickens might call its dark twin at the window, from Pygmalion's grim Romantic parody, *Coppelia*, E. T. A. Hoffmann's story of the dancing doll. In Pygmalion stories an artist makes a thing of stone which his desire transforms into a woman of flesh, a woman who returns his desire. In versions of Coppelia, a man, sometimes an artist, sometimes not, falls in love with a mechanical doll. Deluded by his desire, he for a time believes the invention is real. But always in the end, her creator cruelly reveals her contrivance, and her ownership by the inventor, leaving the suitor awakened, abandoned and ashamed. Coppelia trails Galatea in one version or another through the nineteenth and into the twentieth century, in fiction, in opera and, inevitably, in ballet. Her story is Pygmalion's deconstructed. Pygmalion means that culture depends on there being "some truths it is better not to know" (Hillis Miller 1990: 221): not only that lovers pretty much invent their beloveds, but that readers invent the characters in which they "believe" and critics the texts they "read." Coppelia counter claims that the unreadable will be read, illusion can not be permanently sustained. The other is not only other but usually another's, and all fictions of loving, having, knowing relish declaring themselves finally to be just and only that: fiction.

Obviously, Coppelia provides a sort of sardonic pericope on adaptation. We've danced with the doll made by the man who won't let us call our dream our own. In the end, certainly at the end of this book, the dancing dolls all go home with Dickens. If he'll have them back. And adaptation turns out a branch of the sad science of derivatives. Of course, I feel that, though, I suspect, not as much as I would if what I staged set out any claims for mimetic fidelity or historical authenticity. I knew from the get-go that someone else had supplied the doll whose steps I guided. And that she wasn't going home with me, and certainly would never bear my name. Adaptors are not authors and only delude themselves like poor Hoffmann when they permit themselves to think so.

In fact, that is just the point where I find the Coppelia story so *à propos*, and so attractive. In the Barthesian terms with which we began, the *brio* of the adaptation always depends upon the prior and sustained *brio* of the original text. Barthes insists texts can provide us two kinds of joy: the permitted *pleasures* of the sustained view, and the forbidden *bliss* of the stolen glimpse, adaptation's special elation: fastening on what was intended to be kept out of view. But pleasure and bliss are not mutually exclusive joys. Just the reverse. Each makes the other more piquant, Barthes insists; actually, his word, predictably, is perverse. Same thing. You can't glimpse, unless you face squarely up to what's been displayed. But seeing only what's shown gets you nothing of your own. Which means that for every Hoffmann there's got first to be a Coppelius, if there's to be a Coppelia. And at the end of the exercise she goes home with him.

But doesn't that also only go to show how much the inventor, and the invention, turn out to depend upon the dreamer: how much the author, and the text, turn out to depend upon the adaptor? Real authors don't dance. They merely write. It's Hoffmann not Coppelius who propels the doll. (I'm thinking, obviously, of versions where the doll partners the dreamer, not those deeply incorrect renderings where she's merely a spectacle.) Coppelius only manages at best – authorially – to put the darned gadget in place and wind it up. It's Hoffmann who steps out smartly. Coppelius, then, not Hoffmann stands for the real Pygmalion, but a Pygmalion manqué.

Impotently, the inventor can only love his creation through another's eyes. She won't dance for him: he made her. He knows she's only a machine. So Coppelius trots her around to other people's parties. How else can he see his beloved Coppelia in action? He can credit her reality only when another man is suckered into the illusion, thereby deluding them both. Clearly, then, it's the Hoffmanns, the adaptors, who have chosen the better part.

Authorship means you have to house the machine. You lug it in and out of other people's places, and watch from the sidelines while others enjoy what you've made and can't use yourself. But the adaptor not only gets to, but must, partner, if the dance is to be done – somewhat like readers with fictions, only better. Reading is always finally just some more or less bittersweet rendition of dancing in the dark, solo, a fantasy of partnering. But adaptors, adaptors not only could have danced all night, they do. So long as they remember that what they're doing is not your basic *pas de deux*. Between Pygmalion and Coppelia, then, I'm sure I know which tale carries the truly happy ending. Which tale I suggest that you enter. And which role I advise you to play.

COME UP AND BE DEAD

We begin in the dark.
We hear figures shuffling into the playing space which surrounds us on all sides. They are speaking softly.

VOICES
In these times of ours, though concerning the exact year
there is no need to be precise, between Southwark Bridge
which is of iron and London Bridge which is of stone, as an
autumn evening was closing in . . . In. In. In . . . Closing in.

The movement stops. Silence. And then from stations all through the playing space, the VOICES *resume, softly, beckoningly.*

VOICES
Come up. Come up and be dead. (*Repeat ad lib.*)

The lights come up, dim, crepuscular. The speaking figures have perched themselves atop ordinary schoolroom desks, scattered apparently at random, throughout the playing space. Desks that weren't there before the lights went down. These figures balance, sitting or standing, in attitudes that easily recall the statuary that adorn nineteenth-century graves and mausolea. They are the PUPILS.
BRADLEY is moving from one PUPIL to another, modifying each figure he touches, making it more dramatic, more exaggerated, more extreme. He seems to be walking in his sleep. Everything he does in these early stages of the play has this quality of dreaming.
At one end of the space, perched high on a stepladder, next to a large blackboard, sits a shrewdly imbecile child crone, JENNY, keeping time with a long stick or pointer.

JENNY

Look at this phantom. In the darkness of the entry. A something in the
likeness of a man.

*A male figure, the LIKENESS, appears at the edge of the playing space. In every way he
is BRADLEY'S exact double, except that where BRADLEY is all dreaminess, the
LIKENESS is all crafty watching and care.*
*BRADLEY moves toward him, trying to focus, to pay attention, but stops short when this
LIKENESS moves aside and reveals behind him LIZZIE, absolutely still and doll-like
in her impeccable, impenetrable artifice. The LIKENESS whispers in her ear, and —
after a moment — she speaks. She never speaks without being similarly prompted, and,
whenever she speaks, it is with the same grave calm, entirely without affect.*
BRADLEY is struck dumb by her.

LIZZIE

What place may this be?

GIRL PUPILS

This is a school.

BOY PUPILS

Churchyard.

GIRL PUPILS

Conveniently and healthfully located above the living.

BOY PUPILS

The dead, droopingly inclined.

LIZZIE

Where young folks learn book learning? Who teaches this school?

BRADLEY

I do.

PUPILS

Quite a young man
Expensively educated
Wretchedly paid
Under the necessity of teaching
Accepting the needless inequality
And inconsistency of his life
With a submission almost slavish.

LIZZIE
You are the master here, are you?

BRADLEY
(*as though waking up*)
Yes. I am the master.

The word Master produces a BEDLAM of hoots and jeers from the PUPILS. Gradually the bedlam turns into a choric recitation of the following ODE. Through it all BRADLEY, transfixed, moves slowly toward LIZZIE until he stands facing her a few inches apart, held off by a minatory gesture from the LIKENESS.

ODE
Winter day
Churchyard
a paved square court
a slight fall of snow
a raised bank of earth about breast high
feathering
in the middle, enclosed by iron rails
feathering the sills and frame
iron rails
frame of the
churchyard
schoolroom
churchyard windows
Here
conveniently and healthfully elevated above the level of the living
were the dead
of the schoolroom windows
and the tombstones
feathering the sills and frame
droopingly inclined
a slight fall of snow feathering
as if they were ashamed of the lies they told
churchyard
schoolroom
winter evening
here were the dead
above the level of the living
schoolroom
churchyard
ashamed of the lies they told
living – dead
inclined – drooping
schoolyard
churchroom

feathering
winter
Here.

Half of the PUPILS now suddenly fall "into a state of waking stupefaction." The other half maintain "a monotonous droning noise, as if they were performing on a sort of bagpipe."

BRADLEY
I can restrain myself. And I will.

JENNY
(*to LIZZIE*)

Come up. Come up and be dead.

The LIKENESS leads LIZZIE around BRADLEY, to a vacant desk-chair. She sits on the back of the chair, but in the normal, precisely normal, attitude of the correct schoolgirl. The LIKENESS stations himself behind her.

LIZZIE
Would you be so kind as to write your name, learned governor?

BRADLEY
It cannot concern you much to know.

LIZZIE

True. You are right, Schoolmaster.

JENNY wraps some cloth around the pointer, turning the stick into a sort of puppet.

JENNY
Truth, the honorable Mrs. T.!

Reluctantly, BRADLEY moves to the blackboard and slowly prints his name.

LIZZIE
I should dearly love to hear these young folks read that name off, from the writing.

PUPILS
Bradley Headstone.

LIZZIE
Headstone. Why that's in a churchyard.

PUPILS

Schoolroom.

GIRL PUPILS

The dead healthfully and conveniently elevated above the living.

BOY PUPILS

Droopingly inclined.

LIZZIE

Schoolmaster. Your origin?

BRADLEY

I desire it to be forgotten.

LIZZIE

As you please. Schoolmaster.

JENNY

Truth. Full dressed.

LIZZIE

Schoolmaster, your origin?

BRADLEY

Poor.

JENNY

Oh, what a wolf you are.

LIZZIE

Your birth?

BRADLEY

I desire it to be forgotten.

LIZZIE

As you please, Schoolmaster.

JENNY

Truth!

BRADLEY

Mean.

JENNY

Truth. Truth. Truth.

BRADLEY

Shaming.

LIZZIE

And a lovely thing it must be for to learn young folks what's right.

BRADLEY begins to move among the desks, addressing the PUPILS.

BRADLEY

Myyy Dearrrr Childerrrennnnn. Myyyy Dearrrrr Childerrrrennnnn, beauttttifuullll word – word-word – : sssseppppullllchrrrrre. Sepulchre.

PUPILS

How does it feel to be dead?

This brings on another bedlam. BRADLEY stands chagrined and LIZZIE unfazed as all around them the PUPILS, egged on by JENNY, turn their question into a sort of hysterical fugue.

PUPILS

To be dead, how does it feel. How does it? Dead? To be dead? How does it feel? Feel to be dead?

Suddenly, it is completely quiet.

BRADLEY

I am always wrong when you are in question. It is my doom. Read.

The PUPILS produce small, dog-eared volumes from inside their clothing and together begin to read, some holding the pages upside down, others aslant.

PUPILS
(*reading*)

"The Adventures of Little Margery." The Good Child's Book. Little Margery resided in the village by the mill. She severely reproved and morally squashed the miller, when she was five and he was fifty. She divided – .

The PUPILS have stopped because BRADLEY has come up next to LIZZIE. They watch expectantly. He produces a volume for LIZZIE to take. She does not move. The PUPILS, smiling, put down their books and watch.
BRADLEY tries gently to make LIZZIE accept the book. She makes no response at all.

PUPILS
(*whispering to each other*)

They say she's very handsome.

BRADLEY
When you say they say, what do you mean?

No one answers him. He opens the book for LIZZIE and points out the words as he reads aloud.

BRADLEY
Little Margery resided in the – .

Unexpectedly, he stops, silently mouthing words to LIZZIE, words which will not come. After a moment, to cover his embarrassment, he rounds on the other pupils.

BRADLEY
Part of speech they?

PUPILS
Personal pronoun.

BRADLEY
Person, they?

PUPILS
Plural number.

BRADLEY
(to LIZZIE)
What is the word? The word is village Sound it out. Vii.
Vii.

Holding the book for LIZZIE, BRADLEY directs the others to continue to read aloud.

PUPILS
She divided her porridge with the singing birds. She
denied herself a nankeen bonnet on the ground that the
turnips did not wear nankeen bonnets, neither did the
sheep who ate them.

BRADLEY stops the reading. He waits for LIZZIE to followsuit.

LIZZIE
What have you come here for?

BRADLEY
To be of use. To come here, certain nights of the week,
and give you certain instruction.

LIZZIE
I am scholar enough.

BRADLEY

You are always in my thoughts now.

THE LIKENESS looks to JENNY, and then speaks in a memorable, trained voice.

LIKENESS

In such a night as this, Troilus mounted the Trojan walls
and sighed his soul toward the Grecian tents.

BRADLEY
(to LIZZIE)

I hope that it is not I that has distressed you. I meant no
more than to put the matter in its true light before you. I
am disappointed.

JENNY

On whose account do you come here?

BRADLEY

Her own.

JENNY

O Mrs. T, you hear him.

LIKENESS

In such a night did Thisbe fearfully o'ertrip the dew.

JENNY

And saw the lion's shadow.

BRADLEY

To reason with her for her own sake.

JENNY

Oh Mrs. T.!

LIKENESS

In such a night stood Dido.

BRADLEY

For her own sake, as a perfectly disinterested person.

JENNY

Really, Mrs. T., since it comes to this, we must turn you
with your face to the wall.

*JENNY turns aside the pointer, and as she does so, LIZZIE also turns away from
BRADLEY.*

BRADLEY

No!

BRADLEY tries but cannot turn LIZZIE back round.

LIKENESS

Medea.

The LIKENESS takes from JENNY a large piece of chalk, and coming down makes a chalk mark on the floor. LIZZIE moves gracefully down and takes her place on the mark. A bright, spotlight picks her out, causing her to send a strong shadow. At a gesture from the LIKENESS, BRADLEY comes to stand at the edge of this shadow. JENNY begins to hum. (If you wish to press the point, she can hum "les oiseaux dans la charmille" from Tales of Hoffmann, but it can just as easily be something from Gershwin, or Kern, or Porter.) The PUPILS join in with the various sounds of an accompanying orchestra. LIZZIE begins to turn and whirl, adagio, around the playing space, preceded always be the LIKENESS who chalks on the floor the marks she should reach. BRADLEY, in turn, follows, carefully keeping always on the edge of her shadow.

BRADLEY
(*To LIZZIE*)

Do you suppose that a man, forming himself for the duties I discharge, watching and repressing himself daily, dismisses a man's nature. . . . I entreat you to retract the course you have chosen. . . . Confide in me. Prefer me . . . . I am a man of strong feeling, and I have strongly felt this disappointment. I do strongly feel it. I should like to ask you. . . . I should like to ask you. . . . To ask you. . . . I should like to ask you, if I may without offense.

BRADLEY stops. LIZZIE continues to whirl, guided by the chalk-marking LIKENESS. After a moment, BRADLEY moves to the blackboard. He begins to erase his name, starting with the last letter in Headstone and ending with the B at the beginning of Bradley. Just as he is poised to erase the B, the PUPILS cry out.

PUPILS

B! I love my lover with a B.

BRADLEY

Because she's beautiful.

LIZZIE returns to her desk.

LIZZIE

Who is this in pain?

BRADLEY

You are the ruin of me. You could draw me to fire.

PUPILS

I hate my love with a B.

BRADLEY

Because she's brazen. You could draw me to water.

PUPILS

I took her to the sign of the –

BRADLEY

You could draw me to any good. Every good.

PUPILS

I treated her with Bonnets.

BRADLEY

You could draw me to any exposure and disgrace.

PUPILS

She lives in.

BRADLEY

Bedlam.

PUPILS

And her name is . . .

SILENCE

PUPILS

Her name is . . .

JENNY

Truth!

The word Truth is taken up by the PUPILS and echoes through the room.

JENNY

Full dressed!

BRADLEY

I am fit for nothing.

BRADLEY erases the letter B. The room erupts.

BRADLEY

You are the ruin . . . the ruin . . . the ruin of me.

BRADLEY must cling to JENNY'S ladder to remain erect. The PUPILS happily take out their books and resume reading.

PUPILS

The experience of Thomas Tuppence. Having resolved not to rob, under circumstances of uncommon atrocity, his particular friend and benefactor of 18 pence, he presently came into supernatural possession of 3 and 6 pence and

lived a shining light every afterwards. Note: that the
benefactor came to no good.

> LIZZIE

What a lovely thing it must be for to learn young folks
what's right.

*At a gesture from the LIKENESS, LIZZIE returns to the center of the playing space,
prepared once more to dance. JENNY and the PUPILS softly begin to hum again.
BRADLEY, hearing them, turns to see what is taking place.*

> BRADLEY

I can't play.

> LIZZIE

Have patience.

LIZZIE begins to dance, guided once again by the chalk-marking LIKENESS.

> BRADLEY

Take me up.

> PUPILS

Come play.

> JENNY

Come up. Come up and be dead.

*BRADLEY begins to move with great difficulty toward LIZZIE who is always moving
away from him.*

> BRADLEY

Have pity on me.

> PUPILS

Come play with us.

> BRADLEY

Take me up – .

> PUPILS

Come play.

> BRADLEY

Take me up and make me light.

*BRADLEY falters, then falls into an epileptic fit. LIZZIE continues to dance and the
PUPILS to hum.*

> LIZZIE
> (*dancing*)

What is it like to be dead? Bradley Headstone, Master?
What is it like to be dead? Bradley Headstone? Master.

BRADLEY rushes at the LIKENESS. He wants to seize the chalk. BRADLEY and the LIKENESS grapple. BRADLEY shows a strength he has not used at any earlier moment in the action. The LIKENESS must struggle hard to retain his grasp on the chalk.

The humming and the dancing become particularly delicate and refined. They go on as though in some other area.

BRADLEY

What is your name. Your name.

LIKENESS

I am the Lock.

BRADLEY

The Lock?

LIKENESS

The Deputy Lock –

BRADLEY

The bottom – . The bottom –

LIKENESS

The Deputy Lock on the job.

BRADLEY

The bottom – . The bottom of the raging sea –

LIKENESS

This is the Lock-house.

BRADLEY

The bottom of the raging sea heaved up. On me you
forced it. I have never been here since a lad. Which way?
Which way? Let go. Let go.

The LIKENESS suddenly reverses BRADLEY'S grip. Now it is BRADLEY who is being forced by the LIKENESS to watch the dancing.

BRADLEY

Let go. Let go.

LIKENESS

I'll hold you living.

BRADLEY

Let go.

LIKENESS

And I'll hold you dead.

BRADLEY

What is your name?

JENNY cries out the name. Both dancing and humming stop.

JENNY

Truth.

BRADLEY crumples. LIKENESS pulls up his head so that he is forced to look at LIZZIE. She slowly turns her head, but not her body, so that she is looking directly at BRADLEY.

BRADLEY

I have wronged her in fact. I have wronged her in intention. I am not the schoolmaster, Bradley Headstone. Do you hear me? Twice. I am not the schoolmaster, Bradley Headstone. Do you hear me? Three times. I am not the schoolmaster, Bradley Headstone.

LIKENESS releases BRADLEY who slumps to the ground. LIKENESS comes down to join LIZZIE who lingers a moment, looking at BRADLEY.

LIZZIE

Who is this in pain?

LIZZIE then allows herself to be guided off by LIKENESS. Just before she disappears she turns back.

LIZZIE

I am scholar enough.

After a moment the PUPILS begin to reprise their ODE. BRADLEY forces himself to stand and move toward the board, picking up the chalk the LIKENESS discarded. With the chalk he attempts to write a B. The PUPILS pause. With some difficulty he can manage the vertical stroke but when he tries the first curve, his hand falters and he makes no mark. The chalk falls from his hand. He picks it up and tries again to write. Once more he makes the vertical stroke but nothing more.
The ODE resumes.
Over and over BRADLEY repeats that vertical stroke, but nothing more. He pauses, seeks out another area of the board and there stabs again. His chalking becomes more deliberate, more forceful, more painful as the Ode builds.

ODE
Winter day
Churchyard
a paved square court
a slight fall of snow
a raised bank of earth about breast high
feathering
in the middle, enclosed by iron rails
feathering the sills and frame
iron rails

frame of the
churchyard
schoolroom
churchyard windows
Here
conveniently and healthfully elevated above the level of the living
were the dead
of the schoolroom windows
and the tombstones
feathering the sills and frame
droopingly inclined
a slight fall of snow feathering
as if they were ashamed of the lies they told
churchyard
schoolroom
winter evening
here were the dead
above the level of the living
schoolroom
churchyard
ashamed of the lies they told
living – dead
inclined – drooping
schoolyard
churchroom
feathering
winter
Here.

Even after the ODE is finished BRADLEY continues stabbing at the board. It is covered with white scratches. But we see that, though they do not spell out his or any other name, they bear some sort of relation to each other. He is drawing a kind of floor or site plan. A large, semi-palatial plan. Indeed, if we look attentively, we see that he is drawing a detailed plan of the building in which this performance is taking place, public and private spaces alike. BRADLEY continues to stab as the light dim on the sound of that repeated chalky scratch.

END OF PLAY

*****

NOT QUITE END OF BOOK

LET ME OFFER YOU TO CONCLUDE, ONE LAST ADAPTATION, THIS TIME A VALEDICTORY VERSION OF *Edwin Drood's* INCOMPARABLE SAPSEA EPITAPH.

"STRANGER, PAUSE
And ask thyself the Question
CANST THOU DO LIKEWISE?
Of course you can
And therefore
DO NOT WITH A BLUSH RETIRE
BUT GO THOU
AND DO THOU
OTHERWISE".

Notes

I DICKENS, ADAPTATION AND GROTOWSKI

1 Many of the terms in this section of the argument derive from Merlin Donald (1991). I came upon Donald's work after I had staged the adaptations that generated the argument. But it gave me the theoretical context with which to write about what I had, in effect, already discovered in Dickens, and subverted.

Donald deploys *episodic*, *mimetic*, *mythic* and *theoretical* as ways of classifying the development of human cognition.

> *The Episodic*, a vision of reality limited to event perceptions, human beings share with primates.
>
> *The Mimetic* emerges with homo erectus – pre- and early linguistic self-representations based on the episodic but expressed typically in games, tool-making skills, group rituals and standardized gestures.
>
> *The Mythic-linguistic* charts a move from a primarily *oral* to a primarily *visual* representational system, the system that gives us the notion of narrative. Keyed on the invention of writing.
>
> *The Theoretic*, building on the mythic, predicts and explains through the use of expanded memory systems. It is analytic, paradigmatic, logoscientific.

2 James Kincaid, quoting these lines, argues that "this novel assures us that there is no end to our childhood, to our play, to our desire – certainly no end to our flesh" (Kincaid 1971: 244). Those would not be precisely my emphases. You probably have to be as smart as Kincaid to see things exactly his way. And even then you probably wouldn't. But I entirely accord in his centering Dickens on not merely the idea but on the experience of pleasure.

3 This description comes from Oliver Sacks' profile of the idiot savant Stephen Wiltshire in *The New Yorker* (January 9, 1995), p.65. It was that brilliant analysis that first suggested to me to think about Dickens himself as an idiot savant and that also led me to the work of Merlin Donald.

4 For an elaboration of this model of fiction, see Brooks (1985), especially chapter 1, "Reading for the Plot," pp. 3–36 and chapter 2, "Narrative Desire," pp.37–61.

5 This image comes so close to the moving peroration with which Garrett

Stewart concludes his enduringly important *Dickens and the Trials of the Imagination* that I can't resist quoting it almost in full. "The imagination can be authenticated in Dickens's novels only when it makes an inward space for personality . . . [I] true fancy . . . serves to pluralize reality. It builds alternative places in the mind, fictive chambers like Dickens's own expansive and colorful narrative (there is no better example) where new room is made for the imagination – spacious, airy, and gaily lit" (1974: 227). I think of adaptation as exactly that sort of "new room."

6 Of course, Derrida and many others following Derrida find Lacan insufficiently sensitive on exactly this point. A handy summary of that critique can be found in *The Purloined Poet: Lacan, Derrida and Psychoanalytic Reading*, edited by John P. Muller and William J. Richardson (Johns Hopkins, 1988). In addition to essays by Lacan and Derrida, Barbara Johnson ("The Frame of Reference: Poe, Lacan, Derrida") and Jane Gallop ("The American Other") make, as one might expect, especially valuable contributions.

2 . . . AS UPON A THEATRE

1 All quotations from *Our Mutual Friend* are taken from the 1971 Penguin edition, edited with an introduction by Stephen Gill. Because the chapters are numbered according to the four Books into which Dickens divided the novel, the citation form offers first the book in upper-case roman numerals, followed by the chapter within the book in lower-case roman, followed by the page numbers, in arabic, e.g.(IV: ix, 795).

2 John Dizikes, the Pulitzer-Prize-winning historian of opera, has made this connection in a paper read at The University of California, Santa Cruz, "Charles Dickens and the World of Opera." "On the night of January 31st, 1863, in Paris, Charles Dickens went to the Opera to see and hear Charles Gounod's *Faust*. He was moved by the story – so 'splendid,' 'noble,' 'sad,' – and by the performance, 'so nobly and sadly rendered.' 'The composer must be a very remarkable man indeed,' he wrote in a letter next day." Dizikes then elaborates on an earlier suggestion of Edgar Johnson: "I think Edgar Johnson was right to guess that Marguerite's yielding to Faust had provoked in Dickens a powerful spasm of guilt having to do with his own affair with Ellen Ternan, probably heightened by Dickens identifying himself with the Faust who wielded magical power over the hearts and minds of people but whose power, glimpsing his own mortality, was beginning to fade. 'I could hardly bear the thing,' Dickens wrote. 'It affected me so, and sounded in my ears so like a mournful echo of things that lie in my own heart'" (pp.2–3). I am grateful to Professor Murray Baumgarten for pointing me to Professor Dizikes's fascinating, erudite essay.

3 My reading of the "problematics of representation" in the poem is deeply indebted to Joseph's (1992) magisterial account of the poem's place within the long perspective of our civilization's meditation on the interlinked questions of knowledge and invention.

4 Litvak, (1992) correctly I think, insists on refusing the too easy Foucauldian dichotomy between an eighteenth century of public spectacle and a nineteenth century of private isolation. "Thus, while it may still be true that, as Gillian Beer says, Dickens's 'style is spectacle,' the disjunctive representation of theatricality in *Nicholas Nickleby* at any rate, presents a challenge to the homogenizing tendency of many accounts of the Dickens theater. In place of a total theatrical system which offer itself up for either celebration or condemnation, we discover in that text a set of discontinuous theatrical*ities*" (p.116). In that text, and, I would argue, in all the others also.

Dickens's theatricality seems to combine models of spectacle found in Clark's (1985) study of painting and Booth's (1981) analysis of theatre. In this hybridized sense, spectacle covers not only theatre and painting but also fiction and an inexhaustible variety of other nineteenth-century *realizations*: International Exhibitions, the vistas of urban expansion, museums, railroad termini, botanical gardens: all those sites plate glass turns into sights. I use *realizations* deliberately here to evoke Meisel's remarkable (1983) study of the intersections of painting, fiction, history and performance in the nineteenth century. And for a helpful contextualization of Clark's model of spectacle within the project of the Situationist International, see Jay (1993: 416–432).

For a very different reading of mid-nineteenth-century spectacle, see Richards's incisive (1990) study especially the Introduction (pp. 1–16) and Chapter 1 "The Great Exhibition of Things" (pp. 17–72). Richards forcefully argues that "the spectacle of the Exhibition elevated the commodity above the mundane act of exchange and created a coherent representational universe for commodities" (p. 4), a representational universe that functions as "what Louis Althusser calls 'practical ideology,' or an imaginary way of relating to a real world" (p. 5). Impressive as Richards's arguments undoubtedly are, I would prefer to stress the opposite side of spectacle: its apotropaic function, representing the deadly incoherence of capital in such a way that it seems to neutralize the obvious danger or ward off, for specific audiences, the obvious threat. In this sense, the paradigmatic spectacle is not, say, the palm house at Kew but the lion house at the zoo.

5 The metaphor of theater in the nineteenth-century has been much and well studied. In addition to the work already cited in this chapter, the reader should also see these pioneering texts: Carlisle (1981); Marshall (1986); Auerbach (1990). Examining a slightly earlier but still relevant period in a very readable study, see Agnew. (1986).

6 Professor Murray Baumgarten has pointed out to me the significant connection between this privatization of performance and the nineteenth century's movement to privatize and internalize reading. Reading moves from reading aloud to reading alone, from an earlier cultural and oral practice as communing and communitarian, in family or other groups, to reading alone, for myself, to gain information, to extend the internal life of the self, reading as a form of intellectual capital-formation. I would only add to this illuminating parallel the suggestion that Dickens's public readings nostalgically appear to

return to the world of communitarian readings but actually parody that experience, turning it into a commercial, profit-making enterprise, where the passive audience can only be read to, and never read with. The lecture platform becomes the hearth-manqué.

7 For an authoritative analysis of the scenario of Jewish conversion in the nineteenth-century British culture, see Ragussis (1995).

3 . . . TO BE A SHAKESPEARE

1 All references to *Nicholas Nickleby* come from the Oxford Illustrated Edition (1971). References to *Pickwick Papers* are also to the Oxford Illustrated Edition (1959). For both novels citations give chapter number in roman numerals followed by page numbers in arabic.

2 Significant portions of this reading of *Pickwick* appeared in Glavin (1993).

For a very different way to read Jingle, see Stewart (1974). In this indelibly important study, Stewart starts off in roughly the same place that I do: "from the first, Jingle is a thorough delight, an intentional comedian *at* whom we never laugh. It is as if Dickens wanted to personify, in all its unreined nervous energy, his own comic and creative imagination, and began to do so with Jingle." But Stewart immediately goes on to say that Dickens quickly withdraws his identification with the player when he recognizes "the capacities for evil and lie in his own expressive powers" (p. 68). I credit that withdrawal much more to the unconscious operations of shame than to conscious and conscientious moral scruples. One way to say this is that Garrett Stewart and I are both interested in the trials of Dickens's imagination but Stewart sees Dickens as a much more responsible and on the whole nicer sort of person than I do. Probably because Garrett Stewart is on the whole more responsible and certainly much nicer than I.

3 Edward Eigner uses his unsurpassed knowledge of pantomime to read the Wardle elopement as an explicit and conscious deployment of a typical pantomime plot with Rachel as Columbine, Tupman as Lover, and Jingle as Harlequin: a "typical harlequinade capture and escape, in which the Harlequin as usual proves himself far too nimble for his self-righteous but heavy-footed pursuers" (Eigner 1989: 7–8).

4 My understanding of shame is indebted to Morrison (1989). Morrison argues that Freud, fascinated by guilt, neglected shame, and most of orthodox analysis has followed his lead. For Morrison, however, guilt and shame work in radically different ways: guilt a sense of unworthiness in relation to the other; shame a sense of unworthiness in relation to the self.

For the best reading of shame in Dickens, see Newsom (1983). Newsom's comprehensive and imaginative reading connects Dickens's shame to the twelve-year old's famous humiliation in Warren's blacking factory. I concede the ways in which shame took narrative shape from that experience but, following Heinz Kohut, I would prefer to put the originating trauma much earlier, before the Oedipal scenario completes itself. Such a trauma would not be recuperable by consciousness. Thus, the memory of the blacking factory is in large part painful because it recuperates an even earlier and completely unmanageable pain. Warren's constitutes, in effect, a kind of screen dream.

5 I rely in this discussion of aberration on Stoller's illuminating and enlightened distinction (1975) between variants and perversions. Both variants and perversions are classes of what he calls aberration: "an erotic technique or constellation of techniques that one uses as his complete sexual act and that differs from his culture's traditional, avowed definition of normality." A variant refers to "an aberration that is not primarily the staging of forbidden fantasies, especially fantasies of harming others." The term perversion he limits exclusively to "a habitual, preferred aberration necessary for one's full satisfaction, primarily motivated by hostility." Because variant only makes sense within Stoller's larger nomenclature, my argument prefers to collapse the distinction into two opposing terms: aberration (non-normative, erotic technique free of hostility and hatred) and perversion (non-normative, erotic technique dependent on hostility and hatred). See Stoller 1975: *passim*: for the definition of terms, pp. 3–5.

6 The richest and most resonant reading of the early Dickens's relation to early Victoriana is to be found in Stein's invaluable (1987) study. In its suppleness and willingness not only to tolerate but to tease out complexity, the book is especially useful as an antidote to more univocally and fashionably Foucauldian readings of the period.

7 Dobson (1992) is now the definitive study of the Shakespearean canonization from the Restoration through the eighteenth century. See also the essays in Marsden (1991), particularly: Nany Klein Maguire, "Nahum Tate's *King Lear*: 'The King's Blest Restoration'" (pp. 29–42), and Nicola J. Watson, "Kemble, Scott, and the Mantle of the Bard" (pp. 73–92).

8 Baer's elegantly argued (1992) study is the definitive history of the O. P. riots and of their context in British social and economic tradition. It is worth noting here that Baer argues persuasively that through several sources, notably George Cruikshank, Dickens would have been very familiar with those riots, even though he was born three years later.

4 EXIT: "THE SANGUINE MIRAGE"

1 Dickens divides *A Tale of Two Cities* into three Books. Citations of the text will offer the Book number in upper-case roman, the chapter number in lower-case roman, and the page numbers in arabic. The pages refer to the Penguin edition (1970).

2 In connection with the difficulties involved with *Nickleby* and theatre, it's fun to recall an anecdote from S. J. Adair Fitz-Gerald, author of "Stories of Famous Songs," "The Zankiwank," and "Fame, the Fiddler." *Nicholas Nickleby*, he remembers, was staged in Worthing in the last third of the nineteenth-century as a benefit for the actor Edward Stirling. Unfortunately,

because "Worthing mothers of the poorer classes did not countenance play acting," the theater could not round up enough boys to represent Dotheboys Hall. But then a local barber – also "a performer on the French horn, a bird fancier, newsvender, corn-cutter" – promised easily to produce at least fifty boys without any difficulty:

> Lured from the by-streets and alleys by his horn like the children in the 'Pied Piper of Hamelin,' the small fry followed him to the theatre yard; once there, [this] Figaro closed the gates upon Mr. Squeers's children. Amidst crying and moaning, they were placed on the stage, sitting on benches, and kept in order by Figaro's cane . . . completely bewildered. When the treacle was administered most of them cried. This delighted the audience, thinking it so natural (so it was). At nine o'clock, the act over, [the] cruel barber threw open the gates, driving his flock out. (Fitz-Gerald 1910: 137–138).

3 Kohut's reformulations of Narcissism occur in his 1966 essay "Forms and Transformations of Narcissism," originally delivered to the Fall Meeting of the American Psychoanalytic Association in 1965, and the follow-up to that paper, "Thoughts on Narcissism and Narcissistic Rage" (1972). Both papers have been reprinted, the first as chapter 4 and the second as chapter 5, in Charles B. Strozier's collection of Kohut essays (Kohut 1985).

4 In somewhat different terms, James Kincaid has been arguing this point for almost all of his distinguished career. Happily, these essays have now been collected as "The First Part: Dickensian Jugglers" in his remarkable collection of absurdist interventions (1995: 21–87).

5 Ambiguities in Kohut's "Thoughts on Narcissism and Narcissistic Rage" have been recently and fruitfully explored by Richard H. Marohn, "Rage without Content," and Paul H. Ornstein, "Chronic Rage from Underground: Reflections on Its Structure and Treatment," both in Goldberg (1985).

6 This distinction between performance and absorption deliberately echoes the argument of Fried's important (1981) book. Fried, as his subtitle indicates, is interested principally in the practice and theory of French painting toward the end of the *ancien régime*. Nevertheless, as his title suggests, he is also deeply concerned with the issues of representation and perception that shape the dynamic of theater, particularly the moral and sociopolitical arguments of anti-theatricality. While Dickens is doubtless entirely unaware of the philosophical content and historical context that Fried so skillfully illuminates, it is also clear that the issues that shaped the era of Diderot remained for him psychically charged with enormous and compelling anxiety.

7 The best account of Dickens's relations with Chapman and Hall remains Patten (1978). See esp. pp. 88–89.

8 For a brilliant reading in a completely different direction see the highly influential analysis in Arac (1979).

9 The indispensable study of the monstrous parent in nineteenth-century fiction is Sadoff (1982). The first chapter on Dickens (pp. 10–64) is everywhere incisive, but it's really the entire book that is invaluable. See also Thomas

(1990), esp. pp. 61–69 on *A Christmas Carol*, pp. 170–191 on *Great Expectations*, and pp. 219–237 on *Edwin Drood*.

10 The essential book on Dickens and violence remains, I think, Carey (1973). And of course Collins (1965) continues to be indispensable.

5 HOW TO DO IT

1 Justice demands I make it clear that model of tragedy I've just outlined is Hamlet's, not Kohut's. Kohut is only marginally concerned with how the family dynamic inflects the unfolding of tragedy. It is actually Bennett Simon, commenting on Kohut, who stresses the family as the primary location of the tragic. Kohut is much more intrigued by the intersection of heroism and narcissism in the production of heroism in a more general and historical way. That is: there's a lot he could say, but doesn't, about Horatio and especially about Fortinbras. He is, for instance, fascinated by the narcissism that runs through the career and writing of Winston Churchill. (It was Churchill who said: "All men are worms, but I am a glow-worm."). It is this narcissism which for Kohut grounds the heroic figure and rhetoric Churchill produced in the Battle of Britain. Kohut's analysis thus can touch illuminatingly on figures as various as Othello, Macbeth and Lear, in ways that Hamlet's cannot.

2 Like *A Tale of Two Cities*, *Little Dorrit* is divided into Books (2) and the books are in turn divided into chapters. We cite this novel, then, in the same way: upper-case roman for book, lower-case roman for chapter, arabic for page number.

3 For the transformation of the martial in non-literary formats, see the remarkable chapter "Remember the *Temeraire*" in Stein (1987). Stein's extensive and elegant analysis of Turner's "memorial" painting for Nelson makes clear how impossible it is for the nineteenth century to represent heroism apart from loss. Even victories can not be remembered without becoming "pensive" and "pathetic," "solemn and subdued, rather than grandiosely celebratory" (pp. 257, 256). For even the most glorious triumphs the nineteenth century seems unable to separate memory from mourning (p. 270).

4 Perhaps Clennam should be said more to splinter than split. Showalter (1979) showed how the novel is structured on a fascinatingly complex set of doublings. But these pairings are all versions of what Doris Brothers would call alter ego, figures of opposition and otherness, not of twinned continuity and likeness. Alexander Welch traces the ways in which Clennam's rage gets split off into Rigaud (Welch 1986: 134–135). Showalter sees his "rebellious energies" working themselves out in Pancks (p. 33). I would also locate his wandering eros in Henry Gowan.

References

Agnew, Jean-Christophe. 1986. *Worlds Apart: The Market and the Theaterin Anglo-American Thought 1500–1750*. Cambridge: Cambridge University Press.

Andrews, Malcolm. 1994. *Dickens and the Grown-up Child*. Iowa City: Iowa University Press.

Allen, Shirley S. 1971. *Samuel Phelps and Sadler's Wells Theatre*. Middletown: Wesleyan University Press.

Arac, Jonathan. 1988. "*Hamlet, Little Dorrit* and the History of Character." *South Atlantic Quarterly* 87: 311–328.

1979. *Commissioned Spirits: The Shaping of Social Motion in Dickens, Carlyle, Melville and Hawthorne*. New Brunswick: Rutgers University Press.

Archer, William. 1890. *William Charles Macready*. London: K. Paul, Trench, Trubner.

Artaud, Antonin. 1958. *The Theater and Its Double* (1938), trans. Mary Caroline Richards. New York: Grove Weidenfeld.

Auerbach, Nina. 1990. *Private Theatricals: The Lives of the Victorians*. Cambridge, MA: Harvard University Press.

Baer, Marc. 1992. *Theatre and Disorder in Late Georgian London*. Oxford: Clarendon Press.

Barish, Jonas. 1981. *The Antitheatrical Prejudice*. Berkeley: California University Press.

Barthes, Roland. 1975. *The Pleasure of the Text* (1973), trans. Richard Miller. New York: Hill & Wang.

Benjamin, Walter. 1969. "The Work of Art in the Age of Mechanical Reproduction." In *Illuminations: Essays and Reflections*, trans. Harry Zohn, ed. Hannah Arendt. New York: Schocken.

Berry, Cicely. 1988. *The Actor and His Text*. New York: Scribner's.

Birringer, Johannes. (1991) *Theatre, Theory, Postmodernism*. Bloomington, IN: Indiana University Press.

Blau, Herbert. 1990. *The Audience*. Baltimore: Johns Hopkins University Press.

Booth, Michael R. 1981. *Victorian Spectacular Theatre 1850–1910*. Boston: Routledge & Kegan Paul.

Bouissac, Pierre. 1981. *Circus and Culture*. Bloomington, IN: Indiana University Press.

Bourdieu, Pierre. 1990. *In Other Words: Essays Towards a Reflexive Sociology*. Stanford: Stanford University Press.

Brecht, Bert. 1964. *Brecht on Theatre*, ed. and trans. John Willett. New York: Hill & Wang.

———. 1955. *Mother Courage*, English Version by Eric Bentley. New York: Grove.

Brecht, Stefan, Peter L. Feldman, Donald M. Kaplan, Jan Kott, Charles Ludlam and Donald Richie. 1970. "On Grotowski: A Series of Critiques." *TDR* 14: 178–211.

Brint, Steven. 1994. *In an Age of Experts: The Changing Role of Professionals in Politics and Public Life*. Princeton: Princeton University Press.

Brooks, Peter. 1985. *Reading for the Plot: Design and Intention in Narrative*. New York: Vintage.

Brothers, Doris. 1985. "The Search for the Hidden Self: A Fresh Look at Alter Ego Transferences." In Goldberg 1985:191–207.

Buzacott, Martin. 1991. *The Death of the Actor: Shakespeare on Page and Stage*. London: Routledge, 1991.

Carlisle, Janice. 1981. *The Sense of an Audience: Dickens, Thackeray, and George Eliot at Mid-Century*. Athens: Georgia University Press.

Carr, Jean Ferguson. 1989. "Dickens's Theatre of Self-Knowledge." MacKay 1989:27–44.

Carrigan, Tim, Bob Connell and John Lee. 1987. "Toward a New Sociology of Masculinity." In *The Making of Masculinities: The New Men's Studies*, ed. Harry Brod. Boston: Unwin, pp.63–100.

Castle, Terry. 1986. "Phantasmagoria: Spectral Technology and the Metamorphosis of Modern Reverie." *Critical Inquiry* 15: 26–61.

Clark, T.J. 1985. *The Painting of Modern Life: Paris in the Art of Manet and his Followers*. New York: Knopf.

Collins, Philip. 1965. *Dickens and Crime*. London: Macmillan.

Crary, Jonathan. 1992. *Techniques of the Observer: On Vision and Modernity in the Nineteenth Century*. Cambridge, MA: MIT Press.

Davis, Tracy C. 1991. *Actresses as Working Women: Their Social Identity in Victorian Culture*. London: Routledge.

Derrida, Jacques. 1973. *The Archeology of the Frivolous: Reading Condillac*, trans. with intro. John P. Leavey Jr. Pittsburgh: Duquesne University Press.

Detienne, Marcel and Jean-Paul Vernant. 1978. *Cunning Intelligence in Greek Society and Culture*, trans. Janet Lloyd Sussex. London: Harvester.

Diamond, Elin. 1995. "The Shudder of Catharsis In Twentieth-Century Performance." Parker and Sedgwick 1995: 152–171.

Dews, Peter. 1995. *The Limits of Disenchantment: Essays on Contemporary European Philosophy*. London: Verso.

Dobson, Michael. 1992. *The Making of the National Poet: Shakespeare, Adaptation and Authorship 1660–1769*. Oxford: Clarendon Press.

Donald, Merlin. 1991. *Origins of the Modern Mind: Three Stages in theEvolution of Culture and Cognition*. Cambridge MA: Harvard University Press.

Donohue, Joseph W. Jr. *Dramatic Character in the English Romantic Age*. Princeton:

Princeton University Press.

1975. *Theatre in the Age of Kean*. Totowa, NJ: Rowman and Littlefield.

Eigner, Edwin M. 1989. *The Dickens Pantomime*. Berkeley: California University Press.

Eissler, Kurt. 1971. *Discourse in Hamlet and "Hamlet': A Psychoanalytic Inquiry*. New York: International Universities Press.

Fairbairn, W. Ronald. 1940. *Psychoanalytic Studies of the Personality*. London: Routledge & Kegan Paul, 1952.

Farb, Nigel, ed. 1987. *Arguments Between Language and Literature*. Manchester: Manchester University Press.

Feltes, N.N. 1986. *Modes of Production in Victorian Novels*. Chicago: Chicago University Press.

Fitz-Gerald, S. J. Adair. 1910. *Dickens and the Drama*. New York: Scribner's.

Fogel, Gerald I, Frederick M. Lane and Robert C. Liebert. 1986. *The Psychology of Men: New Psychoanalytic Perspectives*. New York: Basic Books.

Foulkes, Richard, ed. 1986. *Shakespeare and the Victorian Stage*. Cambridge: Cambridge University Press.

Freedman, Barbara. 1991. *Staging the Gaze: Postmodernism, Psychoanalysis and Shakespearean Comedy*. Ithaca: Cornell University Press.

Freud, Sigmund. 1953. "The Splitting of the Ego in the Process of Defense" 1940. *Standard Edition* 23: 275–78. London: Hogarth.

Fried, Michael. 1981. *Absorption and Theatricality: Painting and the Beholder in the Age of Diderot*. Berkeley: California University Press.

Garis, Robert. 1965. *The Dickens Theatre: A Reassessment of the Novels*. Oxford: Clarendon Press.

Glavin, John. 1988. "Bulgakov's Lizard and The Problem of the Playwright's Authority." *TEXT* 4: 385–406.

1993. "Pickwick on the Wrong Side of the Door." *Dickens Studies Annual* 22: 1–20.

Grotowski, Jerzy. 1968. *Towards A Poor Theatre*. New York: Simon & Schuster.

Goldberg, Arnold, ed. 1985. *The Widening Scope of Self Psychology: Progress in Self Psychology*. Vol.9. Hillsdale, NJ: The Analytic Press.

Harbison, Robert. 1988. *Eccentric Spaces*. Boston: Godine.

Heath, Stephen. 1992. "Lessons from Brecht." In *Contemporary Marxist Literary Criticism*, ed. Francis Mulhern. London: Longman. pp.230–257.

Hirschman, Albert. 1970. *Exit, Voice and Loyalty: Responses to Decline in Firms, Organizations and States*. Cambridge, MA: Harvard University Press.

Hobsbawm, Eric. 1994. *The Age of Extremes: A History of the World 1914–1991*. New York: Pantheon.

Huston, Hollis. 1992. *The Actor's Instrument: Body, Theory, Stage*. Ann Arbor: Michigan.

Hutter, Albert D. "Dismemberment and Articulation in *Our Mutual Friend*." *Dickens Studies Annual* 11: 135–164.

Innes, Christopher. 1981. *The Holy Theatre: Ritual and the Avant Garde*. New York: Cambridge University Press.

Iser, Wolfgang. 1993. *Staging Politics: The Lasting Impact of Shakespeare's History Plays*. New York: Columbia University Press.

Jaffe, Audrey. 1991. *Vanishing Points: Dickens, Narrative, and the Subject of Omniscience*. Berkeley: California University Press, 1991.

Jay, Martin. 1993. *Downcast Eyes: The Denigration of Vision in Twentieth-Century French Thought*. Berkeley: California University Press.

Johnson, Edgar. 1952. *Charles Dickens: His Tragedy and Triumph*. New York: Viking.

Johnson, Terrence J. 1972. *Professions and Power*. London: Macmillan.

Johnstone, Keith. 1979. *IMPRO: Improvisation and the Theatre*. New York: Theatre Arts Books.

Joseph, Gerhard. 1992. *Tennyson and the Text*. Cambridge: Cambridge University Press.

Kaplan, Fred. 1988. *Dickens: A Biography*. New York: Avon.

Kincaid, James. 1971. *Dickens and the Rhetoric of Laughter*. Oxford: Clarendon.

1971. "Viewing and Blurring in Dickens: The Misrepresentation of Representation." *Dickens Studies Annual* 16: 95–111.

1992. "Fattening Up on Pickwick." *Novel* 26: 235–244.

1995. *Annoying the Victorians*. London: Routledge.

Kohlmaier, Georg and Barna von Sartory. 1986. *Houses of Glass: A Nineteenth-Century Building Type*, trans. John C. Harvey. Cambridge MA: MIT Press.

Kohut, Heinz. 1984. *How Does Analysis Cure?*, ed. Arnold Goldberg. Chicago: Chicago University Press.

1985. *Self Psychology and the Humanities: Reflections on a New Psychoanalytic Approach*, ed. Charles B. Strozier. New York: Norton.

Kucich, John. 1985. "Dickens' Fanstastic Rhetoric: The Semantics of Reality and Unreality in *Our Mutual Friend*." *Dickens Studies Annual* 14: 167–185.

Kumiega, Jennifer. 1985. *The Theatre of Grotowski*. London: Methuen.

La Capra, Dominick. 1984. "Ideology and Critique in Dickens's *Bleak House*." *Representations* 6: 116–123.

Lacan, Jacques. 1975. *The Seminar of Jacques Lacan. Book I. Freud's Papers on Technique 1953–1954*, trans. John Forrester, ed. Jacques-Alain Miller, ed. New York: Norton: 1991.

Larson, Janet. 1980. "The Arts in These Latter Days: Carlylean Prophecy in *Little Dorrit*." *Dickens Studies Annual* 8: 139–195.

Lefebvre, Henri. 1974. *The Production of Space*, trans. Donald Nicholson-Smith. Oxford: Blackwell, 1991.

Litvak, Joseph. 1992. *Caught in the Act: Theatricality in the Nineteenth-Century*. Berkeley: California University Press.

Lovell, Terry. 1987. *Consuming Fiction*. London: Verso.

MacIntyre, Alasdair. 1984. *After Virtue: A Study in Moral Theory*. South Bend: Notre Dame University Press.

MacKay, Carol Hanbery, ed. 1989. *Dramatic Dickens*. London: Macmillan.

Macready, William Charles. 1967. *The Journal of William Charles Macready 1832–1851*, ed. J.C. Trewin. London: Longmans.

Manning, Sylvia. 1991. "Social Criticism and Textual Subversion in *Little Dorrit.*" *Dickens Studies Annual* 20: 127–147.

Marcus, Steven. 1965. *Dickens From Pickwick to Dombey.* New York: Simon and Schuster.

Marsden, Jean, ed. 1991. *The Appropriation of Shakespeare: Post-Renaissance Reconstruction of the Works and the Myth.* New York: Harvester Wheatsheaf.

Marshall, David. 1986. *The Figure of Theater: Shaftesbury, Defoe, Adam Smith and George Eliot.* New York: Columbia University Press.

Meisel, Martin. 1983. *Realizations: Narrative, Pictorial and Theatrical Arts in Nineteenth-Century England.* Princeton: Princeton University Press.

Meyers, Donald I. and Arthur M. Schore. 1986. "The Male–Male Analytic Dyad: Combined, Hidden and Neglected Transference Paradigms." In Fogel et al. 1986: 245–261.

Michie, Helena. 1987. *The Flesh Made Word: Female Figures and Women's Bodies.* Oxford: Oxford University Press.

Miller, D.A. 1988. *The Novel and the Police.* Berkeley: California University Press.

Miller, J. Hillis. 1958. *Charles Dickens The World of His Novels.* Bloomington, IN: Indiana University Press.

1990. *Versions of Pygmalion.* Cambridge MA: Harvard University Press.

Morrison, Andrew P. 1989. *Shame: The Underside of Narcissism.* Hillsdale, NJ: The Analytic Press.

Mulvey, Laura. 1989. *Visual and Other Pleasures.* Bloomington, IN: Indiana University Press.

Murdoch, Iris. 1977. *The Fire and the Sun: Why Plato Banished the Artists.* Oxford: Clarendon.

Newsom, Robert. 1977. *Dickens on the Romantic Side of Familiar Things: "Bleak House" and the Novel Tradition.* Santa Cruz: The Dickens Project, 1988.

1980. "'To Scatter Dust': Fancy and Authenticity in *Our Mutual Friend.*" *Dickens Studies Annual* 8: 39–60.

1983. "The Hero's Shame." *Dickens Studies Annual* 11: 1–24.

Orgel, Stephen. 1996. *Impersonations: The Performance of Gender in Shakespeare's England.* New York: Cambridge University Press.

Orwell, George. 1954. "Charles Dickens." In *A Collection of Essays.* New York: Doubleday.

Ornstein, Paul H. 1985. "Chronic Rage from Underground: Reflections on Its Structure and Treatment." Goldberg 1985: 143–57.

Ortner, Sherry B. 1996. *Making Gender: The Politics and Erotics of Gender.* Boston: Beacon.

Parker, Andrew and Eve Kosofsky Sedgwick. 1995. *Performativity and Performance.* New York: Routledge.

Parrott, W. Gerrod. 1993. "Beyond Hedonism: Motives for Inhibiting Good Moods and for Maintaining Bad Moods." In *Handbook of Mental Control,* D.M. Wegner and J.W. Pennebaker. Englewood Cliffs, NJ: Prentice Hall, 1993, pp.278–305.

Patten, Robert L. 1978. *Dickens & His Publishers*. Santa Cruz: The Dickens Project, 1991.

Phillips, Adam. 1994. *On Flirtation*. Cambridge MA: Harvard University Press.

Pocock, J. G. A. 1985. *Virtue, Commerce and History*. Cambridge: Cambridge University Press.

Pratt, Mary Louise. 1987. "Linguistic Utopias." In *The Linguistics of Writing: Arguments between Language and Literature*, ed. Nigel Fabb. Manchester: Manchester University Press, pp.48–66.

Ragussis, Michael. 1979. "The Ghostly Signs of *Bleak House*." *Nineteenth-Century Fiction* 34: 253–280.

　　1995. *Figures of Conversion: "The Jewish Question" & English National Identity*. Durham: Duke University Press.

Reader, W. J. 1966 *The Rise of the Professional Classes in Nineteenth-Century England*. New York: Basic Books.

Report from the Select Committee on Dramatic Literature. London, 1832.

Riffaterre, Michael. 1991. "The Mind's Eye, Memory and Textuality." In *The New Medievalism*, ed. Marina S. Brownlee, Kevin Brownlee, and Stephen G. Nichols. Baltimore: Johns Hopkins University Press. pp.29–45.

Richards, Thomas. 1990. *The Commodity Culture of Victorian England: Advertising and Spectacle 1851–1914*. Stanford: Stanford University Press.

Roach, Joseph. 1995. "Culture and Performance in the Circum-Atlantic World." In Parker and Sedgwick 1995: 44–63.

Robbins, Bruce. 1990. "Telescopic Philanthropy: Professionalism and responsibility in *Bleak House*." In *Nation and Narration*, ed. Homi K. Bhabba. New York: Routledge, pp.212–230.

Roberts, Doreen. 1990. "*The Pickwick Papers* and the Sex War." *Dickens Quarterly* 7: 299–311.

Rogers, Philip. 1972. "Mr. Pickwick's Innocence." *Nineteenth-Century Literature* 27: 21–37.

Ross, John Munder. 1986. "Beyond the Phallic Illusion: Notes on Man's Heterosexuality." Fogel *et al.* 1986 49–70.

Rubin, Leon. 1981. *The Nicholas Nickleby Story: The Making of the Historic Royal Shakespeare Company Production*. New York: Penguin.

Sadoff, Dianne F. 1982. *Monsters of Affection: Dickens, Eliot & Bronte on Fatherhood*. Baltimore: Johns Hopkins University Press.

Saunders, Mary. 1989. "Lady Dedlock Prostrate: Drama, Melodrama, and Expressionism in Dickens's Floor Scenes." In Mackay 1989: 68–80.

Sedgwick, Eve Kosofsky. 1985. *Between Men: English Literature and Male Homosexual Desire*. New York: Columbia University Press.

Sedgwick, Eve Kosofsky and Adam Frank, eds. 1995. *Shame And Its Sisters: A Silvan Tomkins Reader*. Durham: Duke University Press.

Showalter, Elaine. 1979. "Guilt, Authority and the Shadows of *Little Dorrit*." *Nineteenth-Century Fiction* 34: 20–40.

Siddons, Henry. 1822. *Practical Illustrations of RhetoricalGestures and Action*. London: Blom.

Simon, Bennett. 1988. *Tragic Drama and the Family: Psychoanalytic Studies from Aeschylus to Becket.* New Haven: Yale University Press.

States, Bert O. 1985. *Great Reckonings in Little Rooms: On the Phenomenology of Theater.* Berkeley: California University Press.

Stein, Richard L. 1987. *Victoria's Year: English Literature and Culture 1837–1838.* Oxford: Oxford University Press.

Stewart, Garrett. 1974. *Dickens and the Trials of the Imagination.* Cambridge, MA: Harvard University Press.

Stoller, Robert J. 1975 *Perversion: The Erotic Form of Hatred.* New York: Random House.

Straub, Kristina. 1992. *Sexual Suspects: Eighteenth-Century Players and Sexual Ideology.* Princeton: Princeton University Press.

Temkine, Raymonde. 1972. *Grotowski*, trans. Alex Szogyi. New York: Avon Books.

Thomas, Ronald R. 1990. *Dreams of Authority: Freud and the Fictions of the Unconscious.* Ithaca: Cornell University Press.

Van Ghent, Dorothy. 1950. "The Dickens World: A View from Todger's." *Sewanee Review* 58: 419–438.

Watkins, Evan. 1989. *Work Time: The English Departments and the Circulation of Cultural Value.* Stanford: Stanford University Press.

Weeks, Jeffrey. 1981. *Sex, Politics and Society: The Regulation of Sexuality Since 1800.* London: Longmans.

Welch, Alexander. 1986. *The City of Dickens.* Cambridge, MA: Harvard University Press.

Wiles, Timothy J. 1980. *The Theatre Event.* Chicago: Chicago University Press.

Wilshire, Bruce. 1991. *Role Playing and Identity: The Limits of Theatre as Metaphor.* Bloomington, IN: Indiana University Press.

Wolin, Richard. 1995. *Labyrinths: Explorations in the Critical History of Ideas.* Amherst: University of Massachusetts Press.

Worthen, William B. 1984. *The Idea of the Actor: Drama and the Ethics of Performance.* Princeton: Princeton University Press.

Index

CAMBRIDGE STUDIES IN NINETEENTH-CENTURY
LITERATURE AND CULTURE

General editor

GILLIAN BEER, *University of Cambridge*

Titles published